Financial Management: BBA, MBA, CFA, CPA, CMA, CFP, and FRM.

Copyright

Copyright © 2024 by Azhar ul Haque Sario

All rights reserved. No part of this book may be reproduced in any manner whatsoever without written permission except in the case of brief quotations embodied in critical articles and reviews.

First Printing, 2024

Azhar.sario@hotmail.co.uk

ORCID: https://orcid.org/0009-0004-8629-830X

Disclaimer: This book is free from AI use. The cover was designed in Microsoft Publisher. This book is general complete guide for BBA, MBA, CFA, CPA, CMA, CFP, and FRM.

Table of Contents

Copyright **2**

A Financial management function **19**

The nature and purpose of financial management **19**

The nature and purpose of financial management **19**

b) Explain the relationship between financial management and financial and management accounting 21

2. Financial objectives and the relationship with corporate strategy **23**

Discuss the relationship between financial objectives, corporate objectives and corporate strategy.[2] 23

2. Financial objectives and the relationship with corporate strategy **25**

b) Identify and describe a variety of financial objectives, including: [2] 25

i) shareholder wealth maximisation 25

ii) profit maximisation 27

iii) earnings per share growth. 29

3. Stakeholders and impact on corporate objectives **31**

Stakeholder Objectives: Range and Identification **31**

Stakeholder Objective Conflicts **33**

Management and Stakeholders: Agency Theory **35**

Measuring Corporate Achievement **37**

i) Ratio Analysis for Corporate Achievement **37**

ii) Changes in Dividends and Share Prices as Part of Total Shareholder Return **39**

e) Encouraging Stakeholder Objectives Achievement **41**

i) Managerial Reward Schemes for Stakeholder Objectives **41**

ii) Regulatory Requirements for Encouraging Stakeholder Objectives **43**

Financial management environment **45**

The economic environment for business **45**

Main Macroeconomic Policy Targets **45**

Fiscal, Monetary, Interest Rate, and Exchange Rate Policies in Macroeconomic Policy Targets **47**

Government Economic Policy and Planning/Decision-making in Business **49**

Planning and Decision-Making in Business **51**

Competition Policy **51**

Government Assistance for Business **53**

Green Policies and Sustainability **55**

Corporate Governance Regulation **57**

2. The Nature and Role of Financial Markets and Institutions **59**

Nature and Role of Money and Capital Markets **59**

The crucial role of Financial Intermediaries in financial markets **61**

The Functions of Stock and Corporate Bond Markets in Financial Markets **63**

Understanding the Nature and Features of Securities in Relation to the Risk/Return Trade-Off **65**

The Transformative Impact of Fintech on the Nature and Role of Financial Markets and Institutions **67**

The Nature and Role of Money Markets **69**

The Essential Role of Money Markets in Providing Short-Term Liquidity to Private and Public Sectors **69**

The Role of Money Markets in Providing Cost-Effective Short-Term Trade Finance **71**

The Role of Money Markets in Allowing an Organization to Manage its Exposure to Foreign Currency Risk and Interest Rate Risk **73**

Role of Banks and Financial Institutions in the Operation of Money Markets **74**

Interest-bearing Instruments **77**

Discount Instruments **79**

Derivative Products **81**

Nature of Working Capital and its Elements **83**

Objectives of Working Capital Management and the Conflict between Liquidity and Profitability **85**

The Central Role of Working Capital Management in Financial Management **87**

Management of Inventories, Accounts Receivable, Accounts Payable and Cash **89**

The Cash Operating Cycle and the Role of Accounts Payable and Accounts Receivable **89**

Current Ratio and Quick Ratio **91**

Inventory Turnover Ratio	**93**
Sales Revenue/Net Working Capital Ratio	**95**
Techniques for Assessing Creditworthiness	**100**
Techniques for Collecting Amounts Owing	**103**
Offering Early Settlement Discounts	**106**
Factoring and Invoice Discounting	**108**
Managing Foreign Accounts Receivable	**110**

Discuss and apply the use of relevant techniques in managing accounts payable, including 111

Trade Credit Effectively	**111**
Evaluating the Benefits of Early Settlement and Bulk Purchase Discounts	**114**
Managing Foreign Accounts Payable	**115**

Explain the various reasons for holding cash, and discuss and apply the use of relevant techniques in managing cash, including 117

Preparing Cash Flow Forecasts to Determine Future Cash Flows and Cash Balances	**118**
Assessing the Benefits of Centralized Treasury Management and Cash Control	**118**
Cash Management Models: The Baumol Model and the Miller-Orr Model	**120**
Investing Short-Term	**122**

Determining Working Capital Needs and Funding Strategies 124

The Length of the Working Capital Cycle and Terms of Trade	**125**
An Organisation's Policy on the Level of Investment in Current Assets	**127**

The Industry in which the Organisation Operates: Factors Influencing Working Capital Investment in Current Assets in Different Industries **128**

Understanding the Difference Between Permanent and Fluctuating Current Assets for Effective Working Capital Management **129**

The Relative Cost and Risk of Short- term and Long-term Finance **131**

Utilizing the Matching Principle for Effective Working Capital Funding Strategies **132**

Working Capital Funding Strategies: Evaluating the Costs and Benefits of Aggressive, Conservative, and Matching Funding Policies **134**

Working Capital Funding Strategies: The Impact of Management Attitudes to Risk, Previous Funding Decisions, and Organization Size **135**

D Investment appraisal 138

Investment appraisal techniques 138

Identifying and Calculating Relevant Cash Flows for Investment Projects: A Critical Analysis **138**

The Payback Period as an Investment Appraisal Method: A Critical Evaluation and Discussion of Its Usefulness **141**

Calculating Discounted Payback and Its Usefulness in Investment Appraisal **143**

Calculating Return on Capital Employed and Its Usefulness in Investment Appraisal **147**

Calculating Net Present Value and Its Usefulness in Investment Appraisal **149**

Internal Rate of Return (IRR) as an Investment Appraisal Method **152**

The Superiority of Discounted Cash Flow (DCF) Methods over Non-DCF Methods in Investment Appraisal **154**

Comparing the Relative Merits of Net Present Value (NPV) and Internal Rate of Return (IRR) Methods in Investment Appraisal **156**

2. Allowing for inflation and taxation in DCF 158

Comparing Nominal-Terms and Real-Terms Approaches to Investment Appraisal **159**

Calculating Taxation Effects of Cash Flows in Investment Appraisal **161**

Calculating and Applying Before- and After-Tax Discount Rates in Investment Appraisal **162**

Adjusting for risk and uncertainty in investment appraisal 164

Distinguishing Between Risk and Uncertainty in Investment Appraisal: Probability and Project Life Considerations **165**

Sensitivity Analysis in Investment Appraisal: Benefits, Techniques, and Limitations **166**

Applications and Effectiveness of Sensitivity Analysis in Investment Projects **168**

Simulation Technique: Applications, Techniques, and Effectiveness in Adjusting for Risk and Uncertainty in Investment Appraisal **169**

Applications and Techniques of Adjusted Payback Method in Investment Appraisal **171**

Risk-Adjusted Discount Rates Technique in Investment Appraisal: Applications and Discussions **173**

4. Specific investment decisions (Lease or buy, asset replacement, capital rationing) 176

Analyzing Leasing and Borrowing to Buy - Before- and After-Tax Costs of Debt **176**

Analyzing Asset Replacement Decisions Using Equivalent Annual Cost and Equivalent Annual Benefit Methods: Five Sample Examples **179**

Calculating Profitability Indexes for Divisible Investment Projects under Single-Period Capital Rationing: Examples and Evaluations **182**

The Calculation of the NPV of Combinations of Non-Divisible Investment Projects under Single-Period Capital Rationing **185**

Reasons for Capital Rationing: Internal and External Factors **187**

Business finance **189**

Sources of, and raising, business finance **189**

Exploring Overdraft as a Short-Term Financing Option for Businesses **189**

Exploring Short-Term Loans as a Financing Option for Businesses **192**

Understanding Trade Credit as a Financing Option for Businesses **193**

Exploring Lease Financing as a Financing Option for Businesses **194**

Equity Finance for Businesses **195**

Debt Finance for Businesses **197**

Lease Finance for Businesses **198**

The Role and Limitations of Rights Issues in Raising Equity Finance **199**

Placing as a Method of Raising Equity Finance for Companies **201**

Public Offers (IPOs) for Companies Looking to Raise Equity Finance **202**

Differences Between Islamic Finance and Conventional Finance: Principles, Practices, and Funding **203**

The Concept of Riba in Islamic Finance and Examples of How Returns are Generated through Shari'ah-Compliant Financing Methods **204**

Understanding Murabaha **206**

Understanding Ijara **207**

Understanding Mudaraba **208**

Understanding Sukuk **210**

Understanding Musharaka **211**

Understanding Retained Earnings **212**

Internal Sources of Finance to Increase Working Capital Management Efficiency **213**

The Relationship between Dividend Policy and Financing Decision **215**

Theoretical Approaches and Practical Influences on Dividend Decisions **216**

Cost of Capital **218**

Estimate the Cost of Equity **219**

Dividend Growth Model **219**

Systematic and Unsystematic Risk **221**

Portfolio Theory and CAPM **222**

The Capital Asset Pricing Model (CAPM) **224**

Estimating the cost of debt **226**

Irredeemable Debt **226**

Redeemable Debt **228**

Convertible Debt **230**

Preference Shares **233**

Bank Debt **235**

Estimating the Overall Cost of Capital **237**

Distinguishing between Average and Marginal Cost of Capital **237**

Calculating Weighted Average Cost of Capital (WACC) Using Book Value and Market Value Weightings **238**

Sources of finance and their relative costs **242**

Relative Risk-Return Relationship and Costs of Equity and Debt **242**

Creditor Hierarchy and Its Connection with Relative Costs of Sources of Finance **243**

The Problem of High Levels of Gearing: Risks and Challenges **244**

Assessing the Impact of Sources of Finance on Financial Position, Financial Risk, and Shareholder Wealth Using Appropriate Measures **245**

Ratio Analysis Using Statement of Financial Position: Exploring Gearing, Operational and Financial Gearing, Interest Coverage Ratio and Other Relevant Ratios **246**

Assessing the Impact of Sources of Finance on Financial Position, Financial Risk, and Shareholder Wealth Using Appropriate Measures ii) Cash Flow Forecasting **248**

Assessing the Impact of Sources of Finance on Financial Position, Financial Risk, and Shareholder Wealth Using Appropriate Measures iii) Leasing or Borrowing to Buy **250**

Impact of cost of capital on investments **251**

The Relationship between Company Value and Cost of Capital **252**

Circumstances Under Which WACC Can Be Used in Investment Appraisal **253**

Advantages of Using CAPM Over WACC in Determining Project-Specific Cost of Capital **254**

The Application of the CAPM in Calculating a Project-Specific Discount Rate **256**

Capital structure theories and practical considerations **258**

The Traditional View of Capital Structure and its Assumptions **258**

Miller-Modigliani Theory of Capital Structure Under Different Tax Regimes **259**

Impact of Capital Market Imperfections on Miller-Modigliani Theory of Capital Structure **261**

The Pecking Order Theory and Its Relevance to the Selection of Sources of Finance **262**

Shareholder Wealth Maximization Assessment Criteria: 264

Net Present Value (NPV) **268**

Internal Rate of Return (IRR) **279**

Return on Investment (ROI) **291**

Earnings Per Share (EPS) **297**

Dividend Yield **299**

Profit Maximization Assessment Criteria: **302**

Total Revenue - Total Cost Approach **304**

Marginal Revenue - Marginal Cost Approach **306**

Average Revenue - Average Cost Approach **308**

Elasticity Approach **311**

Current Ratio **314**

Debt-to-Equity Ratio **314**

Inventory Turnover Ratio **315**

Return on Assets **316**

Gross Profit Margin 317
Debt service coverage ratio 318
Trend Analysis 319
Working Capital Ratio 320
Quick Ratio 321
Interest Rate Impact on Interest Coverage Ratio 322
Price-to-Earnings Ratio 324
Inventory Turnover Ratio 326
Cash Conversion Cycle 328
Return on Equity 330
Trend Analysis on Debt-to-Assets Ratio Prediction 332
Total Shareholder Return (TSR): 333
Problem 1: ABC Inc 334
Problem 2: XYZ Corporation 335
Interest Rate in Macroeconomic Policy Targets: *Problems 337*
Problem 2 337
Problem 3 339
Problem 4 340
Problem 5 341

Exchange Rate in Macroeconomic Policy Targets: 344

Problem 2 345

Problem 3 346

Problem 4 347

Problem 5 348

Stock in Financial Markets: Case Studies 350

Case 2 351

Corporate Bond in Financial Markets: 351

Case 2 353

Manage Exposure to Foreign Currency Risk: Case Studies 354

Case Based on Trade Policy Target 356

Case Based on Monetary Policy Target 357

Interest-Bearing Instruments of the Money Market 359

Case 2: Monetary Policy Target 360

Certificates of Deposit (CDs): 361

Case 2: Expansionary Monetary Policy 361

Commercial paper: 363

Scenario 2: 363

Banker's acceptances: 364

Scenario 2 364

Repurchase agreements (repos): 365

Question 2 365

Federal funds: 367

Question 2 367

Municipal notes: 367

Question 2 368

Negotiable certificates of deposit (NCDs): 368

Question 2 369

Eurodollar deposits: 370

Question 2 370

Money market funds: 371

Question 2 372

Derivative Products: Scenarios 372

Scenario 2 373

Options Contracts: 375

Scenario 2 376

Forward Contracts: 378

Scenario 2 379

Swaps Contracts 380
Interest Rate Derivatives 382
Credit Derivatives 382
Currency Derivatives 384
Commodity Derivatives 385
Investment Appraisal Techniques 387
Net Present Value (NPV) 388
Internal Rate of Return (IRR) 389
Profitability Index 390
Modified Internal Rate of Return (MIRR) 391
Discounted Payback Period 392
Discounted Cash Flow Analysis 394
Question 2 395
Allowing for inflation in Discounted Cash flow 396
Allowing for taxation in DCF 397
Analysis 398
Analyzing Asset Replacement Decisions Using Equivalent Annual Cost and Equivalent Annual Benefit Methods 400
Profitability Indexes for Divisible Investment Projects under Single-Period Capital Rationing 402

NPV of Combinations of Non-Divisible Investment Projects under Single-Period Capital Rationing 403

Cost of Capital 406

Cost of equity 407

Dividend growth model 408

Systematic risk 410

Unsystematic risk 411

Capital Asset Pricing Model (CAPM) 413

Cost of Debt 413

Irredeemable debt 415

Redeemable debt 416

Convertible debt 417

Preference shares 419

Bank debt 421

Average and Marginal Cost of Capital 422

Weighted Average Cost of Capital (WACC) Using Book Value and Market Value Weightings 423

Traditional View of Capital Structure 424

Miller-Modigliani Theory of Capital Structure Under Different Tax Regimes 426

Miscellaneous 427

Problem 2 428

Problem 3 429

Problem 4 429

Problem 5 430

Free cash flow to firm: **430**

Problem 2 431

Problem 3 **432**

Problem 4 **433**

Problem 5 **433**

Firm Cash Flow to Equity: **434**

Problem 2 **435**

Problem 3 **436**

About Author **437**

A Financial management function

The nature and purpose of financial management

The nature and purpose of financial management

Financial management is the process of planning, organizing, directing, and controlling financial activities in a company or organization. It involves making financial decisions to maximize profits and ensure the financial stability of a company. The purpose of financial management is to manage and allocate financial resources to meet the goals of the company or organization. In short, financial management is essential in achieving the financial objectives of the company.

The nature of financial management involves various activities such as financial planning, budgeting, financial analysis, and financial controls. Financial planning involves setting goals and objectives for the company and creating a financial plan to achieve them. It involves forecasting sales, estimating expenses, and setting financial targets. Budgeting involves allocating resources to different departments and projects that require funding. Financial analysis involves evaluating the financial performance of the company, analyzing financial statements, and identifying areas where improvements can be made. Financial controls are implemented to ensure that financial activities are being carried out in compliance with laws and regulations.

The purpose of financial management is to ensure the long-term financial success of the company. This involves managing cash flow, utilizing financial resources effectively, and controlling costs. Financial management helps companies make informed financial decisions based on facts and data analysis. For instance, a company's financial management team may decide to invest in a new project or expand their business after conducting a cost-benefit analysis. Financial management also helps in managing risks by diversifying investments and identifying potential threats to the company's financial well-being.

In conclusion, financial management is an important aspect of any organization or company. It aims to optimize financial resources and ensure the long-term financial stability and success of the organization. It involves various activities, such as financial planning, budgeting, financial analysis, and financial controls, and helps improve decision-making processes. Companies that implement effective financial management practices are better equipped to maximize profits, minimize risks, and achieve their financial objectives.

b) Explain the relationship between financial management and financial and management accounting

Financial management and financial accounting are both important aspects of a business, working together to provide crucial information for decision-making processes. Financial management focuses on making decisions that will benefit the company's financial performance, while financial accounting is focused on recording financial transactions and generating financial statements.

Financial management uses financial accounting information to make strategic financial decisions for the business. Financial accounting produces financial statements that consist of the income statement, balance sheet, and cash flow statement. The income statement shows the company's revenue and expenses over a period of time, revealing whether the company has made a profit or loss. The balance sheet shows the company's assets, liabilities, and equity at a specific point in time. The cash flow statement shows the inflows and outflows of cash over a period of time.

Financial management uses financial accounting to get a clear picture of the company's financial position and performance. For instance, by analyzing the company's financial statements, financial management can determine if the company is profitable or not, if the company is generating cash or burning through it, or if there is a need for additional funding. All these factors are essential in making informed financial decisions.

Management accounting, on the other hand, provides information to internal stakeholders, such as management, employees, and stakeholders, for decision-making processes. Management accounting provides information on how to allocate and use resources, as well as how to optimize performance. Management accountants create reports that provide detailed information about a specific department, cost center, or product line, allowing financial management to make informed decisions about how to allocate resources.

Financial management and management accounting work together to provide a complete financial picture of the company. By combining financial accounting and management accounting data, financial management can make decisions that are aligned with the company's overall strategy, goals, and objectives.

For example, suppose a company wants to invest in research and development. By utilizing the financial and management accounting data, financial management can determine whether the investment will generate a profit, whether alternative methods of investment exist, and whether it's worth the investment at all. Management accounting will provide information on resource allocation and how to optimize performance, while financial accounting will provide information on the financing required for the investment and how it will influence the financial performance of the company.

In conclusion, financial management, financial accounting, and management accounting are closely related and work together in providing a complete financial picture of the company. Financial accounting provides information on the company's financial performance and position, while management accounting provides information to allocate and use resources effectively. Financial management uses the information generated from financial and management accounting to make informed decisions that are aligned with the company's overall strategy and goals. By leveraging this data, businesses can optimize performance, minimize costs and risks, and maximize profitability.

2. Financial objectives and the relationship with corporate strategy

Discuss the relationship between financial objectives, corporate objectives and corporate strategy. [2]

Financial objectives are an integral part of any organization's corporate performance management strategy. These objectives are closely linked to corporate objectives and corporate strategy, as a company's financial objectives are derived from the overall goals and objectives of the organization. Corporate strategy lays the foundation for the company's financial objectives and outlines how the company will achieve its goals. Corporate strategy articulates the overall direction of the organization and the plans for achieving its goals. The strategy sets out the company's vision, mission, objectives, and goals, and outlines the steps that the organization will take to achieve them. Financial objectives are a part of corporate strategy, and they are necessary to ensure that the company has enough resources to support the overall strategy.

Financial objectives are specific financial targets that the organization sets to achieve its broader objectives. For instance, a company's corporate strategy may be to become a market leader in its industry by developing cutting-edge products. The financial objective to support this corporate objective might be to increase revenue by 20% in the next three years. By achieving this financial objective, the company will have the resources it needs to invest in research and development, marketing, and other activities necessary to become a market leader.

The relationship between financial objectives, corporate objectives, and corporate strategy is closely linked. Corporate strategy defines the goals of the organization and outlines the steps needed to achieve them. Financial objectives translate these goals into specific targets related to financial performance. Corporate objectives define the scope and priorities of the organization, while financial objectives set specific targets for measuring progress towards those priorities.

Also, corporate strategy provides a roadmap for how resources will be allocated to support financial objectives. It helps to ensure that financial objectives are aligned with the broader goals of the organization. For instance, if a company's overall corporate goal is to expand into new markets, the financial objective might be to raise capital through a public offering, optimizing the availability of capital resources.

In conclusion, financial objectives are essential to achieve the broader goals and objectives of the organization. They are closely linked to corporate objectives and corporate strategy, forming an integrated system that aligns financial targets with the goals of the organization. By aligning financial objectives with corporate objectives and corporate strategy, companies can ensure that their resources are allocated effectively and that they are on track to achieve their long-term goals.

2. Financial objectives and the relationship with corporate strategy

b) Identify and describe a variety of financial objectives, including: [2]

i) shareholder wealth maximisation

Shareholder wealth maximization is one of the primary financial objectives of a company. It is an explicit and high-priority goal of most companies where the primary objective is of financial nature, such as a profit organization. It is an approach or as an ideology that drives companies to increase shareholder wealth by maximizing the company's profits and value, which in turn increases the stock's price and returns to the shareholders.

Shareholder wealth maximization can be defined as a financial objective that aims to maximize the value of the owners' equity in the company.

The approach of shareholder wealth maximization is often criticized for overlooking other important business goals, such as creating jobs, offering attractive salaries to employees, sustainability, or contribution to society, among others, to prioritize the maximization of profits for the stockholders; hence, sometimes it is seen as a short-term goal.

Companies usually focus on shareholder wealth maximization as a long-term goal, as it keeps shareholders' interests in mind and attempts to ensure sustainable growth for the organization.

To achieve shareholder wealth maximization, companies employ different strategies. First, they develop and implement techniques that increase the company's revenue and margin, such as identifying new business verticals, introducing new products and services, enhancing existing products/services, and being innovative in the market.

The second strategy relates to the management of financial resources. Companies maintain better cash flow by improving working capital management, reducing expenses, and investing in high-return opportunities to generate more significant profits.

Finally, the third strategy is to maximize shareholder value through financial risk management. Companies implement effective financial management techniques to minimize financial risk, such as hedging currency exposure and setting up contractual agreements that offer protection against price and interest rate volatility.

In conclusion, shareholder wealth maximization is an essential financial objective of a company that emphasizes maximizing shareholder equity value. It is an approach that guides companies to promote the long-term interests of the stockholders and ensures reliable growth of the organization. Companies focus on adopting various strategies, including revenue maximization, financial resource management, and risk management, to attain the goal of shareholder wealth maximization, which ultimately benefits the shareholders.

ii) profit maximisation

Profit maximization is another primary financial objective of a company. It is the typical motive for most companies that operate in competitive markets and where the primary objective is of financial nature. Profit maximization is an explicit and understandable objective where the company's aim is to generate maximum profit using all available resources.

Profit maximization deals with a company's ability to earn an income in excess of the expenses it incurs. The concept is quite simple – a company must maximize its profits to be economically sustainable in the long run. Profit maximization is also closely linked with shareholder wealth maximization as it is a fundamental aspect of financial stability that significantly influences shareholder returns.

To achieve profit maximization, companies employ various strategies such as increasing sales and revenue and decreasing costs. By boosting sales and revenues, companies can increase their profits considerably. Reducing expenses is another strategy that companies follow to boost their profits. For instance, reducing staff costs, optimizing manufacturing costs by improving efficiency, and negotiating better prices with suppliers are some examples of cost-cutting measures.

Companies may also introduce pricing strategies to boost their profits. Setting prices below the competition can take significant market share; however, it can eat into profit margins. On the other hand, charging prices above the competition can result in higher profit margins, but it can reduce market share. Companies must determine an optimal pricing structure that maximizes profit.

Profit maximization is not without its criticisms. Critics argue that with profit maximization as the only objective, companies can sometimes overlook other important aspects, such as the social responsibility, long-term sustainability, employee benefits, customer satisfaction, among others. These criticisms highlight the importance of balancing profit maximization with other social and environmental responsibilities.

In conclusion, profit maximization is an essential financial objective for a company. It increases the company's profitability and ensures its long-term financial stability. Through techniques such as increasing sales revenue, decreasing costs, and pricing strategies, companies attempt to maximize their profits. At the same time, it's imperative to balance the profit motive with other responsibilities, such as being socially responsible and being sustainable in the long run. Profit maximization plays an important role in the financial success of a company, but it should not come at the expense of other goals and objectives essential for the organization.

iii) earnings per share growth.

Earnings per share (EPS) growth is a financial objective that is important for investors and firms alike. The earnings per share growth represents the increase in the earnings that shareholders receive for each share of the company's stock they own. The EPS growth is calculated by dividing the company's net earnings by the total number of shares outstanding. The EPS growth rate is expressed as a percentage and helps investors and firms evaluate the company's performance over time.

EPS growth is a crucial factor considered by investors when making investment decisions. Companies that show consistent EPS growth are considered more favorable because a company with increasing EPS means that the company is financially healthy and generating profits. Higher earnings per share translate to higher dividends paid to shareholders, which makes the company's stock more attractive.

There are several methods companies can use to achieve EPS growth. One of the most common methods is through cost-cutting measures such as reducing overhead expenses or increasing production efficiency. For example, a manufacturing company can reduce production costs by investing in better equipment and technology, leading to increased net earnings and eventually an increase in EPS. Another method is through revenue growth, where firms aim to increase their sales volume or prices to ultimately increase their net earnings. For instance, a company that expands to new markets, introduces innovative products and services, or creates a strong brand image can generate more revenue and subsequently, more earnings.

However, achieving EPS growth is not always an easy task for companies. Factors such as market saturation or competition can have a major impact on a company's growth potential. Additionally, companies need to balance the expectations of investors with the reality of their performance. An overemphasis on EPS growth may lead companies to take risks that may jeopardize long-term sustainability.

In conclusion, EPS growth is a financial objective pursued by firms to increase their profitability and attract potential investors. Companies can achieve EPS growth through cost-cutting measures or revenue growth but must balance the expectations of shareholders with the reality of their performance to maintain long-term sustainability. Overall, EPS growth is an important benchmark for a company's financial success and serves as a key factor in investment decisions.

3. Stakeholders and impact on corporate objectives

Stakeholder Objectives: Range and Identification

Stakeholders are individuals or groups who have an interest in an organization and can influence, or be influenced by, its decisions or actions. A range of stakeholders can impact corporate objectives, and understanding their objectives is critical for companies to develop effective strategies that can maximize shareholder value while minimizing potential conflicts with other stakeholders.

1. Shareholders: Shareholders are the owners of a company and are interested in maximizing their return on investment or maximizing the value of their investments. Their primary objective is to see their investments grow or earn dividends. Shareholders are concerned with how well the company is performing financially, how much profit the company is making, and what their return on investment is.

2. Employees: Employees are key stakeholders of a company and play a vital role in achieving its objectives. They are interested in job security, career growth, compensation, benefits, and work conditions. Employees want to work for a company that values their contributions, respects them, and provides a good work-life balance.

3. Customers: Customers are an essential stakeholder for every business, and their objectives are pretty simple: to get a quality product or service at a reasonable price. Customers also expect value for their money, excellent customer service, and clear communication from companies. Customers can play a crucial role in whether a company succeeds or fails based on their feedback and loyalty.

4. Suppliers: Suppliers are also an instrumental stakeholder in a

company's success or failure. They provide raw materials, equipment, and services to companies, and their objective is to maintain a sustainable relationship with companies that are reliable and consistent in their business practices. Suppliers want to be paid on time and treated fairly by their clients.

5. Government and regulatory bodies: Government and regulatory bodies are stakeholders that have a vested interest in the organization and its operations. Their objectives are to ensure that the company complies with all legal requirements, environmental standards, and ethical practices. In some cases, governments and regulatory bodies can influence corporate objectives by imposing regulations or guidelines.

6. Competitors: Competitors are a major stakeholder in the sense that they can impact a company's market share or profitability if they offer better products or services or perform better than the company. Competitors' objective is to increase their market share, improve their products or services, or reduce costs to outperform their business rivals.

In conclusion, identifying the range of stakeholders and their objectives is essential for companies to develop a well-rounded corporate strategy and maintain positive relationships with stakeholders. Each stakeholder group has different objectives and influences on the organization, and corporate objectives should aim for a balanced and sustainable approach that considers the interests of all stakeholders. Companies that adopt a stakeholder-oriented approach can build strong relationships with stakeholders, mitigate risks, and achieve long-term success.

Stakeholder Objective Conflicts

Stakeholders of a company often have different objectives, and conflicts can arise when their objectives are not compatible with each other. The possible conflict between stakeholder objectives can pose significant risks to the organization's reputation, performance, and financial stability, and need to be managed carefully.

One potential area of conflict is between shareholders and other stakeholders such as employees or the wider community. Shareholder objectives are primarily to maximize profits, dividends and the value of their investments, while employees may prioritize job security, wages, benefits, and work conditions. Shareholders may push for cost-cutting measures, such as layoffs or pay cuts, to improve profits, while employees may resist such tactics. This conflict can have a negative impact on workplace morale, productivity, and ultimately the company's performance.

Another area of conflict is between a company's social responsibility and environmental objectives and the share price or profit objectives of shareholders. For instance, a company may invest in sustainable or renewable technologies that have long-term benefits for the environment but may not generate immediate financial returns. Shareholders may become impatient with such investments, potentially leading to a loss of shareholder value, which can create conflicts between the company's short-term profitability objectives and its long-term goals for sustainability.

Stakeholders can also have differing expectations regarding ethical conduct, particularly in regards to corporate social responsibility. A company may have environmental or social commitments that can conflict with shareholder demands for profit maximization. For example, an oil company may have to make difficult choices between balancing the interests of its shareholders and the wider community in regards to commercial developments or practices that are seen as damaging to the environment.

Additionally, the government and regulatory bodies may also have conflicting objectives with shareholders and companies. Regulatory bodies may be concerned with the environmental impact, consumer safety, or illegitimate business practices that can conflict with corporate objectives such as profit maximization.

In conclusion, there can be conflicts between stakeholder objectives that challenge the organization's long-term sustainability, financial health, or reputation. Successfully managing such conflicts requires companies to either align stakeholder interests as much as possible or prioritize stakeholders in a way that minimizes negative consequences. Effective communication, collaboration, and negotiation can be crucial tools to reduce conflict and improve stakeholder engagement. Ultimately, companies that can balance competing stakeholder objectives, while maintaining their core values and executing a well-considered corporate strategy, will reap long-term benefits, such as stronger reputations, increased profitability, and sustained growth, and create superior shareholder value.

Management and Stakeholders: Agency Theory

Management plays a crucial role in meeting the diverse objectives of stakeholders. To achieve this, managers must balance the objectives of different stakeholders while pursuing the overall strategic goals of the organization. In this context, the application of agency theory can guide management in meeting stakeholder objectives through the alignment of interests between the various stakeholders.

Agency theory is a framework that describes the relationship between principals (the stakeholders) and agents (the management) in an organization. According to agency theory, management acts as agents on behalf of the stakeholders, and their interests should be aligned with those of the stakeholders. In this way, management can make decisions that benefit all stakeholders and promote the long-term success of the organization.

To meet stakeholder objectives, management must identify the needs and expectations of each stakeholder group and integrate them into the organization's overall strategy. One way to do this is to prioritize stakeholders based on their relative importance to the organization. For example, management could prioritize shareholders' goals by emphasizing profits while ensuring that the interests of other stakeholders, such as employees or the environment, are not compromised.

Furthermore, agency theory suggests that aligning incentives and compensation is critical for providing management with a sense of accountability to stakeholders. This approach can encourage management to make decisions that maximize stakeholder value, which is fundamental to the long-term success of the organization. For example, managers may be awarded performance-based bonuses, based on metrics that reflect the company's social, environmental, and economic goals.

Moreover, management can also monitor and report engagement with stakeholders through regular communication, reporting disclosure, and accountability procedures. Open communication enables management to understand the diverse needs and expectations of stakeholders, and to respond to any conflict of interest promptly. For example, providing timely reports to regulatory bodies can provide evidence of effective stakeholder engagement and aid regulatory compliance.

In conclusion, the role of management in meeting stakeholder objectives is crucial for the long-term success of any business. Management must align incentives, communicate regularly with stakeholders, and prioritize stakeholder goals to create and maintain a sustainable relationship that supports the company's strategic goals. The application of agency theory, along with other stakeholder theories, can be a useful framework to guide management's decision-making process when dealing with various stakeholder groups. Ultimately, the key to success is the ability of management to balance competing stakeholder interests while executing a sound corporate strategy.

Measuring Corporate Achievement

i) Ratio Analysis for Corporate Achievement

Ratio analysis is a useful tool for measuring the achievement of corporate objectives. It involves analyzing different financial ratios that provide insight into the company's performance, financial position, and profitability. Some of the commonly used ratios for analyzing corporate objectives include return on capital employed, return on equity, earnings per share, and dividend per share.

1. Return on Capital Employed (ROCE): ROCE is an essential ratio that measures how efficiently a company utilizes its capital to generate a profit. ROCE is calculated by dividing earnings before interest and taxes (EBIT) by total capital employed. The ratio indicates how much profit a company generates per unit of capital. The higher the ROCE, the better the company is performing.

2. Return on Equity (ROE): ROE measures how effectively a company is using its equity to generate profit. The ratio is calculated by dividing net income by shareholders' equity. A high ROE means that the company is generating a significant return for shareholders, and investors expect to receive higher returns in the future.

3. Earnings Per Share (EPS): EPS is a vital ratio that measures the amount of profit earned for each outstanding share of a company's common stock. The ratio is calculated by dividing net income by the total number of outstanding shares of common stock. EPS provides valuable insights into the earning power of a company.

4. Dividend Per Share (DPS): DPS is the amount of cash paid per share to common shareholders as dividends. The ratio is calculated by dividing the total dividend paid by the total number of outstanding shares of common stock. DPS is an indicator of the amount of cash that

a company returns to its shareholders.

By analyzing different ratio metrics, a company can identify trends and patterns that help them understand its financial health, identify areas of strength, and pinpoint areas that require improvement. For instance, if ROCE is decreasing while other ratios remain stable, it may indicate ineffective capital utilization.

Moreover, by comparing these ratios to industry benchmarks or historical data, companies can establish whether they are performing well compared to their peers. This data helps senior executives make informed decisions and, if necessary, recalibrate their strategies to improve performance in specific areas.

In conclusion, ratio analysis is a critical tool that can help companies measure their achievement of corporate objectives. The different ratios, such as ROCE, ROE, EPS, and DPS provide valuable insights into the performance, profitability, and financial health of a company. Accordingly, it is essential to undertake a thorough analysis of these ratios regularly to understand how the business is performing and make informed decisions to capitalize on strengths and address weaknesses.

ii) Changes in Dividends and Share Prices as Part of Total Shareholder Return

Measuring achievement of corporate objectives is an essential aspect of evaluating the effectiveness of a company's strategic plans. There are various ways to measure the success of corporate objectives, and one of the common approaches is to assess the changes in dividends and share prices as part of total shareholder return.

Total shareholder return (TSR) is the total return received by a shareholder through stock price appreciation, dividends, and other distributions. TSR provides a measure of how much money an investor has made on their shares over a certain period, including both capital appreciation and income.

Dividends are an important component of TSR, and companies that pay consistent and growing dividends tend to attract more investors. Companies that consistently increase their dividends signal financial strength and operational efficiency, which translates to confidence in the management team's performance. As a result, the shareholders benefit from the positive market sentiment, leading to increased share prices and higher total shareholder returns.

Share prices are also an important indicator of the company's performance, and the changes in the stock prices reflect the market's confidence in the firm's future prospects. A rising share price is an indication that investors are optimistic about the company's future profitability and growth prospects. This optimism is often based on the company's ability to deliver on its objectives, producing stronger financial results, which translate to higher shareholder returns.

For example, consider a pharmaceutical company that invests in research and development in the hope of bringing new drugs to market. The company's strategic objective might be to develop new drugs and increase its market share. If the company achieves its objective, it is likely to generate higher earnings and increased profits. This, in turn, is likely to lead to higher shareholder returns in the form of increased dividends and higher share prices.

In conclusion, changes in dividends and share prices as part of total shareholder return are two essential measures for evaluating the achievement of corporate objectives. Companies that pay consistent dividends and have a rising share price tend to attract more investors, which translates to higher total shareholder returns. Monitoring these metrics closely can provide insight and help management teams make informed decisions to achieve their objectives.

e) Encouraging Stakeholder Objectives Achievement

i) Managerial Reward Schemes for Stakeholder Objectives

The achievement of stakeholder objectives is a vital aspect of corporate governance. Stakeholders, including employees, shareholders, customers, and suppliers, all have different objectives, and it is important to ensure that these objectives are being met by the company. Managerial reward schemes, such as share options and performance-related pay, can encourage the achievement of stakeholder objectives.

Share options are a type of incentive plan that allows employees to purchase company shares at a specific price. The employees who are eligible for these options typically have a vested interest in the company's success and achievement of stakeholder objectives. By providing share options to managers and other employees, companies can motivate them to work towards achieving the objectives that benefit all stakeholders, including shareholders, employees, and customers.

A performance-related pay scheme is another technique that can encourage the achievement of stakeholder objectives. This type of reward system is based on the employee's performance and how well the company has achieved its objectives. The employees who perform well and contribute to the success of the company are rewarded with bonuses or other compensation that is linked to the company's performance. This type of reward system can encourage employees to work hard and to take ownership of their role in achieving the company's objectives.

For example, a company whose primary objective is to increase customer satisfaction may use a performance-related pay scheme to incentivize customer service employees. If the company is successful in improving customer satisfaction, the employees who contribute to this success can receive performance-based bonuses. This approach ensures that employees feel invested in the company's success and that they work hard to achieve the company's objectives.

In conclusion, managerial reward schemes are an effective way to encourage the achievement of stakeholder objectives. By providing incentives such as share options and performance-related pay, companies can motivate their employees to work towards achieving the company's objectives, which benefits all stakeholders. Carefully designed reward schemes can align the interests of employees, shareholders and the other stakeholders, creating a win-win situation. It is important to ensure that the reward schemes are aligned with the company's long-term goals and values to avoid any short-term focus at the expense of the company's sustainability.

ii) Regulatory Requirements for Encouraging Stakeholder Objectives

Encouraging the achievement of stakeholder objectives is one of the primary responsibilities of any company's management. Consequently, regulatory requirements such as corporate governance codes of best practices and stock exchange listing regulations set by governing bodies can go a long way in promoting corporations' commitment to achieving these objectives.

Corporate governance codes of best practice outline the principles of good governance and best practice standards that companies should adopt. These guidelines ensure that the company's management has a framework that enables them to balance competing stakeholder interests and enhances their long-term value creation. These codes address issues such as board structure, risk management, executive compensation, and stakeholder engagement. By complying with these codes, companies can promote transparency and accountability, which helps to gain the trust of stakeholders.

Stock exchange listing regulations are another way that regulators can promote corporate accountability to stakeholder objectives. These regulations are set in place to ensure that companies listed on the stock exchange maintain good governance standards and adhere to disclosure requirements. By listing on a stock exchange, the company is making a commitment to operate transparently and in accordance with high standards of governance. Some of the regulations that contribute to achieving stakeholder objectives include the requirement to publish financial reports regularly, disclose significant corporate events, and maintain a board remuneration policy that aligns with the interests of shareholders.

For example, the UK Corporate Governance Code, developed by the Financial Reporting Council (FRC), provides a framework for companies to adhere to regarding corporate governance. The code advocates for the effective engagement with stakeholders, including shareholders, employees, customers, suppliers, and communities, and provides guidance on board structures that can ensure that competing stakeholder interests are balanced.

In conclusion, regulatory requirements such as corporate governance codes of best practice and stock exchange listing regulations are vital tools for promoting accountability and encouraging the achievement of stakeholder objectives. These regulations provide guidance on what good corporate governance entails and help companies adopt best practices. While compliance with these regulations does not guarantee that a company will always meet its stakeholders' objectives, they establish a framework of ethical principles, transparency and accountability that will create trust among stakeholders ultimately. By aligning their activities with stakeholder interests, companies can gain a competitive advantage and enhance their long-term sustainability.

Financial management environment

The economic environment for business

Main Macroeconomic Policy Targets

The economic environment is the framework in which businesses operate. It is comprised of various macroeconomic variables such as inflation, interest rates, exchange rates, and employment levels. Governments and central banks use macroeconomic policies to achieve specific targets in the economy. In this context, this essay identifies and explains the main macroeconomic policy targets.

Macroeconomic policy targets are the broad goals that governments and central banks set to guide their interventions in the economy. The main macroeconomic policy targets include:

1. Price Stability:

Price stability refers to the level of inflation in the economy. Governments and central banks aim to achieve low and stable inflation rates to ensure that prices of goods and services remain stable. High inflation rates can create economic uncertainty, reduce investment, reduce purchasing power, and lower the standard of living. For example, to maintain price stability, central banks may increase interest rates, which reduces borrowing and spending, thus curbing inflation.

2. Full Employment:

The full employment goal seeks to ensure that there are enough job opportunities available for all who wish to work. High levels of employment contribute to the growth of the economy by increasing consumption and improving living standards. Through macroeconomic policies such as fiscal policies, governments can create job opportunities by investing in public infrastructure, providing tax incentives to businesses, and offering programs that promote entrepreneurship.

3. Economic Growth:

Economic growth represents the increase in the production and output of goods and services in an economy. Governments aim to achieve sustainable economic growth rates to improve living standards, job opportunities, and returns on investments. Macroeconomic policies such as monetary and fiscal policies can be used to stimulate economic growth by increasing money supply, reducing taxes, or increasing government spending.

4. External Balance:

International trade plays a vital role in the economy. Maintaining external balance seeks to ensure that exports and imports remain balanced. Governments aim to achieve a balance in the current account balance while enhancing economic growth. For example, exchange rate policies can be used to improve export competitiveness, boosting economic growth while maintaining external balance.

In summary, macroeconomic policy targets are set by governments and central banks to guide their interventions and manage the performance of the economy. The primary macroeconomic policy targets include price stability, full employment, economic growth, and external balance. Effective macroeconomic policies that achieve these targets promote economic stability, increase investment, boost consumption and improve the overall living standards in the society.

Fiscal, Monetary, Interest Rate, and Exchange Rate Policies in Macroeconomic Policy Targets

When it comes to achieving macroeconomic policy targets, fiscal, monetary, interest rate, and exchange rate policies all play a critical role. These policies are enacted by governmental authorities to influence the overall performance of the economy.

Fiscal policy refers to the use of government spending and taxation to regulate the economy. When the government increases its spending, it puts more money into circulation, which can have a positive effect on economic growth. On the other hand, when the government increases taxes, it reduces disposable income, which can slow down the economy. Fiscal policy can be used to promote job creation, stabilize prices, and encourage economic growth. For example, during the 2008 financial crisis, the US government implemented a fiscal stimulus package that included tax rebates and infrastructure spending to boost economic activity.

Monetary policy is the process of controlling the money supply and interest rates to achieve macroeconomic objectives. Central banks, such as the Federal Reserve in the US, use monetary policy to influence interest rates, which can affect borrowing, lending, and investment decisions. The Federal Reserve can decrease interest rates to encourage borrowing and business investment, which can stimulate economic growth. Conversely, the central bank can increase interest rates to control inflation and slow down an overheating economy. For instance, in response to the COVID-19 pandemic, the US Federal Reserve lowered interest rates to near zero in an effort to increase borrowing and stimulate the economy.

Interest rate policy refers to the manipulation of interest rates to influence economic growth. By adjusting interest rates, central banks can boost economic activity or slow down inflation. A lower interest rate stimulates lending, spending, and investment, whereas a higher interest rate makes borrowing more expensive, which can slow down economic activity. For example, a country experiencing high inflation may increase interest rates to control inflation, while a country experiencing declining economic growth may reduce interest rates to stimulate economic activity.

Exchange rate policy refers to the management of a country's currency to achieve macroeconomic objectives. A country with a weak currency may want to strengthen its currency to reduce the cost of imported goods and services, while a country with a strong currency may want to maintain that strength to encourage foreign investment. For example, China actively manages its currency to keep its value artificially low, which makes its exports cheaper and more attractive to foreign buyers.

In conclusion, fiscal, monetary, interest rate, and exchange rate policies all play an essential role in achieving macroeconomic policy targets. These policies, which are often implemented through the actions of central banks and governments, are vital tools in regulating the overall performance of the economy. When used effectively, they can promote job creation, stabilize prices, encourage economic growth, and control inflation.

Government Economic Policy and Planning/Decision-making in Business

Government economic policy plays a crucial role in shaping the business environment. As businesses operate within a larger economic context, they are inevitably impacted by the government's economic policies. In turn, businesses can also influence government economic policy through political lobbying and advocacy.

Businesses must consider government policies and regulations when making planning and decision-making in order to stay compliant with the law while also achieving their own goals.

For instance, government policies and regulations can significantly impact business operations in many areas. For example, policies related to environmental protection and labor laws may restrict business operations, increasing operational costs or reducing the potential for profit. Furthermore, trade policies, such as tariffs or quotas, can change the cost of importing raw materials or exporting finished products, affecting the supply chain and price points.

In addition, government policies can impact market demand for certain products or services. For example, legislation that promotes renewable energy can encourage businesses to develop new technology and invest in green energy production.

On the other hand, government investment in certain sectors or industries can also provide new opportunities for businesses. Governments may incentivize businesses to invest in specific areas that are deemed to benefit the national interest. For example, a government may provide tax breaks for businesses that invest in research and development or offer subsidies to industries important to national security.

Moreover, businesses can also influence government economic policy. For instance, businesses may engage in political lobbying to influence policymakers, and provide feedback on government policies or regulatory changes that impact their operations.

In conclusion, government economic policies can significantly impact planning and decision-making in business. Businesses need to be aware of, and comply with, government policies and regulations that pertain to their operations. They must also be proactive in engaging with policymakers and shaping government policy to benefit their interests, ultimately promoting economic growth, and creating a stable and competitive business environment.

Planning and Decision-Making in Business

Competition Policy

The need for competition policy arises from the recognition that competition is a critical driver of economic growth and innovation. Without effective competition, businesses may engage in anti-competitive behavior that can harm consumers, restrict innovation, and distort markets. Competition policy is enforced by regulatory agencies to ensure that competition is fair and open and that businesses operate within the confines of the law.

Competition policy interacts with planning and decision-making in business in various ways. By enforcing rules that regulate market structures and conduct, competition policy creates a level playing field, enabling businesses to compete on merit rather than through anti-competitive practices. This promotes decision-making that is focused on the provision of high-quality goods and services, rather than on anti-competitive manipulation or exploitation.

Businesses must also consider competition policy when making planning and decision-making. For instance, if a business is considering a merger with another firm, it must take into account the potential impact of the merger on competition in the market. A merger that significantly reduces competition could be blocked by regulatory authorities. Similarly, businesses must comply with competition law and regulations to avoid sanctions or legal action.

In application, competition policy can help prevent businesses from dominating a market and exploiting their position to the detriment of customers. Regulatory agencies can investigate complaints of anti-competitive behavior such as price fixing, monopolistic collusion, and abuse of dominant market position, and impose measures such as fines, remedies, or divestitures as necessary.

An example of competition policy in action is the European Commission's investigation of large technology companies for potential anti-competitive practices. The commission is examining whether these companies have abused their market power to unfairly restrict competition in areas such as online advertising or app stores. If the commission finds evidence of anti-competitive behavior, it could impose penalties or require changes to the companies' business practices.

In conclusion, competition policy is an essential component of creating a healthy business environment. Its enforcement enables businesses to compete on merit and without anti-competitive behavior. It is critical for businesses to consider competition policy when making planning and decision-making, and to comply with competition law and regulations to avoid legal action. Ultimately, competition policy helps foster innovation, economic growth, and consumer welfare.

Government Assistance for Business

The need for government assistance for business arises from the recognition that businesses may require additional support or resources to achieve their goals or stay competitive. This support can come in various forms, such as grants, tax incentives, subsidies, or loans.

Government assistance for business interacts with planning and decision-making in business in several ways. For instance, businesses can use government assistance to help finance research and development, expand their operations, or adopt new technologies. This assistance can also help businesses through difficult periods or economic downturns.

Government assistance can also impact planning and decision-making by incentivizing businesses to invest in certain industries, regions, or activities. For example, a government may provide tax incentives to businesses that invest in renewable energy, while another may offer subsidies to promote employment growth in a particular region. These incentives can encourage businesses to make decisions based on the perceived benefits of operating in certain sectors or regions.

In application, government assistance can come in different forms, depending on the needs of businesses and the priorities of policymakers. For instance, in response to the COVID-19 pandemic, many governments provided financial assistance to small businesses affected by the economic fallout of the pandemic. This assistance included grants, loans, and wage subsidies to help businesses remain open and retain workers.

Another example is the US government's small business administration (SBA) that provides assistance to small businesses to help them grow and expand operations. The SBA provides loan guarantees, counseling, and education services to help businesses better understand the market and the risks involved in growing their operations.

Businesses need to consider government assistance when making planning and decision-making because it can impact their operations, growth potential, and profitability. For instance, businesses need to consider the eligibility criteria for assistance, the type of support provided, and the potential obligations associated with receiving government assistance such as meeting compliance requirements.

In conclusion, government assistance can play a vital role in helping businesses grow and remain competitive. Its provision helps businesses through difficult periods, incentivizes investment in priority areas, and fosters economic growth. However, businesses must consider the terms and conditions associated with assistance to make informed decisions about their operations and growth ambitions.

Green Policies and Sustainability

The need for green policies and sustainability in business arises from the recognition that businesses have a responsibility to contribute to a sustainable future. This means operating in a way that minimizes negative environmental impacts while promoting social welfare and economic growth. Green policies and sustainability require businesses to develop strategies that consider the long-term effects of their activities on the environment, society, and the economy.

Green policies and sustainability interact with planning and decision-making in business in various ways. For instance, businesses must consider environmental impacts when developing new products or services. This requires analyzing the potential effects of their activities on the environment, including energy use, water consumption, greenhouse gas emissions, and waste generation. Based on this analysis, businesses can make informed decisions about the feasibility, profitability, and environmental impact of their activities.

Green policies and sustainability can also impact planning and decision-making by influencing business strategy development. Businesses can use sustainability as a basis for developing competitive advantages or improving operational efficiency. For example, a business that reduces energy consumption and greenhouse gas emissions may achieve cost savings and improved reputation compared to a competitor that does not prioritize sustainability.

In application, green policies and sustainability can come in different forms, such as the development of circular economies, cleaner production processes, and sustainable sourcing of materials. Businesses can also adopt environmental management systems, such as ISO 14001, to monitor and reduce their environmental impact.

An example of green policies and sustainability in action is the European Union's Circular Economy Action Plan, which aims to promote more sustainable production and consumption patterns within the EU. This includes measures such as promoting extended producer responsibility, reducing waste, and encouraging the re-use and recycling of materials.

In conclusion, green policies and sustainability are increasingly important for businesses. They require businesses to consider the long-term environmental, social, and economic impact of their activities, and to develop strategies that align with sustainability goals. In doing so, businesses can enhance their reputation, achieve cost savings, and develop competitive advantages while contributing to the well-being of society and the environment.

Corporate Governance Regulation

Corporate governance regulation refers to the rules and guidelines that companies must follow to ensure transparency, accountability, and ethical behavior in their decision-making processes. It is a critical component of business planning and decision-making, serving as a framework for ensuring that companies operate in the best interests of their stakeholders, including shareholders, employees, customers, and the wider community.

One of the primary needs for corporate governance regulation is the prevention of unethical behavior and the protection of stakeholders' interests. In the absence of such regulation, companies may act in ways that benefit a small group of individuals or pursue short-term gains at the expense of long-term sustainability. This can result in reputational damage, economic instability, and a loss of public trust.

Proper corporate governance also supports decision-making by ensuring that companies have a clear framework for assessing risks and opportunities while staying within established ethical and legal boundaries. This helps to prevent poor decision-making and can lead to better outcomes for the company and its stakeholders.

Regulation also provides a clear set of guidelines for companies to follow, which can help achieve a more level playing field for all organizations, regardless of size or industry. This can serve as an equalizer and encourage a more competitive business environment that promotes innovation, productivity, and a focus on creating value for all stakeholders.

Corporate governance regulation often includes codes of ethics, laws, and regulations at both the national and international levels. For example, laws such as the Sarbanes-Oxley Act in the United States, the ASX Corporate Governance Principles in Australia, and the UK Corporate Governance Code all aim to promote transparency, accountability and responsibility in decision-making while discouraging fraudulent activities.

In conclusion, corporate governance regulation plays a vital role in business planning and decision-making by providing a framework for ethical behavior, accountability, transparency, and risk management. With the right regulatory environment in place, companies can operate more efficiently, effectively, and sustainably, benefitting all involved.

2. The Nature and Role of Financial Markets and Institutions

Nature and Role of Money and Capital Markets

Money and capital markets are two significant parts of the financial market, and they play a crucial role in the functioning of the economy. These markets are essential in facilitating the flow of capital between savers and investors and providing access to financing for individuals and companies.

Money markets refer to the financial markets for short-term borrowing and lending, typically for a duration of fewer than 12 months. Money markets provide liquidity to financial institutions or corporations with short-term funding needs. Participants in the money market can include banks, governments, and corporations, among others. The primary function of the money market is to facilitate the short-term borrowing and lending of funds between participants at competitive interest rates.

Capital markets, on the other hand, refer to the financial markets for long-term borrowing and lending. These are the markets that provide companies with access to equity and debt financing through the issuance of stocks, bonds, and other securities. Participants in capital markets include investors, corporations, governments, and other institutions. Capital markets help companies to raise large amounts of capital over longer terms to support their operations, expansion plans or to finance infrastructure, among others.

In the national context, the role of money and capital markets is to facilitate the efficient allocation of capital within a country's borders. By providing liquidity to financial institutions and facilitating access to financing for companies, the markets can help to promote economic growth and development. For example, effective functioning of the money market plays a crucial role in ensuring an adequate supply of credit to individuals and businesses, keeping the cost of borrowing low, and ensuring that interest rate fluctuations are kept in check.

In the international context, the role of money and capital markets is to facilitate international trade and investment. The international capital markets provide a platform for companies to access financing from investors around the world. The foreign exchange market, for example, facilitates global transactions by providing a medium for the exchange of one currency for another, reducing the risk and cost of cross-border transactions.

Moreover, the bond market provides governments and corporations with access to financing from global investors, enabling poorer countries and companies to borrow at lower interest rates than they might obtain locally.

In conclusion, money and capital markets play a critical role in the functioning of the economy, both nationally and globally. By providing liquidity and facilitating access to financing for individuals and corporations, these markets support economic growth, development, and international trade. Their efficient functioning is vital in promoting economic stability while ensuring that financial markets remain fair and transparent for all participants.

The crucial role of Financial Intermediaries in financial markets

Financial intermediaries play a crucial role in facilitating the flow of funds between savers and borrowers in financial markets. They act as a link between the two parties by collecting funds from savers and reallocating them to borrowers who need capital to finance their business operations, investments, or other expenses.
Essentially, financial intermediaries are institutions that channel funds from parties with a surplus of funds (e.g. savers) to parties with a shortage of funds (e.g. borrowers). These intermediaries include banks, credit unions, insurance companies, mutual funds, and pension funds, among others.

One key role of financial intermediaries is risk management. They pool the money of many savers to create a diversified portfolio of investments, reducing the risk for each individual saver. They also use their expertise and resources to conduct risk assessments for borrowers, thereby reducing the risk of loan defaults.

Furthermore, financial intermediaries provide a range of financial services, such as deposit-taking, loans, insurance, and investment products. For example, banks receive deposits from savers and offer loans to borrowers, earning income on the difference between the interest rates charged on loans and paid on deposits. Insurance companies offer policies that protect individuals and businesses against financial losses. Mutual funds pool the investments of many individuals to purchase a diversified portfolio of securities, providing investors with access to a wider range of investment options.

Financial intermediaries also play a critical role in promoting economic growth and development. By channeling funds efficiently to profitable investments, they help to finance new technologies, businesses, and infrastructure, which can create jobs and stimulate economic activity.

In summary, financial intermediaries are essential players in financial markets, providing critical services such as risk management, financial intermediation, and promoting economic development. They play a vital role in ensuring efficient allocation of capital, which is crucial for the growth and stability of an economy.

The Functions of Stock and Corporate Bond Markets in Financial Markets

Stock markets and corporate bond markets are two of the most important financial markets, which offer various financial instruments for investors to invest in. In this section, we will explain the functions of both markets.

The primary function of a stock market is to provide a platform for companies to raise capital by selling shares of their stock to investors. When a company issues equity shares, it is essentially selling a part of its ownership in exchange for capital. Investors who purchase these shares are entitled to a portion of the profits of the company, known as dividends, as well as to vote in shareholder meetings to make decisions about the company's future.

Besides, stock markets offer investors the opportunity to buy and sell shares of publicly traded companies easily. This is in contrast to private companies, where it is harder to sell shares or acquire them as they are not traded on stock markets. With stock markets, investors can quickly buy or sell shares at any time during market hours. This provides investors with liquidity, which is the ease with which they can convert their investments into cash.

On the other hand, corporate bond markets are debt markets that allow corporations to issue bonds to raise capital. Corporate bonds are debt instruments that pay investors a fixed rate of interest on a regular basis, with the principal amount repaid upon maturity. The primary function of corporate bond markets is to provide companies with access to capital from a broad range of investors at a lower cost than bank loans. For investors, corporate bonds offer a relatively low-risk investment with a predictable return.

The corporate bond market also provides flexibility in terms of the type of bonds a company can issue. For example, companies can issue bonds with different maturities, ranging from short-term bonds with a maturity of less than one year to longer-term bonds with a maturity of 10 or more years. Companies can also issue bonds with different levels of risk, from investment-grade bonds to high-yield or junk bonds.

Overall, both stock and corporate bond markets play important roles in the financial system. By providing companies with access to capital while also offering investors a range of financial instruments to choose from, these markets help to support business growth and stability in the economy.

Understanding the Nature and Features of Securities in Relation to the Risk/Return Trade-Off

The financial securities market is a crucial component of the financial system, providing individuals and institutions with investment opportunities to find the right balance between risk and reward. The trade-off between risk and return is a concept that is central to understanding the nature and features of different securities.
In general, securities with higher risk levels typically offer higher returns, while securities with lower risk levels offer lower returns. This is because investors require compensation for taking on additional risk.

One type of security is stocks or equities. Stocks represent ownership in a company, and their values fluctuate based on factors like the company's performance, industry conditions, and broader economic trends. Investing in stocks can offer the potential for high returns, but also comes with a high level of risk. Because the value of the stock can fluctuate widely, investors need to be prepared to tolerate substantial losses if the investment does not perform well.

Another type of security is bonds. A bond is a debt instrument that represents a loan from the bondholder to the borrower, which is typically a company or government. Bonds can offer investors a lower-risk investment than stocks, but also typically have lower returns. Investors earn interest payments from bonds, and the bondholder is repaid the face value of the bond at its maturity.

Government bonds are typically lower risk than corporate or municipal bonds, as the risk of the government defaulting on its obligations is perceived to be lower. However, the returns on government bonds are generally lower than on corporate or municipal bonds.

Other types of securities include options, futures, and derivatives. These are financial contracts whose value is derived from the underlying assets such as stocks, bonds, or commodities. These securities are riskier than traditional stocks or bonds, but they can offer investors the potential for higher returns.

In summary, the nature and features of different securities have a significant impact on the risk/return trade-off. Higher-risk securities generally offer higher returns, while lower-risk securities offer lower returns. By understanding the characteristics and performance of different securities, investors can make informed decisions about how to balance their portfolios and optimize the risk/return trade-off.

The Transformative Impact of Fintech on the Nature and Role of Financial Markets and Institutions

Fintech refers to the use of technology and innovation in financial services. In recent years, the impact of fintech has been significant, changing the nature and role of financial markets and institutions by disrupting traditional business models, improving customer experience, and increasing access to financial services.

One of the most significant impacts of fintech has been to democratize financial markets and institutions. Fintech companies have created new digital platforms that offer financial services at a lower cost and with greater convenience, such as peer-to-peer lending, crowdfunding, and digital payments. These platforms enable access to financial services to previously underserved markets, such as small businesses, low-income households, and emerging economies.

Moreover, fintech has also facilitated innovation in financial markets and institutions. For example, robo-advisory services have emerged as a new, automated form of investment management, utilizing artificial intelligence (AI) and machine learning to provide personalized recommendations at a lower cost than traditional financial advisors. Blockchain technology, the underlying technology behind cryptocurrencies like Bitcoin, has the potential to revolutionize the way financial transactions are conducted, offering faster, cheaper, and more secure transactions.

Another key impact of fintech is that it has enhanced the customer experience in financial services. Fintech companies are leveraging technologies like mobile apps, digital wallets, and chatbots to provide 24/7 customer service, simplified account management, and personalized recommendations. This personalized experience is crucial in building customer trust and loyalty, which is essential in a highly competitive financial market.

Finally, fintech has also posed challenges for traditional financial institutions, which must adapt to remain competitive in the market.

Large banks, for example, have responded by developing their own fintech capabilities, investing in startups, or acquiring existing fintech firms. By improving their digital platforms, banks can offer better customer experiences, reduce costs, and increase efficiency.

In summary, fintech has had a significant impact on changing the nature and role of financial markets and institutions. By democratizing access to financial services, fostering innovation, and improving customer experience, fintech has opened up new opportunities while also posing challenges for traditional financial institutions.

The Nature and Role of Money Markets

The Essential Role of Money Markets in Providing Short-Term Liquidity to Private and Public Sectors

Money markets are an essential component of the global financial system, providing a platform for short-term borrowing and lending between financial institutions, companies, and governments. The primary role of money markets is to provide short-term liquidity to the private and public sectors to help meet their immediate funding needs. The private sector uses money markets to finance their operations and manage their short-term cash flow needs. Financial institutions like banks and corporations use money market instruments such as commercial paper, certificates of deposit, and repurchase agreements to borrow funds at low-interest rates. This allows them to meet their short-term funding needs, expand their business operations, or invest in new opportunities.

For example, a corporation could issue commercial paper, which is a type of unsecured, short-term debt instrument that is sold to investors. By issuing commercial paper, the corporation can raise funds that can be used to finance its day-to-day operations, such as paying suppliers or employees, without having to resort to more expensive sources of funding.

Similarly, governments also use money markets to finance their short-term funding needs, such as managing their deficits or financing the day-to-day operations of their government. Governments issue treasury bills, which are short-term debt securities that are used to fund government operations. Treasury bills are considered safe, low-risk investments because they are backed by the full faith and credit of the government, and are therefore popular investments for individuals, corporations, and other financial institutions.

Besides, money markets play a crucial role in providing short-term liquidity to financial institutions during times of market stress. In periods of financial turmoil, interbank lending may become more challenging, making it more expensive for institutions to borrow funds. Money markets provide an alternative source of funding for these institutions, allowing them to manage their liquidity needs and maintain their business operations.

In summary, money markets play a critical role in providing short-term liquidity to the private and public sectors, helping them manage their cash flow needs and fund their operations. The instruments traded in these markets, such as commercial paper, certificates of deposits, and treasury bills, offer borrowers low-cost, short-term funding options while providing investors with a safe and liquid investment option.

The Role of Money Markets in Providing Cost-Effective Short-Term Trade Finance

The money markets play a crucial role in facilitating global trade by providing short-term trade finance. Trade finance refers to the financing of international trade transactions and is essential for businesses that import and export goods and services. The primary function of money markets in trade finance is to provide short-term loans to companies for the purpose of managing their working capital needs.

Money market instruments such as commercial paper, certificates of deposit, and bankers' acceptances provide companies with a cost-effective way to raise short-term funding. These instruments are typically issued for terms ranging from a few days to several months, making them ideal for financing trade transactions that have a relatively short maturity.

For example, a manufacturer that imports raw materials from overseas can use a bankers' acceptance to finance the transaction. A bankers' acceptance is a short-term draft issued by a bank on behalf of a customer that represents the bank's promise to pay a specified amount on a specified date. The importer can use the bankers' acceptance to pay the exporter for the goods, and then repay the loan when they sell the finished products.

Likewise, companies that export goods can also use money market instruments to finance their operations. Exporters can use commercial paper to raise funds to cover the cost of producing and shipping their products. By issuing commercial paper, exporters can finance their operations without having to rely on more expensive sources of funding such as traditional bank loans.

Moreover, the money markets also provide a platform for currency exchange transactions that are essential for international trade. Trade finance transactions often involve multiple currencies, and exchange rates can fluctuate significantly. The money markets provide a way for companies to exchange currencies at competitive rates, thereby mitigating the risks associated with fluctuations in exchange rates.

In summary, the money markets play a crucial role in providing short-term trade finance to companies engaged in international trade. The instruments traded in these markets, such as commercial paper and bankers' acceptances, offer cost-effective sources of funding for trade transactions. With the help of money market instruments, businesses can efficiently manage their working capital needs and achieve their trade financing objectives.

The Role of Money Markets in Allowing an Organization to Manage its Exposure to Foreign Currency Risk and Interest Rate Risk

Introduction: The money market is a crucial component of the financial system, as it serves as a platform for short-term borrowing and lending of funds between financial institutions and corporations. The money markets facilitate efficient and effective management of financial resources and liquidity in the economy. This article aims to discuss how the money markets can be utilized to manage exposure to foreign currency and interest rate risks.

Role of Money Markets in Managing Foreign Currency Risk:

Foreign currency risk arises due to the impact of exchange rate fluctuations on the value of an organization's assets, liabilities, and cash flows when converted into domestic currency. One way to manage foreign exchange risk is through the use of money markets. The money markets allow companies to borrow foreign currencies to fund international transactions and to issue commercial paper denominated in foreign currencies. This allows companies to match their liabilities in the same currency as their revenue sources.

For instance, consider a US-based company outsourcing production to China. The company will incur expenses in Chinese Yuan and will have to convert US dollars to Chinese Yuan to pay bills. If the US dollar strengthens against the Yuan, the company will bear a loss. To mitigate this risk, the company can borrow Chinese Yuan from the money market and use this to pay its expenses. Thus, by using the money market, the company can reduce its foreign currency risk.

Role of Money Markets in Managing Interest Rate Risk:

Interest rate risk is the risk of loss arising from fluctuations in interest rates. Organizations face interest rate risk when they borrow funds on a variable interest rate basis or when they have investments generating cash flows at a fixed rate of interest. Money markets are helpful in managing interest rate risk through various instruments.

One of these instruments is interest rate swaps, which enable firms to exchange a fixed rate of interest for a variable rate of interest or vice versa. Companies can use interest rate swaps to manage their exposure to interest rate risk, with the goal of achieving financial flexibility. For example, if a company has issued debt with floating rate interest payments, it may seek to reduce its interest rate exposure by entering into interest rate swaps to exchange the floating rate payments for fixed rate payments.

Conclusion:

The effective management of foreign currency and interest rate risks is critical for companies to maintain their financial stability and profitability. Money markets serve as a vital platform for managing such risks, providing companies with flexibility and cost-effective ways to access short-term funding and enter into derivative transactions such as foreign currency and interest swaps. By utilizing money markets to manage risks, companies can concentrate on their core business activities while maintaining financial stability.

Role of Banks and Financial Institutions in the Operation of Money Markets

Money markets are an integral part of the financial market that deals with short-term borrowing and lending of funds. In this market, financial instruments such as treasury bills, certificates of deposits, commercial paper, and repurchase agreements are traded. Banks and other financial institutions play a significant role in the operation of the money markets. Banks play a vital role in providing the necessary liquidity for the money markets. They lend and borrow funds from the market, acting as intermediaries between the investors and borrowers. Banks act as a source of funding for deposits and lend funds to borrowers in the form of loans. The interbank market is an example of the money market where banks lend to each other to manage their short-term liquidity needs.

Financial institutions also play an important role in the money markets by providing a range of financial products and services to investors and borrowers. These institutions include mutual funds, brokerage firms, hedge funds and insurance companies. They provide a range of financial instruments such as money market funds, commercial paper, and certificates of deposit.

Money market funds are mutual funds that invest in a range of short-term securities such as treasury bills and commercial paper. These funds are an attractive investment for small investors as they provide easy liquidity and low-risk investment opportunities.

Commercial paper is another important instrument traded in the money markets. It is an unsecured promissory note issued by companies to raise short-term funds. Banks actively participate in the trading of commercial paper by providing liquidity to the companies by purchasing the notes.

Repurchase agreements or repos are short-term loans in which a borrower pledges a security to a lender and agrees to repurchase it at a higher price at a later date. This instrument is commonly used by banks to borrow funds from the money markets.

In conclusion, banks and other financial institutions play a prominent role in the operation of the money markets. They provide the necessary liquidity, lending and borrowing funds, and offer a range of financial products and services to investors and borrowers. The money market provides an efficient platform for short-term lending and borrowing of funds, and thus, contributes to the overall functioning of the financial system.

c) Explain and apply the characteristics and role of the principal money market instruments:

i) interest-bearing instruments

ii) discount instruments

iii) derivative products

Interest-bearing Instruments

Interest-bearing instruments are an essential component of the money market that enables investors to gain returns on their investments through interest payments. Interest-bearing instruments are financial instruments that provide a fixed or variable return on the investment. These instruments trade in the money markets and play a crucial role in reflecting market conditions and changes in interest rates.

The principal money market instruments that fall under the category of interest-bearing instruments include Treasury Bills, negotiable certificates of deposit (CDs), and commercial paper. Treasury Bills, created by the US government, are short-term securities that come in maturity periods of 4, 13, 26, and 52 weeks, with the returns coming from the difference between the initial purchase price and final redemption. Treasury Bills are known for their low default risk and high liquidity, making them an ideal investment option for investors looking for a low-risk investment.

Negotiable CDs are another commonly traded interest-bearing instrument, where an investor agrees with a financial institution on a fixed interest rate for a set period. CDs are similar to savings accounts in nature, but with higher interest rates, and many investors invest in them to achieve a more stable investment. CDs are also known to have a higher deposit minimum, but they provide advantages over savings accounts since the interest rate of a CD is locked in and guaranteed for the life of the instrument.

Commercial paper, issued by corporations, is a type of unsecured, short-term promissory note that enables companies to obtain short-term financing. Commercial paper generally has a maturity period of 270 days or less and ranges in size from $100,000 to millions of dollars, with the interest rate of commercial paper varying depending on market conditions and risks.

The role of interest-bearing instruments in the money market is to provide a way for investors to gain returns on their investments and for borrowers to access short-term funding. Interest-bearing instruments are essential for managing short-term liquidity needs, and the interest rates they offer are closely linked to the prevailing rate in the market. The high liquidity and low-risk nature of these instruments make them ideal for investors looking for a safe but stable return on their investments.

In conclusion, interest-bearing instruments play a crucial role in the money market, providing opportunities for investors to gain returns on their investments through interest payments. Treasury Bills, negotiable CDs, and commercial paper are examples of interest-bearing instruments with different structures and features that make them suitable for different types of investors. Understanding the roles and characteristics of these instruments is important for investors and businesses looking to access and utilize liquidity in the money market.

Discount Instruments

Discount instruments are an essential component of the money market that enables investors to purchase securities at a discount to their face value. Discount instruments trade in the money markets, and they are often used to fund short-term liquidity needs. These instruments are similar to interest-bearing instruments, but they differ in that they are sold at a discount to the face value and, upon maturity, the investors receive the full value of the instrument.

The principal money market discount instruments include Treasury Bills, repurchase agreements (repos) and zero-coupon bonds. Treasury Bills are short-term securities created by the US government to finance the national debt. They come in maturity periods of 4, 13, 26, and 52 weeks, and they are sold at a discount to their face value, with the full value being paid out at maturity. The return on investment comes from the difference between the purchase price and the face value at maturity. Treasury Bills are known for their high liquidity, low default risk, and competitive returns.

Repurchase agreements (repos) are short-term loans that are collateralized by securities. In a repo, a dealer will sell securities to an investor and agree to buy them back at a slightly higher price on a specified date. These instruments are commonly used by banks to borrow funds from the money markets to meet short-term liquidity needs.

Zero-coupon bonds are another type of discount instrument that does not pay interest but instead relies on the difference between the purchase price and its face value at maturity. The investor purchases the bond at a significant discount to its face value, and then receives the full value of the bond when it matures. Zero-coupon bonds differ from traditional bonds in that they do not have periodic interest payments.

The role of discount instruments in the money market is to enable investors to purchase securities at a discount and receive the full value of the instrument at maturity. These instruments are important for managing short-term liquidity needs, and they reflect market conditions and changes in interest rates. The high liquidity and low default risk of discount instruments make them a popular form of investment for investors looking for low-risk, short-term investment opportunities.

In conclusion, discount instruments play an essential role in the money market by enabling investors to purchase securities at a discount and receive the full value of the instrument at maturity. Treasury Bills, repurchase agreements, and zero-coupon bonds are examples of discount instruments with different structures and features that make them suitable for different types of investors. Understanding the roles and characteristics of these instruments is important for investors and businesses looking to access and utilize liquidity in the money market.

Derivative Products

Derivative products are an important class of financial instruments that are traded in the money market. Derivatives are complex financial instruments whose value derives from an underlying asset, with their value fluctuating based on changes in the underlying asset. Derivatives are used to hedge risk or speculate on changes in asset prices, making them an essential component of the money market.

The principal money market derivative products include futures, options, and swaps. Futures contracts are agreements that require the buyer to purchase an underlying asset at a future date at a specified price. Futures contracts are often used by businesses as a hedging strategy to control commodity prices, allowing them to lock in the price of a commodity at a future date.

Options are another derivative product that gives the buyer the option, but not the obligation, to buy or sell an underlying asset at a future date at a specified price. Options are often used by investors as a hedging strategy to mitigate risk or as a speculative instrument to take advantage of movements in the underlying asset's price.

Swaps are agreements between two parties to exchange cash flows based on an underlying asset. These agreements are often used by businesses to adjust the terms of their debt to a more favorable rate. An example is interest rate swaps, where one party agrees to pay a fixed interest rate in exchange for another party paying a variable rate.

The role of derivative products in the money market is to provide investors with a way to manage risk and speculate on future market conditions. Derivatives also play a central role in the price discovery process, allowing the market to reflect the true value of an underlying asset. Derivatives are used as a hedging strategy to mitigate the impact of market volatility on investment portfolios.

In conclusion, derivative products are an essential component of the money market, allowing investors to hedge risk, speculate on changes in asset prices, and manage their portfolios effectively. Futures contracts, options, and swaps are examples of derivative products with different features and structures, making them suitable for different types of investors. Understanding the characteristics and roles of these instruments is crucial for investors and businesses looking to participate in the money market.

C Working capital management
The nature, elements and importance of working capital

C Working capital management
The nature, elements and importance of working capital

Nature of Working Capital and its Elements

Working capital refers to the amount of funds that a company has at its disposal to meet its daily operational requirements. It is the difference between current assets and current liabilities of a company. Working capital is essential for businesses as it helps them in carrying out their daily operations in a smooth and efficient manner. In simple terms, it is the liquid funds available with a company for day-to-day expenses.

The most critical elements of working capital include cash, accounts receivable, inventory, accounts payable, and short-term debt. Let us go into detail about the various components of working capital:

1. Cash: Cash is one of the most crucial elements of working capital. It is the most liquid asset that a business possesses. Having a sufficient amount of cash in hand ensures that the company can pay off its creditors, employees, suppliers, and other operating expenses on time.

2. Accounts Receivable: Accounts receivable is the amount of money that a company is entitled to receive from its customers for goods or services sold. It is an essential component of working capital because it reflects the creditworthiness of a business. The company's ability to collect its receivables promptly is critical to maintain adequate working capital.

3. Inventory: Inventory is the stock of finished goods or raw materials that a company holds for sale or production. It is a fundamental component of working capital, as it ties up a significant portion of the

company's funds. A company needs to balance between holding enough inventory to satisfy customer demand and reducing the inventory holding costs.

4. Accounts Payable: Accounts payable is an obligation in which a company owes to its suppliers for goods or services received on credit. It is another critical component of working capital. A company needs to manage its accounts payable efficiently to avoid any cash flow problems.

5. Short-term Debt: Short-term debt is the borrowing that a company takes from its creditors to finance its operations. It comprises of loans or credit lines that mature within a year. Companies use short-term debt to finance short-term needs or to meet their working capital requirements.

Effective management of working capital requires a deep understanding of the various elements mentioned above. Companies must maintain a balance between their current assets and current liabilities to ensure that they have adequate working capital to meet their daily operational needs.

In conclusion, working capital is crucial for the efficient functioning of a business. It represents the funds available to the company to meet its daily operational requirements. The primary components of working capital are cash, accounts receivable, inventory, accounts payable, and short-term debt. Effective management of these components helps companies to maintain adequate working capital and avoid any cash flow problems.

Objectives of Working Capital Management and the Conflict between Liquidity and Profitability

The primary objectives of working capital management are to ensure the availability of adequate cash flow to meet the short-term liabilities and to maximize profitability by utilizing the resources efficiently. However, the achievement of these objectives is not always easy, and there is a constant conflict between the two goals.

1. Liquidity Objective: The liquidity objective of working capital management refers to the ability of a company to meet its short-term obligations when they become due. In other words, it is the company's ability to convert its short-term assets into cash quickly. The primary objective of liquidity is to ensure that the company has enough funds to meet its commitments while maintaining its creditworthiness. A company with sufficient liquidity can take advantage of opportunities or overcome unexpected emergencies.

Example: A company might keep additional cash on hand to ensure that it can pay off its immediate bills, such as rent and utilities, on time.

2. Profitability Objective: The profitability objective of working capital management aims to maximize the profit by optimizing the utilization of resources effectively. The goal is to use the company's available resources efficiently to maximize sales, minimize expenses, and increase profits. Maximizing profits leads to additional cash inflows, which, in turn, helps maintain liquidity.

Example: A company might lease or rent equipment, take out additional financing, or negotiate better payment terms with suppliers to increase its cash inflows and profits.

Conflict between Liquidity and Profitability:
The liquidity and profitability objectives of working capital management

are often conflicted with each other. To understand this conflict, let us take two situations:

1. A company with high liquidity but low profitability might have too much cash tied up in low-return assets. This situation can lead to the company's failure to take advantage of investment opportunities, resulting in missed opportunities for growth and profit.

2. A company with low liquidity but high profitability might be taking too much risk and relying too heavily on short-term borrowing to meet its cash requirements. This situation can lead to the company's inability to meet its financial obligations, resulting in shut down or bankruptcy.

Thus, an optimal balance between liquidity and profitability is required to ensure the growth, stability, and success of the company. The appropriate working capital management strategy, therefore, is one that maintains a balance between them.

Conclusion:
Working capital management is an essential aspect of any company's financial management. The primary objectives of working capital management are to ensure liquidity and profitability. However, each objective faces inherent conflicts with the other. It is critical to strike the right balance between these two objectives and maintain the appropriate working capital levels to ensure the company's stable growth and success. Maintaining an optimal balance between liquidity and profitability requires careful planning and monitoring of the company's operating cycle, inventory levels, accounts receivable, accounts payable, and cash balances.

The Central Role of Working Capital Management in Financial Management

Working capital management plays a central role in financial management as it is concerned with the management of a company's current assets and liabilities. It involves ensuring that a company has enough cash, accounts receivable, inventory, and other liquid assets to meet its short-term obligations while also maintaining its long-term financial goals. Proper working capital management is vital to the smooth functioning and growth of a business.

The following points elaborate on the central role of working capital management in financial management:

1. Maintaining Adequate Liquidity: One of the primary goals of working capital management is to ensure that a company has sufficient liquidity to meet its obligations when they are due. Lack of liquidity can lead to unfavorable creditworthiness, which can harm the company's reputation and credit rating. A company that engages in proper working capital management can meet its short-term and unexpected obligations without relying on external sources, which can be costly.

2. Managing Cash Flow: Having an efficient working capital management system can help a company manage its cash flow effectively. This involves managing the company's accounts receivable and accounts payable, controlling inventory levels, and managing short-term debt. Effective cash flow management can help a business avoid cash flow problems, maintain positive cash flows, and avoid the need for costly external financing.

3. Maximizing Profitability: Working capital management plays a vital role in maximizing a company's profitability. By effectively managing its current assets and liabilities, a company can optimize cash flows, minimize costs, and enhance profitability. A company that manages its

working capital efficiently can reduce expenses, improve production efficiency, and negotiate better terms with suppliers, helping to improve the bottom line.

4. Supporting Growth and Expansion: Proper working capital management and liquidity planning can help businesses support growth and expansion plans. By investing in infrastructure, equipment, or talent, a company can expand operations and enter new markets. Proper working capital management can help ensure that a company has the necessary funds to take advantage of opportunities as they arise.

The central role of working capital management in financial management can be seen in its impact on business operations, profitability, cash flows, and long-term growth. A company that fails to manage its working capital properly is more likely to experience financial difficulties, cash flow problems, and even bankruptcy.

In conclusion, working capital management plays a critical role in financial management. It involves the management of current assets and liabilities to ensure adequate liquidity, efficient cash flow, and maximum profitability. Proper working capital management is vital to the smooth functioning and growth of a business, as it provides the necessary funds to meet short-term obligations and pursue long-term expansion plans. Effective working capital management is a prerequisite for a healthy and successful business.

Management of Inventories, Accounts Receivable, Accounts Payable and Cash

The Cash Operating Cycle and the Role of Accounts Payable and Accounts Receivable

The cash operating cycle is a critical aspect of working capital management that involves the management of the operating expenses and revenue of a business. It is a measure of the time it takes for a business to convert its current assets, such as inventory, into cash. Effective management of the cash operating cycle can help a business maximize its cash flow and optimize profitability.

The cash operating cycle involves three primary components: accounts payable, accounts receivable, and inventory. Here's how each component plays a role in the cash operating cycle:

1. Inventory: Inventory is a company's stock of goods that are ready for sale or in production. The longer inventory remains unsold, the more cash it ties up. A company must manage its inventory efficiently to reduce the time taken to sell the inventory and obtain cash. This involves controlling inventory levels, improving production efficiency, and ensuring that the inventory does not expire or become obsolete.

2. Accounts Receivable: Accounts receivable is the outstanding amount owed to a business by its customers for goods and services sold on credit. Collecting receivables on time is a critical aspect of the cash operating cycle, as it is necessary to convert the receivables into cash. A company must have an efficient system in place to manage outstanding receivables, such as customer reminders, cash incentives for early payments, and credit checks for new customers.

3. Accounts Payable: Accounts payable is the amount of money that a

business owes to its suppliers for goods and services received on credit. Managing accounts payable is essential for effective cash flow management, as it enables a company to stretch its available cash further. A business may negotiate longer payment terms with its suppliers, delay payments without penalties, or opt for installment payments.

Here's a step-by-step illustration of how the cash operating cycle works:

1. A company purchases inventory on credit from suppliers, creating an account payable for the amount owed.
2. The company uses the inventory to produce products, which are then sold to customers on credit, resulting in accounts receivable.
3. Over time, the accounts receivable are collected and converted into cash, which is then used to repay the accounts payable.

Effective management of the cash operating cycle requires companies to balance their inventory levels, accounts payable, and accounts receivable to maintain sufficient liquidity and optimize profitability. Too much inventory or slow collection of receivables can result in cash shortages, while delaying accounts payable beyond the agreed upon terms can harm relationships with suppliers.

In conclusion, the cash operating cycle plays a vital role in working capital management by converting current assets into cash. Effective management of accounts payable, accounts receivable, and inventory is necessary to ensure sufficient liquidity and optimize profitability. A company must balance its various operating expenses and revenue streams to manage the cash operating cycle effectively.

b) Explain and apply relevant accounting ratios, including:
   i) current ratio and quick ratio
   ii) inventory turnover ratio, average collection period and average payable period
   iii) sales revenue/net working capital ratio.

Current Ratio and Quick Ratio

Current ratio and quick ratio are two essential financial ratios used to evaluate a company's liquidity and ability to meet its short-term obligations. These ratios indicate how well a company can convert its current assets into cash to pay off its current liabilities when they become due. Here's an in-depth analysis of each ratio:

1. Current Ratio: The current ratio measures a company's ability to pay off its current liabilities using its current assets. It is calculated by dividing the company's current assets by its current liabilities. A ratio of 1:1 or higher indicates that a company has sufficient liquid assets to meet its short-term financial obligations.

Formula: Current Ratio = Current Assets / Current Liabilities

Example: ABC Corporation has current assets worth $500,000 and current liabilities worth $200,000. The current ratio of the company can be calculated as follows:

Current Ratio = Current Assets / Current Liabilities
Current Ratio = $500,000 / $200,000
Current Ratio = 2.5

Interpretation: A current ratio of 2.5 means that ABC Corporation has $2.50 of current assets against every $1 of current liabilities, indicating that the company has sufficient liquid assets to meet its short-term obligations.

2. Quick Ratio: The quick ratio, also known as the acid-test ratio, is a more stringent measure of a company's liquidity. It indicates the ability of a company to pay off its current liabilities quickly without relying on the sale of inventory. The quick ratio is calculated by dividing the sum of a company's cash, marketable securities, and accounts receivable by its current liabilities. A quick ratio of 1:1 or higher is considered favorable.

Formula: Quick Ratio = (Cash + Marketable Securities + Accounts Receivable) / Current Liabilities

Example: XYZ Corporation has cash of $100,000, marketable securities worth $50,000, and accounts receivable of $200,000. The current liabilities of the company are worth $125,000. The quick ratio of the company can be calculated as follows:

Quick Ratio = (Cash + Marketable Securities + Accounts Receivable) / Current Liabilities
Quick Ratio = ($100,000 + $50,000 + $200,000) / $125,000
Quick Ratio = 2.4

Interpretation: A quick ratio of 2.4 means that XYZ Corporation has $2.40 of quick assets against every $1 of current liabilities, indicating that the company has the ability to pay off its short-term obligations quickly without relying on sales of inventory.

Application of Current Ratio and Quick Ratio:

- These financial ratios are used by investors, creditors, and financial analysts to evaluate a company's liquidity and financial health.
- A company with a high current ratio is considered financially stable and capable of paying off its short-term liabilities.

- A quick ratio is more stringent than the current ratio and gives a clearer picture of a company's ability to pay off its current liabilities quickly.
- High current or quick ratios might indicate that a company is not effectively utilizing its assets or has poor inventory management.
- Low current or quick ratios might indicate that a company is relying heavily on short-term borrowing to finance its operations.

In conclusion, the current ratio and quick ratio are essential financial ratios used to evaluate a company's liquidity and ability to pay off its current liabilities. The ratios provide valuable insights into a company's financial health and stability and are widely used by investors, creditors, and financial analysts. It is necessary to use these ratios along with other financial metrics to make well-informed investment and lending decisions.

Inventory Turnover Ratio

The inventory turnover ratio is a financial measure used to assess a company's efficiency in managing its inventory. It's calculated by dividing the cost of goods sold by the average inventory level over a given period. A higher inventory turnover ratio indicates that the company is selling its inventory more quickly, whereas a lower ratio can imply that the company is holding on to inventory for too long or has an excess of inventory.

For example, suppose a company has $500,000 in cost of goods sold over a year and an average inventory of $100,000. The inventory turnover ratio for that particular period would be 5, which means that the company sold its inventory five times over the course of the year.

The inventory turnover ratio can be useful to investors and creditors as it can provide insight into a company's profitability and liquidity. A higher inventory turnover indicates that the company is in a better position to meet its financial obligations and generate profits.

Average Collection Period

The average collection period is a financial measure that indicates the amount of time it takes for a company to collect payment from its customers after issuing an invoice. The average collection period is calculated by dividing the number of days in a given period by the ratio of accounts receivable to sales.

For example, suppose a company's accounts receivable is $100,000 and sales for a month amount to $500,000. The ratio of accounts receivable to sales is 0.2. Assuming a 30-day month, the average collection period would be (0.2 x 30) = 6 days.

The average collection period is important for businesses as it directly affects their cash flow. A longer collection period can result in a cash flow shortfall, which can lead to liquidity issues, while a shorter period can help to maintain positive cash flow and improve liquidity.

Average Payable Period

The average payable period is a financial measure that indicates the amount of time it takes for a company to pay its suppliers after receiving an invoice. The average payable period is calculated by dividing the number of days in a given period by the ratio of accounts payable to purchases.

For example, assume a company's accounts payable is $50,000, and total purchases for a month were $200,000. The ratio of accounts payable to purchases is 0.25. The average payable period would be (0.25 x 30) = 7.5 days.

The average payable period is important to businesses as it affects their cash flow and determines their creditworthiness. A longer payable period can help to improve cash flow by providing additional time to pay suppliers, while a shorter period can improve the company's credit rating.

In conclusion, these three financial measures - inventory turnover ratio, average collection period, and average payable period - provide crucial indications of a company's efficiency in managing its inventory, collecting payment from customers, and paying its suppliers. By understanding these measures, businesses can make informed decisions to maintain positive cash flow and profitability.

Sales Revenue/Net Working Capital Ratio

The sales revenue to net working capital ratio is a financial measure used to assess a company's ability to generate sales revenue in relation to the amount of investment in its working capital. This ratio compares a company's sales revenue to its net working capital, which is calculated as the difference between current assets and current liabilities.

The formula for the sales revenue to net working capital ratio is:

Sales revenue / Net working capital

For example, assume a company has sales revenue of $1,000,000 and net working capital of $200,000. The sales revenue to net working capital ratio would be (1,000,000 / 200,000) = 5.

A higher sales revenue to net working capital ratio indicates that the company is generating more revenue with a smaller investment in working capital. This can be a positive indication of efficiency in managing its working capital.

Applications of this ratio include using it as a tool for comparing companies in the same industry. By comparing the ratio of two similar companies, an investor can determine which one is generating more revenue per unit of net working capital invested. This ratio can also be used to monitor a company's performance over time to detect trends in the efficiency of managing its working capital.

In-depth Analysis:

A high sales revenue/net working capital ratio suggests that a company is managing its working capital efficiently by generating more sales revenue with less investment in working capital. This means that the company is producing more output per unit of input, which can increase profitability.

However, an excessively high ratio may suggest that the company is not investing enough in its working capital to support its sales activities. This may lead to cash flow and liquidity issues, which can hamper the company's ability to meet its financial obligations.

On the other hand, a low sales revenue/net working capital ratio may suggest that the company is investing too much in working capital, which can increase the risk of holding excessive inventory or having a large number of unpaid invoices. This can result in a lower return on investment for shareholders.

Therefore, it is important to analyze this ratio in conjunction with other financial measures to gain a more complete understanding of a company's financial performance. In addition, it is essential to evaluate this ratio in the context of the company's industry and past performance to make informed investment decisions.

Managing inventory is a crucial part of a business's operations, as it can have a significant impact on its profitability and cash flow. Managing inventory includes techniques like Economic Order Quantity (EOQ) and Just-In-Time (JIT) techniques. In this write-up, we'll discuss these techniques, their applications, and evaluate their use in managing inventory.

Economic Order Quantity (EOQ) Model:

The Economic Order Quantity (EOQ) model is a technique used to determine the optimal inventory order quantity that can minimize inventory holding costs and ordering costs. The formula for EOQ is:

$$EOQ = \sqrt{(2DS/H)}$$

Where:
- D = Annual demand for the product
- S = Cost of placing an order
- H = Annual holding cost per unit of inventory

For example, suppose a company estimates an annual demand of 10,000 units, an ordering cost of $50 per order, and an annual holding cost of $5 per unit. The EOQ for that product would be:

$$EOQ = \sqrt{(2 \times 10{,}000 \times \$50 / \$5)} = 1{,}000 \text{ units}$$

Applications of EOQ:

The EOQ model provides a useful tool for businesses to manage their inventory efficiently. The formula can be adjusted to fit different inventory management needs, such as safety stock levels or backorders.

Just-In-Time (JIT) Techniques:

Just-In-Time (JIT) is an inventory management technique that involves ordering and receiving inventory only when it is needed in the production process; it's a pull-based system that minimizes inventory holding costs. This technique requires close coordination between the inventory supplier and the company's production team to ensure that inventory arrives precisely when needed, in the required quantities.

Applications of JIT:

The JIT technique is popular among manufacturing companies that have fast production times and limited storage space. It helps manufacturers reduce their inventory holding costs, minimize waste, and increase efficiency.

Evaluation of EOQ and JIT:

Both the EOQ and JIT techniques have their advantages and disadvantages. EOQ is useful in determining an optimal order quantity, and it offers a straightforward method to balance inventory holding costs and ordering costs. However, it doesn't take into account dynamic market factors such as market demand changes, supplier lead times, or raw material shortages.

On the other hand, JIT offers real-time inventory management, which reduces holding costs and helps in streamlining the production process. It can also reduce waste and optimize supply chains, but it requires a high level of coordination between suppliers and the production team. Furthermore, JIT can make the company vulnerable to supply chain disruptions since it depends on the timely delivery of inventory from suppliers.

In conclusion, managing inventory is an essential aspect of a business's operations and can significantly impact its financial performance. EOQ and JIT are two proven techniques that businesses can use to manage inventory efficiently. A successful inventory management strategy must consider a range of factors, such as market demands, supplier dynamics, and production capacity. Therefore, it's essential to evaluate these techniques in conjunction with other relevant factors before implementing a decision to manage inventory.

d) Discuss, apply and evaluate the use of relevant techniques in managing accounts receivable, including:
 i) assessing creditworthiness
 ii) managing accounts receivable [1]
 iii) collecting amounts owing
 iv) offering early settlement discounts
 v) using factoring and invoice discounting
 vi) **managing foreign accounts receivable**

Techniques for Assessing Creditworthiness

Managing accounts receivable, including assessing creditworthiness, is an essential part of financial management for any business. This involves a range of techniques for evaluating and monitoring credit risk, billing and payment policies, and collections procedures. In this write-up, we will discuss the relevant techniques in managing accounts receivable and evaluate their use in assessing creditworthiness.

Assessing Creditworthiness:

Assessing creditworthiness is a critical component of managing accounts receivable. It involves evaluating the creditworthiness of customers to minimize the risk of non-payment, and potential financial loss. There are several techniques that businesses use to assess creditworthiness:

1. Credit Reports:
Credit reports are an important tool for assessing creditworthiness. It's a detailed report of a customer's payment history, credit accounts, and credit score. Credit reports can be obtained from a credit bureau or a company that specializes in conducting credit checks.

2. Financial Statements:
Companies can also evaluate a customer's financial statements to assess their creditworthiness. Financial statements such as balance sheets, income statements, and cash flow statements, can provide insight into a customer's financial stability and ability to pay their bills.

3. Payment History:

Payment history is also a useful way to gauge a customer's creditworthiness. It provides a clear indication of the customer's payment patterns and whether they make payments on time.

Applications of Creditworthiness Techniques:

By using creditworthiness techniques, businesses can reduce their risk of non-payment and identify customers who may require additional monitoring. With the right evaluation techniques in place, a company can offer credit terms to customers that have a lower risk of defaulting, while being more cautious with customers who may have a higher risk.

Evaluation of Creditworthiness Techniques:

The use of creditworthiness techniques has its advantages and disadvantages. Credit checks are helpful, but they may not provide a complete picture of a customer's financial situation. Financial statements may also be limited in their usefulness, especially if a customer has a history of poor financial management. Payment history is a useful tool, but it may not be helpful in identifying customers who have recently experienced financial trouble.

Furthermore, the process of assessing creditworthiness can be time-consuming, and it can delay the sales process. In some cases, businesses may be too cautious in their evaluation, deterring potential customers from buying their products or services.

In conclusion, assessing creditworthiness is an essential component of managing accounts receivable. There are several techniques businesses can use to evaluate a customer's creditworthiness, including credit reports, financial statements, and payment history. However, the usefulness of these techniques depends on the specific customer and whether they provide a complete picture of their financial stability. It's important to use a combination of techniques to evaluate creditworthiness to reduce the risk of non-payment and potential financial loss. A successful accounts receivable management strategy should balance the benefits and drawbacks of assessing creditworthiness and ensure that the process does not hinder the sales process.

Techniques for Managing Accounts Receivable

Managing accounts receivable is a critical aspect of financial management for any business. Accounts receivable refer to the money owed by customers to a business for products or services sold on credit. This write-up will discuss the relevant techniques used in managing accounts receivable and evaluate their effectiveness.

Techniques for Managing Accounts Receivable:

1. Invoicing and Billing:
Invoicing and billing are vital techniques in managing accounts receivable. They entail sending accurate and timely invoices to customers and following up on any delays or non-payments. Invoicing and billing processes must be clear, concise, and easy to understand, with payment terms stated explicitly.

2. Offering Payment Options:
Another strategy for managing accounts receivable is to offer convenient payment options to customers. This includes accepting credit card payments, online payments, automated payments, and other payment options. The more payment options available, the more convenient it is for customers to make payments on time.

3. Collections:
Effective collections procedures are crucial in managing accounts receivable. Businesses should set up a clear procedure for following up on late or unpaid invoices, including sending reminders or making phone calls to customers. At the same time, the business should have a policy for handling situations where a customer consistently fails to pay.

Applications of Managing Accounts Receivable Techniques:

By using these techniques, businesses can reduce their risks of facing cash flow shortages, improve their customer relationships, and improve profitability by minimizing the cost of managing accounts receivable.

Evaluation of Managing Accounts Receivable Techniques:

The effectiveness of managing accounts receivable techniques can vary depending on the type of business and the customers they serve. For example, invoices may need to be more detailed and comprehensive for complex transactions or large clients, while payment options may not be significant for cash-based customers.

Collections procedures may also have their disadvantages, including the cost of collections and potential harm to customer relationships. Therefore, it's essential to balance the benefits and drawbacks of collections procedures and ensure that they are non-intrusive.

In conclusion, managing accounts receivable is an essential component of financial management for any business. The techniques for effective accounts receivable management include billing and invoicing, offering payment options, and effective collections procedures. It is necessary to review these techniques periodically to ensure that they align with customers' expectations and keep up with changing times. By efficiently managing accounts receivable, businesses can improve profitability, minimize the risk of cash flow shortages, and improve customer satisfaction.

Techniques for Collecting Amounts Owing

Accounts receivable is an essential part of a company's financial management. It is an asset that represents the amount of money owed by customers for goods or services that have been provided on credit.

Managing accounts receivable is crucial for any business and demands an understanding of various techniques and processes to streamline collections and ensure positive cash flow.

One such technique to manage accounts receivable is to implement appropriate credit policies. Credit policies provide guidelines on how to evaluate customers' ability to pay and the limits of credit that can be extended to them. Proper credit screening helps to reduce the risk of bad debts and ensures timely collections of receivables. Monitoring credit limits also prevents customers from exceeding their credit threshold, reducing the likelihood of non-payments.

Another technique commonly used in managing accounts receivable is the creation of efficient invoicing systems. Reliable, and timely invoicing process minimizes payment delays and ensures that clients receive a detailed record of their purchase. The invoices should be sent promptly and should include payment terms, discounts for early payment, and a clear breakdown of what is owed. Prompt responding to customer inquiries, addressing discrepancies promptly, and acknowledging the receipt of payment help to maintain a positive relationship between the business and its customers.

Additionally, a proactive collections process is essential in managing accounts receivable. Businesses can set up reminders through automated systems, which notify customers before the payment is due or invoice becomes overdue. If the account remains unpaid, follow-up emails or calls can be made to remind customers of their outstanding payment. It is important to maintain a professional but firm approach in such reminders, avoiding the risk of damaging customer relationships.

Moreover, companies may consider factoring or selling their accounts receivable to specialized financing firms to meet immediate cash needs. Factoring can help companies receive cash quickly while avoiding the time and cost associated with formal collections. However, factoring also comes with added costs and risks that need to be weighed against benefits.

Another technique used to manage accounts receivable is the establishment of a reserve for doubtful debts. This involves setting aside funds for anticipated non-payments for accounting purposes. It provides a realistic view of the company's financial position, ensuring that the company does not overstate its financial health.

In conclusion, managing accounts receivable is crucial for any business to maintain a steady cash flow. Implementing an efficient credit policy, a reliable invoicing process, proactive collections strategy, factoring or selling receivables to finance firms and establishing reserves for doubtful debts are various techniques that businesses can use to manage their accounts receivable. However, choosing the right technique depends on the nature of the business and its customers. It is important to evaluate all options and implement them strategically to ensure that the business functions optimally.

Offering Early Settlement Discounts

Another important technique used in managing accounts receivable is the offering of early settlement discounts. This involves giving customers an incentive to pay their bills early by offering a discount if they pay before the due date. Early settlement discounts help to reduce receivable balances and speed up the collections process, resulting in improved cash flows.

Offering early settlement discounts works by offering a small discount to customers who make payments within a specified period, which is typically less than 30 days. The discount percentage usually ranges between 1-3% of the total invoice amount. This level of discount is enough to incentivize customers to make early payments but not so significant that it would affect the business's profitability.

For example, if a company sells goods worth $1,000 with payment terms of net 30 days, they may offer a 2% discount if the invoice is paid within 10 days. This means that if the customer pays the invoice within ten days, they only pay $980 rather than $1,000, effectively saving them $20.

The benefits of offering early settlement discounts are numerous. For one, it encourages prompt payments, reducing the likelihood of extended payment terms or overdue receivables. It also frees up cash flow, enabling businesses to invest in other areas or pay their own bills more quickly. Additionally, it helps to maintain good relationships with customers, who, in turn, may be more likely to return as repeat customers.

However, offering early settlement discounts must be undertaken strategically to avoid losses and minimize the impact on the business's bottom line. The discount percentage offered must be carefully calculated to ensure that the discount does not surpass the cost of capital. If the discount percentage is too high, the business risks losing money, which may result in reduced margins or, in extreme cases, financial instability.

Furthermore, the cost of discounting must be compared to the benefits of prompt payment. The cost of finance and opportunity costs of foregone revenue must be factored in to evaluate the financial benefits of the discount. Similarly, it should be noted that not all customers will take advantage of the early payment discount. Therefore, a balance must be struck between offering enough incentive to encourage early payment but also ensuring profitability.

In conclusion, offering early settlement discounts is a useful technique to manage accounts receivable. It is an effective way to accelerate payments and maintain good customer relationships. However, the discount percentage offered must be carefully calculated to ensure that it does not result in a loss to the business. Businesses must undertake strategic evaluations to determine the optimal discount percentage for their operations.

Factoring and Invoice Discounting

Factoring and invoice discounting refer to the sale of accounts receivable to third-party finance firms that provide immediate funding in return for a percentage of the invoice amount (minus a fee). These techniques offer an alternative to the conventional method of waiting months for payment.

Invoice factoring involves the outright sale of receivables to a factoring company, whereby the company provides upfront cash, typically a percentage of the value of the invoices, in exchange for ownership of the invoices. The factoring company, in turn, then takes over the responsibility of collecting payment from customers. In contrast, invoice discounting involves using receivables as collateral for a loan. The company still retains ownership of the invoices and is responsible for collecting payment from customers.

Factoring and invoice discounting have several benefits and drawbacks that must be weighed before implementation. One of the main benefits is that they provide immediate cash flow, enabling businesses to invest in other areas or pay their own bills more quickly. Additionally, they eliminate the need for credit checks, making it an excellent option for small businesses that lack the ability to conduct thorough credit evaluations. Factoring and invoice discounting are also faster and more efficient than traditional collections methods, reducing the time and cost of maintaining receivables.

However, factoring and invoice discounting also come with significant costs. For one, the factoring or discounting company will typically charge a fee, which may range from 2-10% of the invoice value. This cost can impact profitability, particularly for companies with already thin margins. Moreover, factoring and invoice discounting require close scrutiny of the terms and contract with the third party in terms of receivables, obligations and potential liability issues.

Additionally, factoring and invoice discounting can negatively affect business-customer relationships as it is an indication that the business is in trouble financially or facing a cash flow crisis. Customers may view factoring negatively and derive the impression that the company is not creditworthy.

In conclusion, factoring and invoice discounting are valid techniques for managing accounts receivable. They can help improve cash flow, provide an alternative to traditional collections methods, and enable businesses to invest in other areas or pay their own bills more quickly. However, the costs and liabilities associated with these methods should be weighed against potential benefits. The business must evaluate the startup, legal and contractual aspects while taking into consideration its relationship with customers. Hence, businesses must have a clear understanding of their financial situation and thoroughly evaluate their options before implementing factoring or invoice discounting.

Managing Foreign Accounts Receivable

Managing foreign accounts receivable can be a complex and challenging process for companies doing business in foreign countries. Several factors can affect the collection of these receivables, including language barriers, currency exchange rates, and cultural differences.

One useful technique for managing foreign accounts receivable is conducting a thorough credit evaluation. This involves evaluating the creditworthiness of foreign customers before granting credit. Credit evaluations can involve conducting credit checks, verifying references, and conducting a thorough analysis of payment histories. Proper credit evaluations can help mitigate the risk of non-payment and enable businesses to make informed decisions on credit limits and payment terms.

In addition, employing the services of local agents can be an effective way to manage foreign accounts receivable. Local agents can provide valuable insights into the market and customs of the foreign country, offer language translation services, and help manage collections. However, it is essential to do proper research to ensure that the local agents are reputable and reliable.

Another effective technique for managing foreign accounts receivable is to develop clear and concise payment terms. These terms should include payment methods, payment due date, and any applicable penalties for late payment. Businesses must also ensure that payment terms comply with foreign regulations and customs. Furthermore, businesses must be prepared to respond promptly to customer inquiries or payment discrepancies. Prompt attention to such issues can prevent payment delays and maintain a positive relationship with foreign customers.

Moreover, businesses must also consider hedging foreign exchange risks when managing foreign accounts receivable. Fluctuating exchange rates can affect the value of receivables and have a significant impact on cash flow. To mitigate these risks, businesses can use foreign exchange hedging techniques like forward contracts, futures contracts, and options contracts. These techniques can help lock in exchange rates and reduce the risk of currency fluctuations.

In conclusion, managing foreign accounts receivable requires careful consideration of the challenges posed by language and cultural differences, currency exchange rates, and foreign regulations. Employing techniques such as credit evaluations, local agents, clear payment terms, prompt attention to customer inquiries, and hedging foreign exchange risks can help businesses manage these challenges and maintain a healthy cash flow. Businesses must evaluate their options and develop effective strategies for managing their foreign accounts receivable to ensure their continued success.

Discuss and apply the use of relevant techniques in managing accounts payable, including

Trade Credit Effectively

Trade credit is a financing technique that allows businesses to purchase goods and services on credit from suppliers. It is an important tool for managing accounts payable, enabling businesses to access goods and services while conserving cash flow. However, managing trade credit effectively requires a careful consideration of suppliers, payment terms, and cash flow requirements.

One technique for managing trade credit effectively is to negotiate favorable payment terms with suppliers. Payment terms refer to the period between the receipt of goods or services and the due date for payment. Longer payment terms may allow businesses to conserve cash flow, but they also increase the risk of late payments, penalties, and damage to supplier relationships. Therefore, it is vital to negotiate payment terms that consider both the business's cash flow requirements and the supplier's needs.

In addition, businesses must establish a system for monitoring and managing trade credit. This involves developing a clear understanding of the terms and obligations of trade credit agreements and keeping track of payment due dates, invoice amounts, and any discounts offered for early payment. Management of trade credit also involves communication with suppliers and proactive measures to address any payment difficulties, including agreements for payment plans in case of issues.

Another technique for managing trade credit effectively is to use supply chain financing. Supply chain financing involves leveraging the creditworthiness of the supply chain to secure financing from third-party financial institutions. This helps reduce the cost of borrowing and may also enable businesses to extend payment terms while providing suppliers with immediate cash flow.

Moreover, businesses can also manage trade credit by consolidating supplier relationships. Consolidating supplier relationships can reduce the complexity of managing trade credit, simplifying payment terms, and reducing the risk of late payments. It also helps to build stronger relationships with suppliers, enabling businesses to negotiate favorable payment terms and access discounts for early payment.

In conclusion, trade credit is an essential tool for managing accounts payable, providing access to goods and services while conserving cash flow. Effective management of trade credit requires a careful consideration of payment terms, supplier relationships, and cash flow requirements. Negotiating favorable payment terms, establishing systems for monitoring and managing trade credit, using supply chain financing, and consolidating supplier relationships are some of the techniques businesses can use to manage trade credit effectively. Businesses must evaluate their options and develop effective strategies to ensure they manage trade credit effectively and maintain a healthy cash flow.

Evaluating the Benefits of Early Settlement and Bulk Purchase Discounts

Managing accounts payable is an essential part of any business, as it affects the financial health of the organization. One technique that can be used in managing accounts payable is early settlement. Early settlement involves paying off your bills before their due dates. Early settlement can improve the financial standing of a company by reducing the amount owed to the supplier or service provider. In doing so, the company can enhance its credit rating as it will have a better payment history.

Another technique in managing accounts payable is bulk purchase discounts. Bulk purchase discounts are discounts that are offered when a company purchases large quantities of goods or services. This technique can be beneficial in reducing costs and increasing profits since it allows companies to purchase goods or services at a reduced cost.

For example, consider a company that purchases stationery items for employees. If the company purchases items in bulk, it can benefit from bulk purchase discounts. Let's say the company usually purchases 100 pens for $10. If the bulk purchase discount is 10%, the company can purchase 150 pens for $13.50, resulting in a discount of $1.50.

It is essential to evaluate these techniques to determine their effectiveness in managing accounts payable. Early settlement can be advantageous to a company as it can reduce the amount owed to the supplier or service provider, and it can result in better payment history for the company. However, this technique may not be useful if the company is facing cash flow problems.

Bulk purchase discounts, on the other hand, can be advantageous for companies that require a considerable number of goods or services. However, companies must ensure that they have the storage and security space to store the purchased items. Additionally, companies should evaluate if the bulk purchase quantity is necessary for the business's needs, as buying more than what is required can lead to wastage.

In conclusion, managing accounts payable requires companies to evaluate various techniques, such as early settlement and bulk purchase discounts. These techniques can result in cost savings for companies, provided that they are applied appropriately. It is crucial to consider the benefits and limitations of each technique and evaluate them based on the needs of the company. By doing so, companies can manage their accounts payable effectively while optimizing their financial standing.

Managing Foreign Accounts Payable

Managing foreign accounts payable can be complex and challenging, as it involves dealing with different currencies, exchange rates, and regulations. Despite these challenges, managing foreign accounts payable is crucial for companies that have international business operations. In this section, we will discuss and apply techniques relevant to managing foreign accounts payable.

One technique in managing foreign accounts payable is using currency hedging strategies. Hedging is a risk management strategy that helps protect companies from potential losses due to changes in the foreign currency exchange rates. Hedging can involve buying or selling currency to reduce the impact of currency fluctuations on a company's finances.

For example, consider a US-based company that has operations in the UK. The company has a purchase order for widgets worth £10,000 that is due in three months. The current exchange rate is 1 US dollar is equivalent to 0.75 pounds. To protect themselves from potential currency fluctuations, the company can use a currency hedging strategy to lock in the exchange rate. The company can either buy forward contracts or options to lock in the exchange rate, reducing the uncertainty and potential losses due to currency volatility.

Another critical technique in managing foreign accounts payable is negotiating with suppliers for favorable payment terms. Negotiating payment terms that align with a company's cash flow can help manage foreign accounts payable better. For example, if a company is facing cash flow problems, it can negotiate with its suppliers to extend payment deadlines or offer partial payments. This can help avoid late payment fees or disruptions in the supply chain, which can affect the company's financial standing.

Lastly, it is essential to maintain accurate and up-to-date records of foreign accounts payable. Maintain detailed records of payments, exchange rates, and communication with suppliers to ensure that payment obligations are met on time while complying with regulations. Using accounting software that can handle multiple currencies and exchange rates can help streamline the process of managing foreign accounts payable.

In conclusion, managing foreign accounts payable requires companies to apply relevant techniques such as hedging currency, negotiating payment terms, and maintaining accurate records. These techniques can help companies mitigate risks and manage the complexities of managing foreign accounts payable. It is crucial to evaluate the benefits and limitations of each technique and apply them based on the company's international business operations' specific needs.

Explain the various reasons for holding cash, and discuss and apply the use of relevant techniques in managing cash, including

Holding cash is essential for any business to meet its day-to-day operating expenses or to make strategic investments. Having sufficient cash reserves can enhance a company's liquidity and flexibility, allowing it to respond to unforeseen events, such as economic downturns or unexpected expenses. In this section, we will discuss the various reasons for holding cash and the relevant techniques in managing cash effectively.

One reason for holding cash includes having sufficient funds available to meet short-term obligations and expenses. Short-term expenses can include paying rent, salaries, utility bills, or unforeseen emergencies. Having cash reserves on hand can help companies avoid late payment fees, poor credit ratings, or a disruption in the supply chain. Companies can use accounting software to manage the inflows and outflows of cash, helping identify any potential cash shortfalls.

Another reason for holding cash includes having funds available for investment opportunities. Having cash reserves can provide companies with the funds they need to make strategic investments or take advantage of new opportunities. For example, if a company identifies an acquisition opportunity, having cash reserves can help fund the acquisition instead of borrowing from external sources.

To manage cash effectively, companies can utilize various techniques, one being preparing cash flow forecasts. Cash flow forecasts involve projecting a company's incoming and outgoing cash flows over a specified period. By analyzing cash flow forecasts and determining future cash flow and cash balances, companies can plan for any potential shortfalls or surpluses, adjust their cash management strategies accordingly and invest any excess funds in viable opportunities.

For example, consider a company that projects an upcoming cash shortfall that will impact its ability to meet its short-term obligations. By preparing a cash flow forecast, the company can identify potential sources for generating cash, such as reducing inventory, negotiating with suppliers or collecting outstanding payments, to avoid disruption in the supply chain or tarnishing the company's credit rating.

In conclusion, holding cash is vital for any business for various reasons, including meeting short-term obligations and expenses and investing in strategic opportunities. Effective management of cash requires companies to utilize relevant techniques such as preparing cash flow forecasts, enabling them to anticipate potential shortfalls or surpluses, adjust their cash management strategies accordingly, and invest any excess funds in viable opportunities. By managing cash effectively, companies can enhance their liquidity and flexibility, improve their financial health, and maximize their potential for growth.

Preparing Cash Flow Forecasts to Determine Future Cash Flows and Cash Balances

Assessing the Benefits of Centralized Treasury Management and Cash Control

Centralized treasury management is the process of consolidating cash management activities within a single, central entity of an organization. By implementing centralized treasury management, organizations can gain several benefits, including improved control over cash and enhanced cost savings. In this section, we will discuss the benefits of centralizing treasury management and cash control, and assess its advantages and disadvantages.

One significant advantage of centralized treasury management is that it facilitates improved control over cash. Centralizing treasury management activities can enable organizations to gain greater visibility of their cash inflows and outflows, which can help them better manage their cash position. For example, suppose an organization has multiple units or subsidiaries that undertake different cash management activities. In that case, centralizing treasury management can help ensure that all units are following best practices, minimize instances of overpayment or late payment fees and improve the accuracy of cash flow forecasts.

Additionally, centralizing treasury management can enable organizations to consolidate their bank accounts, reducing account maintenance fees and operational costs. By reducing administrative tasks such as multiple bank reconciliations and payment processing, organizations can optimize their cash management efficiency.

Centralized cash control also enables organizations to access cash more efficiently. By pooling cash resources into a single account, organizations can improve their bargaining power with banks and access better interest rates or financing options. Additionally, having centralized control of cash can facilitate faster decision-making and improve the responsiveness of organizations to changes in the business environment.

However, centralizing treasury management can have disadvantages. Some organizations may find that centralizing treasury management activities increases operational costs or disrupts existing workflow processes. Organizations may also face challenges in balancing the need for centralized control with the operational requirements of individual units or subsidiaries.

In conclusion, centralizing treasury management and cash control can offer several benefits to organizations, including improved control over cash, enhanced efficiency in cash management, and cost savings. However, organizations must weigh the advantages and disadvantages before implementing centralized treasury management, to ensure that it is the most appropriate solution for their business needs. By assessing the benefits of centralizing treasury management and cash control, organizations can optimize their cash management activities, streamline their cash management activities more effectively, and enhance their capacity for sustained growth.

Cash Management Models: The Baumol Model and the Miller-Orr Model

Cash management models are tools that organizations can use to estimate the optimal size and timing of cash transactions. Two such models are the Baumol model and the Miller-Orr model. In this section, we will discuss these models in detail and how they can be applied to manage cash effectively.

The Baumol model is a cash management model that helps organizations determine the optimal size and frequency of cash transactions. The model assumes that organizations have a constant cash demand rate and costs for holding and transacting cash. By analyzing these variables, the Baumol model can provide an estimate of the optimal cash balance that an organization should hold.

For example, consider a small business that has a monthly cash demand of $20,000 and a $100 transaction cost. Using the Baumol model, the optimal cash balance is $10,000, which minimizes the total costs of holding and transacting cash.

The Miller-Orr model is a cash management model that helps organizations determine the optimal cash balance and the timing of transactions. The model assumes that cash balances follow a normal distribution and that organizations incur transaction costs for moving cash between the optimal and target cash balances. Using these variables, the Miller-Orr model can provide an estimate of the optimal cash balance and the transaction timing that minimizes cash management costs.

For example, consider a company that has a daily cash demand of $50,000 and incurs a transaction cost of $100. Using the Miller-Orr model, the optimal cash balance and transaction timing is $60,000, and cash should be transferred when the cash balance exceeds $66,000 and stop when it falls below $54,000. This model ensures that the company maintains liquidity while minimizing transaction costs.

Organizations can apply these cash management models to determine the optimal level of cash balances, minimize transaction costs, and invest excess cash effectively. However, it is important to note that these models provide estimates based on assumptions and require constant re-evaluation and adjustment to reflect changing business conditions.

In conclusion, cash management models such as the Baumol model and the Miller-Orr model can provide organizations with valuable insights into their cash management strategies. By estimating the optimal cash balance, frequency, and timing of transactions, organizations can manage cash more efficiently, reduce transaction costs and optimize their investment returns. However, organizations should use caution when applying these models and ensure that they regularly evaluate the assumptions on which they are based to reflect current business conditions.

Investing Short-Term

Effective techniques for managing cash require businesses to invest in short-term securities that provide a quick return on investment to maximize the potential benefits of corporate cash holdings. The concept of investing short-term means investing money for a shorter duration, typically less than a year, in securities that offer a higher rate of return, including certificates of deposit, Treasury bills, commercial paper, and money market funds. These short-term investments ensure that the company can earn some interest on their idle cash balance while also ensuring that the cash remains available to be used whenever needed. The objective of managing cash through short-term investing is to optimize the cash balance by minimizing transaction costs, the opportunity cost of holding idle balances, and maximizing interest earnings. The Baumol model and the Miller-Orr model are popular cash management techniques that help companies achieve this objective.

The Baumol model focuses on identifying the optimal cash balance amount needed to ensure that the daily operations remain unaffected. This model divides the cash held by a company into two categories: transaction balance and idle balance. Transaction balance is the minimum cash balance required to run the operations daily. Idle balance refers to the excess cash that can be invested in securities that yield short-term interest. The model establishes a trade-off between the cost of converting securities back into cash and the opportunity cost of holding idle balances by investing excess cash in securities.

The Miller-Orr model is used when cash flows fluctuate and is focused on maintaining a minimum and maximum cash balance limit. When the cash balance approaches the upper limit, some money is shifted to a short-term investment account that earns interest. On the other hand, when the cash balance falls to the lower limit, some of the short-term investments are liquidated, and the cash is transferred back into the company account. This model works well in conditions where cash flow is relatively consistent.

For instance, a car dealership with seasonal sales could benefit from using cash management techniques. By analyzing their entire year's business operations and seasonal sales trends, they could determine the optimal cash balance required to ensure smooth transactions. During the peak sales season, the dealership would use their idle cash to purchase short-term investments that yield higher interest. This approach allows the dealership to earn a return on their cash balances while ensuring that they have enough money to run their daily operations. During the off-season, the investments are liquidated, and money is transferred back to the company account.

In conclusion, investing short-term is a valuable cash management technique that maximizes corporate cash reserves. Companies employ cash management models such as the Baumol Model and Miller-Orr Model which help them balance their idle cash holdings with transaction balances and earn additional interest. These techniques ensure companies remain financially stable and have sufficient liquidity to run daily operations.

Determining Working Capital Needs and Funding Strategies

Working capital investment is the amount of financial capital that is invested to support the daily operational expenses and requirements of a business. It is often measured in terms of the difference between the company's current assets and current liabilities. The level of working capital investment in current assets is a critical aspect of a company's financial management, as it can impact various aspects of the business, including its cash flow, liquidity, and profitability.

There are several key factors that determine the level of working capital investment in current assets. These factors can include the company's size, market demand, operating cycles, lead times, and the capital requirements for financing the business operations. Other factors may include the production process, the industry, competition, economic conditions, and customer creditworthiness. Understanding these factors is essential for determining the optimal level of working capital investment in current assets and the long-term health of the company.

The calculation of the working capital investment in current assets is done by deducting the current liabilities from the current assets. Current assets include cash, inventory, accounts receivables, and other assets that can be converted into cash within a year. Current liabilities refer to obligations that the business is required to pay within a year. The resulting figure represents the working capital investment in current assets, and this amount should be sufficient to manage the day-to-day expenses of the business.

The Length of the Working Capital Cycle and Terms of Trade

The length of the working capital cycle and terms of trade are crucial aspects of a business's financial management because they affect the cash flow and liquidity of a company. The working capital cycle involves the company's operational activities, i.e., how long it takes to sell products or services and collect payment from customers while paying suppliers, and the time duration of the entire process until they receive cash again after the initial outlay. This includes three distinct stages: inventory stage, accounts receivable stage, and accounts payable stage.

The inventory stage is the time needed for a business to acquire inventory, to store it in the warehouse, and then convert it into finished products. The length of the inventory stage is dependent on the type of industry and the business's suppliers. For example, it may take longer for a clothing retailer to receive the latest fashion designs compared to a business selling electronics.

The accounts receivable stage is the time required for a business to collect payment from its customers after products and services have been sold. This stage is typically determined by the payment terms agreed with the customer, and it is important to keep track of the accounts receivable turnover ratio to ensure that the time taken to collect payments is optimal.

The accounts payable stage is the time allowed by suppliers for payment of goods and services. This period is critical as it provides the business with the opportunity to make optimal use of its financial resources by holding cash for longer periods while taking advantage of payment discounts. However, there is a risk that suppliers may stop a business's credit lines if payment terms are breached.

In addition to the working capital cycle, the terms of trade are also important in managing a company's cash flow. The terms of trade refer to the payment terms agreed upon by suppliers and customers. A company must ensure that it has the necessary cash flow to match these terms. A business must pay suppliers within the agreed-upon time frame to avoid the risk of limiting trade credit.

For example, if a company agrees to buy raw materials from a supplier on credit terms of 30 days, they must ensure that they can pay their suppliers within this period. Companies that agree to long payment terms without the necessary liquidity could be at risk of negatively impacting their credit score or damaging their relationships with suppliers.

In conclusion, managing the length of the working capital cycle and the terms of trade is critical to a business's financial stability. Companies must ensure that they have sufficient liquidity to manage their operational needs and that they negotiate payment terms with suppliers in a way that optimizes their cash flow. Effective management of working capital can ultimately maximize profits and improve the long-term health of a business.

An Organisation's Policy on the Level of Investment in Current Assets

Organizations need a clear policy on the level of investment in current assets because it has significant implications for their financial management, affecting the business's ability to function efficiently and maintain positive cash flow. The level of investment in current assets is determined by various factors such as the size of the organization, industry, market demand, supplier payment or receipt of payment, production process, competition, among others. Understanding these factors and formulating an effective policy on the level of investment in current assets can help an organization achieve its financial objectives.

A policy on current asset investment sets guidelines that help finance teams maintain the optimal inventory levels, the optimum cash balance, and efficient accounts receivable management. Organizations must strike a balance between ensuring availability of adequate liquid cash reserves and avoiding excess cash build-up that may lower the return on investment.

For example, a business with a fast inventory turnover rate should invest in inventory management tools, such as tracking software, to prevent overstocking and reduce the risk of holding obsolete inventory. The finance team could also review and reduce the organization's inventory carrying costs, such as storage and insurance fees, to reduce costs and increase profitability.

In addition, effective accounts receivable management is essential in facilitating the organization's cash flow, and organizations must adopt strategic policies that reduce the time it takes to collect payment from customers. This may include implementing a discount policy for early payment or establishing more favorable payment terms.

Organizations can also implement policies on sustainable cash flow management, such as measuring the working capital ratio and cash conversion cycle, to ensure that adequate liquid resources are available for daily operational activities. The policy should keep up with market trends and ensure it aligns with the organization's financial goals.

It is important for organizations to evaluate and adjust their polices regularly to reflect changes in the business environment. For instance, during a period of economic hardship, an organization may adopt more stringent collections policies or cut back on inventory. Similarly, during a period of growth, cash flow forecasting models could be updated to reflect the increased resources required to fund additional inventory or accounts receivable balances.

In conclusion, an organization's policy on the level of investment in current assets is critical in achieving its financial objectives. An effective policy should consider key factors such as the size of the organization, industry, market demand, supplier payment or receipt of payment, production process, and competition, among others. By implementing best practices in inventory management, accounts receivable and cash flow management, and regularly evaluating polices, an organization can optimize its investment in current assets to maintain cash flow and increase profitability.

The Industry in which the Organisation Operates:
Factors Influencing Working Capital Investment in Current Assets in Different Industries

The level of working capital investment in current assets is an important aspect for any organization as it affects the organization's liquidity, profitability, and overall financial stability. Working capital is the difference between a company's current assets and its current liabilities. Current assets are short-term assets such as cash, inventory, and accounts receivable that can be easily converted to cash, while current liabilities are short-term debts such as accounts payable, taxes payable, and short-term loans that must be paid soon.

The level of working capital investment in current assets is affected by various factors, and one of the key factors determining this level is the industry in which the organization operates. Different industries have unique characteristics that affect the level of working capital investment in current assets required to maintain profitability and stability.

For example, industries such as retail and manufacturing require significant investments in current assets due to the need for maintaining inventory levels to meet customer demand. In the retail industry, inventory turnover is critical to maintaining profitability and keeping up with competitors. Therefore, retailers invest in current assets such as inventory to ensure they can meet customer needs.

In contrast, the service industry requires lower levels of current asset investment as the services provided are intangible and do not require significant investment in inventory. For instance, consulting firms require very little inventory investment and may maintain a more flexible approach to payables and receivables.

Furthermore, the industry's payment terms and payment cycles affect the level of working capital investment in current assets. The length of payment terms and payment cycles in any industry can result in a significant investment in accounts receivable, affecting the level of working capital investment in current assets. The construction industry, in particular, has long payment cycles that can be as long as six months, and as a result, requires a higher level of working capital investment in current assets.

In conclusion, the level of working capital investment in current assets is crucial to the financial stability and profitability of any organization. Several factors affect the level of current asset investment required, and one of the key factors is the industry in which the organization operates. Understanding the industry's characteristics, payment terms, and payment cycles can help organizations optimize their working capital investment in current assets to ensure long-term profitability and financial stability.

Understanding the Difference Between Permanent and Fluctuating Current Assets for Effective Working Capital Management

Permanent and fluctuating current assets are two main types of current assets that require different funding strategies. Permanent current assets refer to those current assets that remain fixed and constant over time, whereas fluctuating current assets refer to those that change with time and business needs.

Examples of permanent current assets include property, plant, and equipment, which are necessary for day-to-day business operations. These assets represent a long-term investment in the business and are expected to remain in the business for an extended period. They are not expected to be sold but rather used repeatedly in the day-to-day operations of the business. Permanent current assets are funded through long-term financing sources such as long-term debt or equity financing.

Fluctuating current assets, on the other hand, are short-term in nature and are expected to change over time. These assets include inventories, accounts receivables, and cash, which are used to support day-to-day business operations. The levels of these assets fluctuate according to business cycles and operational needs. They are funded through short-term financing sources such as trade credit, short-term bank loans, and other flexible financing options.

Understanding the difference between permanent and fluctuating current assets is important to ensure that a business can adequately fund its day-to-day operations. Overinvestment in permanent current assets reduces the company's liquidity and may lead to the misallocation of resources. Conversely, inadequate funding of fluctuating current assets may lead to cash flow problems and affect the company's ability to meet its short-term obligations.

One way to manage the funding of these assets is to use the operating cycle to measure the time it takes to turn inventory into cash. This helps in estimating the amount of working capital funding required to meet the business needs. For example, if the operating cycle takes 30 days, the company may require 30 days of funding for its working capital.

In conclusion, permanent and fluctuating current assets are two essential components of working capital that require different funding sources. By understanding the difference between these assets, businesses can optimize their working capital funding strategies, ensuring financial stability and profitability while maintaining adequate liquidity. Effective management of permanent and fluctuating current assets is critical for businesses to achieve their financial goals while meeting their operational needs.

The Relative Cost and Risk of Short- term and Long-term Finance

When planning their financing strategies, businesses must decide whether to use short-term or long-term financing options. Short-term financing is typically for a duration of one year or less, while long-term financing is for more than one year.

The main factor that businesses consider when deciding between short-term and long-term financing is the cost and risk associated with each option. Short-term financing typically has lower interest rates, but it is considered a more expensive and riskier option. This is because businesses using short-term financing must frequently rollover their debt obligations, which can be costly and create cash flow difficulties.

Another risk associated with short-term financing is the potential for interest rate fluctuations, which can significantly affect the cost of debt obligations. This can result in higher debt-servicing costs and negatively impact the business's profitability. Having a large percentage of short-term debt obligations also exposes businesses to the risk of short-term interest rate hikes.

Long-term financing options generally have higher interest rates but are considered less risky as they are for a fixed period. Long-term financing provides businesses with the benefit of having predictable cost and more stable cash flows. Also, long-term financing is often used when businesses require large amounts of capital, such as when expanding operations.

An important consideration when choosing between short-term and long-term financing is the nature of the business activities. For example, seasonal businesses may require short-term financing to meet peak demand during their busy season. On the other hand, businesses requiring long-term investments in fixed assets such as infrastructure, machinery, buildings may require long-term financing options.

In conclusion, businesses must carefully evaluate the cost and risk associated with short-term and long-term financing options. Factors such as the business's nature, cash flow requirements, and investment needs play a vital role in determining which financing options to use. Short-term financing may be appropriate for short-term needs, and long-term financing options may be more suited for long-term investments. Ultimately, choosing the right financing option is critical to ensure a stable and healthy future for any given organization.

Utilizing the Matching Principle for Effective Working Capital Funding Strategies

The Matching Principle is an essential consideration when determining a company's working capital funding strategies. This principle states that a company must match its expenses to its revenues to accurately reflect its profitability over a given period. In practice, this means that a business should only fund its long-term assets with long-term financing options and its short-term assets with short-term financing options. As an example, suppose a business needs to invest in a new piece of equipment. The cost of this equipment, including all related expenses, is $200,000. The business has two financing options available at the time: a short-term loan with a 6-month repayment plan or a long-term loan with a repayment period of 5 years. Based on the Matching Principle, if the equipment generates revenue over a more extended period, the business should fund it with a long-term loan. Long-term loans have lower interest rates but longer repayment periods. In contrast, a business should only use a short-term loan to fund the equipment if the equipment generates revenue in the short term.

Applying the Matching Principle helps businesses to avoid being overburdened with long-term debt in the future. Funding short-term assets with long-term funding can lead to a mismatch in the company's earnings and its financing expenses, resulting in negative cash flows. On the other hand, paying back short-term obligations with long-term financing sources will result in higher interest rates and long-term costs to the company.

Additionally, the Matching Principle is beneficial when it comes to assessing a business's overall risk. By matching its financing with the duration of its assets, a business can align its earning and financing streams effectively. This means that the business can pay for its operating activities without having to rely on external financing sources.

In conclusion, applying the Matching Principle is a crucial factor in determining the optimal working capital funding strategies for businesses. Matching long-term financing sources to long-term assets and short-term financing options to short-term assets ensures that a company has an optimal financing structure that aligns its earnings and financing streams. This helps businesses avoid negative cash flows, higher costs, and ensures they can pay for operating activities without compromising on their long-term profitability.

Working Capital Funding Strategies: Evaluating the Costs and Benefits of Aggressive, Conservative, and Matching Funding Policies

Working capital funding strategies are crucial for companies that aim to maintain a balance between their current assets and liabilities. These strategies include the aggressive, conservative, and matching policies that companies use to determine their funding sources.

An aggressive funding policy is one where companies rely more heavily on short-term funding sources, such as bank overdrafts, to finance their current liabilities. This policy aims to maximize profits and increase the return on investment by investing in high-yield assets. However, an aggressive funding policy can be risky as it could lead to higher interest costs and the possibility of defaulting.

On the other hand, a conservative funding policy involves relying more heavily on long-term funding sources, such as bonds and equity, to finance their assets. This policy aims to minimize risk by reducing the possibility of defaulting on short term liabilities. However, it could also lead to a decline in profitability and a lower return on investment as these sources of funding are often associated with higher interest rates.

A matching funding policy aims to maintain a balance between short and long-term funding sources. A company with this policy will match assets that will generate cash flows in the short term with short-term funding sources and those that will generate long-term cash flows with long-term funding sources. This policy reduces the risks associated with an aggressive funding policy and enhances return on investment by matching the yield on assets with the yield on liabilities.

Each funding strategy has its own set of costs and benefits. An aggressive funding policy may lead to higher profits and return on investment, but could also lead to higher interest costs and the possibility of defaulting. A conservative funding policy may reduce the risk of defaulting on short term liabilities, but could also lead to lower profitability and return on investment. A matching funding policy offers a balanced approach that reduces the risks associated with aggressive policies while also enhancing profitability and return on investment.

For example, a company operating in a highly competitive industry with abundant short-term investment opportunities may prefer to adopt an aggressive funding policy to maximize profits. However, a company operating in a stable industry may prefer to adopt a conservative funding policy to minimize risks. A matching funding policy will be suitable for companies with diverse assets and liabilities that require a balance between short-term and long-term funding sources.

In conclusion, companies should carefully evaluate and consider the relative costs and benefits of aggressive, conservative, and matching funding policies before adopting any funding policy. Companies should also take into account their industry, asset-liability structure, and investment opportunities, among other factors, when choosing a funding policy.

Working Capital Funding Strategies: The Impact of Management Attitudes to Risk, Previous Funding Decisions, and Organization Size

When organizations choose their working capital funding strategies, they consider several factors, including management attitudes to risk, previous funding decisions, and organization size.
Management attitudes to risk are a critical factor in determining funding policies. Some businesses' management may take a more aggressive approach to risk and could adopt an aggressive funding policy.

Conversely, other organizations' management may take a more conservative approach to risk and opt for a conservative funding policy. The management attitude towards risk determines how the organization handles risk and how its financing policy may be structured.

Previous funding decisions are also important because they provide insights into which policies have worked and which have not in the past. If a company has a history of successful aggressive funding policies, they may choose to continue this strategy in the future. Contrarily, if an organization has experienced defaults or liquidity issues as a result of borrowing aggressively, they may choose to become more conservative. Previous funding decisions can inform future strategies and ensure funding policies align with their financial goals.

Organization size is another crucial factor that impacts funding decisions. Larger businesses may be able to access more diverse resources and a variety of funding sources, which smaller organizations may not have access to. Additionally, larger organizations may have bigger investment opportunities, higher profits, and more extensive markets. This advantage may influence a well-established company to adopt a more aggressive funding policy, as they have operational and financial leverage. Smaller organizations, on the other hand, may have more limited liquidity, so they may choose more conservative options, ensuring that their cash resources are not over-depleted.

For example, a small startup may choose a conservative funding policy to achieve its goals without raising concerns about liquidity. A company with a long history of profitability and a highly diversified client base may choose an aggressive approach to reduce the probability of underutilizing resources. In contrast, a company that has experienced previous funding issues may prefer a matching funding policy.

In conclusion, organizations consider management attitudes towards risk, previous funding decisions, and organization size when determining their working capital funding strategies. Management attitudes towards risk must be weighed in conjunction with previous funding decisions and organizational size. Making informed working capital funding decisions demand serious considerations and the use of industry expertise to understand the risks, costs, and benefits. The right funding strategy should align with the business's goals and reflect its potential financing options.

D Investment appraisal

Investment appraisal techniques

Identifying and Calculating Relevant Cash Flows for Investment Projects: A Critical Analysis

When assessing the feasibility of an investment project, it is essential to determine the relevant cash flows accurately. Relevant cash flows are the cash inflows and outflows associated with the project and exclude any sunk costs or external factors. Proper identification and calculation of these cash flows are important to assess the project's profitability and consistency with the business's goals.

The basic approach to calculating cash flows involves subtracting expected cash inflows from expected cash outflows for each year of the project's life. Generally, cash inflows comprise of revenues from sales or rental, interest-generated cash flows connected to investments, royalties, and suchlike. Cash outflows comprise of capital costs, operating expenses such as salaries, taxes, and ongoing maintenance and repair costs. It is crucial to only include cash flows that are a direct result of the proposed investment and exclude any indirect, sunk or irrelevant costs.

Calculating Relevant Cash Flows for Investment Projects

Let's say you want to invest in a small restaurant. You estimate that the initial investment for the restaurant will be $100,000. You anticipate that the restaurant will make $30,000 in profits in the first year, and that the profits will increase by 10% each year after that.

To calculate the relevant cash flows, you would need to consider both the inflows (profits) and outflows (initial investment).

Here's how you could calculate the cash flows over a five-year period:

Year 0 (initial investment):
-100,000 (outflow)

Year 1:
+30,000 (inflow)

Year 2:
+33,000 (inflow)
-10,000 (outflow for additional equipment or repairs)

Year 3:
+36,300 (inflow)
-10,000 (outflow for additional equipment or repairs)

Year 4:
+39,930 (inflow)
-10,000 (outflow for additional equipment or repairs)

Year 5:
+43,923 (inflow)
-10,000 (outflow for additional equipment or repairs)

To calculate the relevant cash flows, you would add up the inflows and outflows for each year. The net cash flow is the difference between the inflows and outflows.

For example, in Year 1, the net cash flow would be $30,000 - $100,000 = -$70,000 (a negative number means a cash outflow).

In Year 2, the net cash flow would be $33,000 - $10,000 - $100,000 = -$77,000.

After you calculate the net cash flows for each year, you could use them to calculate other financial metrics like the payback period, net present value (NPV), and internal rate of return (IRR). These metrics can help you evaluate whether the investment is a good one or not.

For example, when evaluating the cash flows for a new product launch, the relevant cash inflows would include projected sales revenue, while the relevant cash outflows would include fixed costs such as research and development expenses, marketing expenses, and variable costs such as raw material costs or labor costs. This calculation will give a net cash flow for each year of the project.

In addition, it is essential to factor in the time value of money when calculating cash flows to adjust for the impact of inflation and reinvestment. The discounted cash flow (DCF) method measures the present value of future cash flows and should be assessed and considered in the calculations to account for the funds' time value.

By comparing the net present value (NPV) of the project's cash flows with the initial outlay, the investment project's profitability can be measured. A positive NPV indicates that the project's expected cash inflows are greater than the expected cash outflows. Conversely, a negative NPV suggests that the project may result in a loss.

Lastly, sensitivity analysis is another critical aspect of evaluating investment projects. It is vital to identify the assumptions used in calculating the relevant cash flows and estimate how significant these assumptions are on the overall cash flow calculations. Capital investments, as with all aspects of business, involve some degree of uncertainty, sensitivity analysis provides a framework for evaluating how different scenarios can affect the project's profitability.

In conclusion, identifying and calculating relevant cash flows associated with an investment project represents one of the most critical aspects of assessing its feasibility. By using the DCF method and sensitivity analysis, businesses can estimate the expected cash inflows and outflows over time and evaluate the project's overall profitability. Understanding how the project is expected to contribute to the business's bottom line ensures making informed investment decisions aligned with its goals.

The Payback Period as an Investment Appraisal Method: A Critical Evaluation and Discussion of Its Usefulness

The payback period refers to the amount of time it takes for an investment to recoup the initial investment. It is a widely used investment appraisal method that aims to evaluate an investment's suitability by measuring its feasibility to generate cash flows covering the initial investment. The payback period is expressed in years and is calculated by dividing the initial investment by the annual cash inflows.

let's assume a scenario:
A small business owner has invested $50,000 in new equipment, and the expected annual cash flows are $15,000 for each of the next six years. To calculate the payback period, we divide the initial investment by the annual cash inflows.

Payback Period = Initial Investment / Annual Cash Inflows
Payback Period = $50,000 / $15,000
Payback Period = 3.33 years

Therefore, the payback period for this investment is 3.33 years or approximately 3 years and 4 months. This means that it will take just over three years for the investment to recoup the initial investment of $50,000, with the remaining cash inflows from the fourth year onwards being pure profit.

It's worth noting that payback period considers only time that it takes to recoup the initial investment, not the overall profitability of the investment. Therefore, it is important to use payback period alongside other investment appraisal methods such as net present value and internal rate of return to get a comprehensive understanding of the potential investment.

While payback period is useful for assessing the time required to recoup the initial investment, it also has several limitations. The most significant limitation is that it disregards the time value of money, meaning that it assumes that cash flows received are of the same value regardless of when they are received. This could result in a lack of meaningful evaluation of the investment's profitability over the course of its life.

Another limitation of the payback period as an investment appraisal method is that it is solely focused on cash inflows generated, which may not provide an accurate representation of an investment's profitability. The method ignores the cash outflows, such as capital expenditures, operational costs, and inflation, which may negatively impact a project's overall profitability in the long run.

Despite these limitations, the payback period has several advantages as an investment appraisal method. The payback period is easy to calculate, understand and interpret. Business owners and investors rely on this method because it provides them with a relatively quick and straightforward analysis of a potential investment project. It helps in determining an investment's feasibility based on the time taken to recoup the initial investment, which is a critical factor in many situations.

For example, a company may use the payback period method when deciding whether to invest in a new production technology. If the company's management team determines that the payback period is within an acceptable range for their business objectives, the investment may be considered favorable. Discrepancies between the anticipated payback period and the desired range may require more extensive financial analysis.

In conclusion, while the payback period has limitations as an investment appraisal method, it is still beneficial in specific situations as an initial screening tool for potential investments. It can identify whether an investment may be worthwhile before more in-depth financial analysis. It remains a popular technique for evaluating investment projects because of its simplicity and ease of understanding. However, it should not be used as the sole investment appraisal method, and should be supplemented with other techniques such as net present value and internal rate of return that allow for consideration of the time value of money and the project's overall profitability.

Calculating Discounted Payback and Its Usefulness in Investment Appraisal

Discounted payback is a capital budgeting method that considers the time value of money by discounting future cash flows. It is an extension of the traditional payback period and measures the time required for a project to break even in terms of discounted cash flows.

To calculate the discounted payback period, you need to discount each year's net cash flow back to its present value using a discount rate (such as the cost of capital). You then add up the discounted cash flows until the cumulative sum equals the initial investment. The discounted payback period is the number of years it takes for the total discounted cash flows to equal the initial investment.

The usefulness of discounted payback as an investment appraisal method lies in the fact that it considers both the time value of money and the liquidity of an investment. By incorporating the concept of discounted cash flows into the analysis, the method is able to provide a more accurate picture of how long it will take an investment to create value.

However, there are some limitations to discounted payback. First, it may not fully capture the long-term profitability of an investment. Second, it does not take into account the cash flows beyond the payback period. Third, it assumes that cash flows remain constant after the payback period, which may not be the case in reality.

To better understand the application of discounted payback, let's consider an example.

Suppose you are considering an investment in a new manufacturing facility. The initial investment is $10 million, and the estimated net cash flows for the first five years are as follows:

Year 1: $2 million
Year 2: $2.5 million
Year 3: $3 million
Year 4: $3.5 million
Year 5: $4 million

Assuming a discount rate of 8%, the present value of the cash flows would be as follows:

Year 1: $1.85 million
Year 2: $2.18 million
Year 3: $2.43 million
Year 4: $2.59 million
Year 5: $2.65 million

Using the discounted cash flows, the discounted payback period for the investment would be approximately 3.72 years. Therefore, it would take almost 4 years for the investment to generate enough discounted cash flows to cover the initial investment.

Calculating Discounted Payback

Let's say you're considering an investment in a new product line for your company. The initial investment is $200,000, and you expect the project to generate net cash flows of $60,000 per year for the next six years. To calculate the discounted payback period, you would need to discount each year's net cash flow back to its present value using a discount rate of 10%.

Here's how you could calculate the discounted payback:

Year 0 (initial investment):
-$200,000 (outflow)

Year 1:
-$200,000 + ($60,000 / (1 + 0.10)^1) = -$146,487.60 (cumulative discounted cash flow)

Year 2:
-$200,000 + ($60,000 / (1 + 0.10)^2) = -$115,740.74 (cumulative discounted cash flow)

Year 3:
-$200,000 + ($60,000 / (1 + 0.10)^3) = -$91,429.16 (cumulative discounted cash flow)

Year 4:
-$200,000 + ($60,000 / (1 + 0.10)^4) = -$72,790.08 (cumulative discounted cash flow)

Year 5:
-$200,000 + ($60,000 / (1 + 0.10)^5) = -$58,648.40 (cumulative discounted cash flow)

Year 6:
-$200,000 + ($60,000 / (1 + 0.10)^6) = -$47,085.14 (cumulative discounted cash flow)

The discounted payback period would be between Year 3 and Year 4 since the cumulative discounted cash flows become positive in Year 4. We can calculate the exact discounted payback period by figuring out how much of Year 4's cash flow is needed to reach the initial investment.

To do this, we calculate the cumulative discounted cash flows for Year 4:
-$200,000 + ($60,000 / (1 + 0.10)^4) = -$72,790.08

We then subtract this from the initial investment:
$200,000 - (-$72,790.08) = $272,790.08

Next, we divide the amount needed for recovery by the Year 4 cash flow:
$272,790.08 / $60,000 = 4.5465

This means that the discounted payback period would be approximately 4.55 years (between Year 3 and Year 4). It would take almost 4.55 years to generate enough discounted cash flows to cover the initial investment.

By using discounted payback, we have incorporated the concept of time value of money into our analysis and have a more accurate picture of how long it will take for our investment in the new product line to provide a return on our investment.

In conclusion, discounted payback is a useful investment appraisal method that can provide insights into the liquidity and profitability of an investment. However, it is important to be aware of its limitations and to supplement it with other methods such as net present value (NPV) and internal rate of return (IRR) to achieve a more comprehensive analysis of investment decisions.

Calculating Return on Capital Employed and Its Usefulness in Investment Appraisal

Return on Capital Employed (ROCE), also known as the accounting rate of return, is an investment appraisal method that measures the profitability of an investment by comparing the net operating income (profit) to the amount of capital used to generate that profit. The ROCE calculation can be expressed as a percentage by dividing the net operating income by the capital employed.

ROCE is a simple yet powerful financial metric that is useful in evaluating the financial performance of an investment. It is particularly useful when presenting the investment opportunity to financial managers for approval. ROCE can assist in measuring the efficiency of capital investment, evaluating different projects, and prioritizing investments.

The benefits of ROCE also include its ability to evaluate capital deployment, assess the performance of an investment, and aid in forecasting future returns on investment. By using ROCE to analyze an investment, managers can get a good indication of the investment's viability. They can also use ROCE to compare different potential investment projects, evaluate different scenarios, and make investment decisions accordingly.

However, the ROCE has some limitations, such as not considering the time value of money while calculating the cash flows' profits. Therefore, it cannot provide a clear insight into the cash inflows and outflows. It also cannot show how quickly capital invested in any project will capitalize.

To better understand the application of ROCE, consider an example. Suppose you are considering investing in a new project. You expect the investment to generate $400,000 in net operating income over the next 3 years. Further, you require an initial investment of $1,000,000. To calculate the ROCE, you would need to divide the net operating income by the capital employed, and multiply by 100 to give the answer as a percentage.

Here's how you can calculate ROCE:
ROCE = (Net operating income / Capital employed) x 100
ROCE = ($400,000 / $1,000,000) x 100
ROCE = 40%

This means your investment has an ROCE of 40%, indicating that for every dollar invested, you will earn $0.40.

Calculating using a sample example

Let's say you are considering investing in a new machine for your manufacturing company. The initial investment is $500,000, and you expect the machine to generate net operating income of $100,000 per year for the next five years.

To calculate the ROCE, we need to first determine the capital employed, which represents the total investment required to generate the net operating income. In this case, the capital employed is the initial investment of $500,000.

Next, we need to determine the average net operating income for the investment period. To do this, we take the total net operating income for the five years and divide by five:
Average net operating income = (5 x $100,000) / 5 = $100,000

Finally, we divide the average net operating income by the capital employed, and multiply by 100 to obtain the ROCE as a percentage:
ROCE = ($100,000 / $500,000) x 100 = 20%

This means that the investment has an ROCE of 20%, indicating that for every dollar invested, you will earn 20 cents.

In conclusion, ROCE is a useful investment appraisal method that provides an indication of the efficiency of capital investment and the viability of a project. It can be used to evaluate different projects, forecasting future returns, assessing the performance of an investment, and making informed decisions about investment opportunities. However, it's only one metric and managers should use it in conjunction with other methods, such as net present value (NPV) and internal rate of return (IRR), to make well-informed investment decisions.

Calculating Net Present Value and Its Usefulness in Investment Appraisal

Net present value (NPV) is a capital budgeting method that calculates the present value of expected cash inflows and outflows of an investment. The NPV calculation accounts for the time value of money, as it discounts future cash flows back to their present value using a discount rate that reflects the investment's risk.

NPV is a powerful investment appraisal method that determines the difference between the present value of an investment's cash inflows and outflows. It is used to determine the overall value and viability of an investment and is an essential tool for making informed investment decisions.

In NPV calculations, cash inflows are positive while cash outflows are negative values. If the NPV of an investment is positive, it means that the investment generates more cash inflows than outflows, indicating a profitable investment. If the NPV is negative, it means that the investment generates fewer cash inflows than outflows, indicating that it is a loss-making investment.

The usefulness of NPV as an investment appraisal method lies in its ability to consider the time value of money, as well as its flexibility to incorporate changes in interest rates, cash flows, and investment timelines. By incorporating these factors in the analysis, NPV provides a more accurate picture of the investment's potential profitability.

For example, if you are considering investing in a new project with an initial investment of $10,000 and cash inflows of $2,000, $4,000, $4,500, and $5,000 in each year for the next four years, the NPV calculation would look like this:

$$NPV = -\$10{,}000 + (\$2{,}000 / (1+r)^1) + (\$4{,}000 / (1+r)^2) + (\$4{,}500 / (1+r)^3) + (\$5{,}000 / (1+r)^4)$$

Assuming a discount rate of 6%, the NPV would be:
$$NPV = -\$10{,}000 + (\$2{,}000 / 1.06^1) + (\$4{,}000 / 1.06^2) + (\$4{,}500 / 1.06^3) + (\$5{,}000 / 1.06^4) = \$1{,}221.09$$

This indicates that the investment is profitable and will generate a positive NPV of $1,221.09.

An example of calculating net present value (NPV) for an investment.
Suppose you are considering investing in a project that requires an initial investment of $100,000. You expect to receive $30,000 in cash flows for the next five years. Assuming a discount rate of 10%, we can calculate the NPV of the investment as follows:

Year 0 (initial investment): -$100,000
Year 1: $30,000 / (1 + 0.10)^1 = $27,273
Year 2: $30,000 / (1 + 0.10)^2 = $24,793
Year 3: $30,000 / (1 + 0.10)^3 = $22,539
Year 4: $30,000 / (1 + 0.10)^4 = $20,485
Year 5: $30,000 / (1 + 0.10)^5 = $18,614

Next, we add up the Present Value (PV) of all the cash inflows and outflows, which is $113,704.

Finally, we subtract the initial investment from the total present value of cash flows to derive the net present value of the investment. In this case, the NPV of the investment is $13,704:

NPV = PV of cash flows - initial investment
NPV = $113,704 - $100,000
NPV = $13,704

Therefore, based on this calculation, the investment has a positive NPV of $13,704, which indicates that the investment is profitable and will generate a positive return over time.

In conclusion, NPV is a powerful investment appraisal method that is useful in determining the overall value and viability of an investment. It considers the time value of money, is flexible to changes in interest rates, cash flows, and investment timelines, and allows for a more accurate evaluation of an investment's potential profitability. However, managers should use NPV in conjunction with other investment appraisal methods, such as internal rate of return (IRR), to make well-informed investment decisions.

Internal Rate of Return (IRR) as an Investment Appraisal Method

Internal Rate of Return (IRR) is a widely used investment appraisal method which measures the profitability of an investment project. The IRR is the rate at which the net present value of a project becomes zero. In other words, it is the discount rate that equates the present value of the cash inflows from a project with the initial investment.

The usefulness of IRR as an investment appraisal method is due to its simplicity and ease of use. Unlike other methods such as payback, net present value or profitability index, IRR is a straightforward method. As long as the cash flows for a project are determined, IRR can be calculated relatively easily using mathematical software or calculators. Therefore, it can be useful for individuals or small businesses who do not have access to advanced financial tools or the expertise of a financial expert.

Furthermore, the IRR method takes into account the time value of money in a project. By discounting the future cash flows at the prevailing discount rate, the IRR method adjusts for the risk associated with the investment. This means that an investment project with a higher IRR is more likely to be accepted since it generates higher cash inflows relative to the initial investment.

let's assume we are considering an investment project that requires an initial investment of $10,000 and is expected to generate cash flows of $2,000 per year for the next six years. To calculate the IRR of this project, we need to use a financial calculator or software that can solve for the discount rate that equates the present value of the cash inflows to the initial investment.

Here are the cash flows for the investment project:

Year 0: -$10,000 (initial investment)
Year 1: $2,000
Year 2: $2,000
Year 3: $2,000
Year 4: $2,000
Year 5: $2,000
Year 6: $2,000

To calculate the IRR, we can use a financial calculator or software to solve for the discount rate that makes the net present value (NPV) of the cash flows equal to zero. The NPV is calculated by discounting the cash flows at the prevailing discount rate, which we do not know yet.

Using a financial calculator, we can enter the cash flows into the calculator and solve for the IRR, which turns out to be 16.2%. This means that the project generates a return of 16.2% per year, which is higher than the required rate of return for the investor. Therefore, this project may be considered a good investment opportunity.

However, there are some limitations to the IRR method that need to be addressed. Firstly, IRR assumes that the cash inflows from a project are reinvested at the same rate as the IRR itself. This is not always realistic, particularly if the project's cash flows are used for other purposes. Secondly, IRR does not take into account the scale of the investment, and therefore, it may not be applicable to larger and complex projects that have different cash flows during different periods. Thirdly, IRR may generate multiple solutions, especially when the cash flows are non-conventional.

Nonetheless, IRR is an important investment appraisal method that has a wide range of applications in various financial and non-financial sectors. For instance, it can be used to evaluate investments in real estate, capital equipment, and research and development projects. It can also be useful for investors who seek to maximize their returns while minimizing their risks. By comparing the expected IRR of different investment opportunities, investors can make better-informed decisions about where to allocate their funds.

In conclusion, IRR is a popular and valuable investment appraisal method that has many advantages. While it has some limitations, it remains a powerful tool for evaluating the profitability of investment projects. By considering the time value of money and the risk involved, the IRR method offers a more comprehensive analysis of investment opportunities that can help individuals and businesses make better investment decisions.

The Superiority of Discounted Cash Flow (DCF) Methods over Non-DCF Methods in Investment Appraisal

Discounted Cash Flow (DCF) methods are commonly used in investment appraisal because they consider the time value of money. This method calculates the present value of future cash inflows by discounting them to the present using a discount rate. Non-DCF methods, on the other hand, do not consider the time value of money and only focus on the raw data of cash inflows and outflows. In this subheading, we will discuss the superiority of DCF methods over non-DCF methods in investment appraisal.

One of the main advantages of DCF methods over non-DCF methods is that they consider the time value of money. This means that the cash flows from an investment project are discounted at a rate that reflects the opportunity cost of the investment. This allows investors to assess the potential profitability of a project and compare it to other investment opportunities. For example, suppose we are comparing two investment projects that require the same initial investment and generate the same cash flows. The first project generates the cash flows in one year, while the second project generates the cash flows over five years. By using DCF methods, we can see that the first project has a higher net present value since all the cash flows are received earlier, and there is less uncertainty that comes with longer-term investments.

Another advantage of DCF methods is that they allow for more accurate decision-making. By adjusting for the time value of money, investors can make informed decisions about the profitability of a project. Non-DCF methods, such as payback or accounting rate of return, do not take into account the expected return on investment or the risk of the project. For example, a project may have a shorter payback period, but it may not generate as much profit as another project that has a longer payback period. Using DCF methods, we can compare the net present value of each project and determine which investment opportunity is more profitable.

DCF methods are also widely used in various industries, such as real estate, finance, and capital investments. In real estate, DCF methods are used to evaluate the profitability of rental properties, while in finance, DCF methods are used to value stocks and bonds. Capital investments, such as the purchase of new equipment or machinery, are also evaluated using DCF methods to determine the feasibility of the investment.

In conclusion, while non-DCF methods provide a quick and easy way to analyze investment opportunities, DCF methods are far superior in investment appraisal. By accounting for the time value of money, DCF methods allow for more accurate and informed decision-making. They are also widely used in various industries and provide a comprehensive way to evaluate the profitability of investment projects. Consequently, DCF methods should be the preferred method used by investors and analysts when evaluating investments.

Comparing the Relative Merits of Net Present Value (NPV) and Internal Rate of Return (IRR) Methods in Investment Appraisal

Net Present Value (NPV) and Internal Rate of Return (IRR) are two widely used discounted cash flow methods in investment appraisal. While both methods seek to evaluate the profitability of investment opportunities, they differ in their approach and output. In this subheading, we will discuss the relative merits of NPV and IRR, and how they differ in their application and interpretation.

Net Present Value (NPV) is the present value of cash inflows minus the present value of cash outflows, discounted at an appropriate rate. In other words, it calculates the value of an investment project in today's dollars, taking into account the expected cash inflows and outflows over its lifetime. An investment project with a positive NPV indicates that it is profitable, while a negative NPV indicates that it is not.

Internal Rate of Return (IRR) is the discount rate that makes the net present value of a project equal to zero. The IRR method allows investors to evaluate the potential profitability of investment projects by determining their expected rate of return. If the IRR of a project is greater than the required rate of return, it is considered to be profitable, while if IRR is less than the required rate of return, it is not profitable.

The relative merits of NPV and IRR can be seen in their application and interpretation. The main advantage of NPV over IRR is that it provides a more accurate measure of the profitability of an investment project. Since NPV takes into account the size of the investment, the cash flows over time, and the discount rate, it is a more comprehensive measure of investment profitability. For example, in a case with mutual exclusive projects, the project with the highest NPV may not have the highest IRR. Therefore, NPV is preferred for large, long-term investments where accuracy is of the utmost importance.

On the other hand, the main advantage of IRR over NPV is that it is easier to interpret and communicate to others. The IRR represents the percentage return that investors can expect to receive from a project, which is easier to understand than NPV. Furthermore, IRR is a helpful way for investors to benchmark the project against other investment opportunities. For instance, a project with a higher IRR is a better investment compared to an alternative project with a lower IRR.

It is important to note that both NPV and IRR have limitations, and they should be used in conjunction with other evaluation methods. For example, when evaluating complex investments, such as real estate, both NPV and IRR are commonly used together.

2. Allowing for inflation and taxation in DCF

When conducting a discounted cash flow analysis, it is essential to consider the effects of inflation and taxes on cash flows. Inflation and taxes affect the purchasing power of cash over time, and thus, they can significantly impact the profitability of an investment project. Therefore, it is important to account for these factors when calculating the present value of future cash flows. In this subheading, we will discuss how inflation and taxation can be accounted for in DCF analysis. Inflation is a measure of the increase in the general price level of goods and services in an economy over time. When inflation occurs, the purchasing power of cash decreases, and the value of future cash flows declines. Therefore, it is necessary to adjust the cash flows for inflation when calculating the present value of future cash flows. This can be done by using an inflation rate or a real interest rate, which takes into account the inflation rate. The real interest rate is calculated by subtracting the rate of inflation from the nominal interest rate.

Taxes are also an important factor in investment appraisal, as they can significantly impact the net cash flows from an investment project. Taxes can be incorporated into the DCF analysis by using an after-tax discount rate, which accounts for the effects of taxation on the expected cash inflows. This involves subtracting the tax rate from the discount rate to obtain an after-tax discount rate. Similarly, the cash flows can be adjusted for taxes by subtracting the applicable tax rate from the nominal cash inflows.

Incorporating inflation and tax rates into DCF analysis can make the analysis more complex, but it provides a more accurate measure of the profitability of an investment project. By accounting for the effects of inflation and taxes on cash flows, investors can better understand the expected returns from the project and adjust their investment strategies accordingly.

Comparing Nominal-Terms and Real-Terms Approaches to Investment Appraisal

There are two approaches to accounting for inflation in investment appraisal: real-terms and nominal-terms approaches. Both approaches have different approaches to calculating the present value of future cash flows, and each has its advantages and limitations. In this subheading, we will apply and discuss these two approaches to investment appraisal. Nominal Terms Approach The nominal terms approach is the simplest approach to accounting for inflation in investment appraisal. It uses the nominal cash flows, which are the cash flows stated in current dollars without any adjustment for inflation. The nominal discount rate is also the rate stated in current dollars without any adjustments. For example, suppose we are evaluating an investment project that requires an initial investment of $10,000 and is expected to produce nominal cash flows of $2,000 per year for the next five years. Assuming a discount rate of 10%, the nominal terms approach would discount the cash flows at 10% without any adjustments for inflation. Real Terms Approach The real terms approach is a more comprehensive approach to accounting for inflation in investment appraisal. It involves adjusting the cash flows for inflation and discounting them with a real discount rate, which is the nominal discount rate adjusted for inflation. For the same example, suppose the inflation rate is estimated at 3%. To calculate the real cash flows, we need to deflate the nominal cash flows by the inflation rate to adjust for the effects of inflation. The real cash flows would be $1,942 for year one ($2,000/1.03), $1,887 for year two ($1,942/1.03), and so on. The real discount rate, which accounts for inflation, would be 6.8% (10% - 3%), which would be used to discount the real cash flows. Comparison and Analysis The main difference between the two approaches is how they account for inflation. The nominal-terms approach does not adjust for inflation, and thus, it is not as accurate as the real terms approach in evaluating an investment opportunity. The real terms approach, on the other hand, considers the effects of inflation on the cash flows and provides a more accurate measure of the profitability of an investment project over time. There are some limitations to the real terms approach. For instance, it assumes that the cash inflows and outflows are adjusted for inflation equally over time, which is not always the case. It also assumes that inflation rates are predictable, which is not always accurate. Furthermore, the real-terms approach requires more data because it involves additional calculations such as the estimation of inflation rates. Despite these limitations, the real terms approach is widely used in investment appraisal because it provides a more accurate measure of profitability. The nominal terms approach is simple to use, and it may be helpful in simpler situations, and it may not be appropriate for complex investments or long-term projects. In conclusion, the real-terms and nominal-terms approaches to investment appraisal both have different benefits and limitations. The real-terms approach provides a more accurate measure of profitability, but it requires additional data and calculations. The nominal-terms approach, on the other hand, may be helpful in simpler situations, but it is not as accurate as the real terms approach. Therefore, investors should choose the approach that is most suitable for their investment project and take into account the effects of inflation when evaluating investment opportunities.

Calculating Taxation Effects of Cash Flows in Investment Appraisal

Calculating the taxation effects of relevant cash flows is an essential aspect of investment appraisal. It involves evaluating the tax benefits and liabilities associated with an investment project. When evaluating the profitability of an investment opportunity, the cash flows must be adjusted for tax implications. This subheading will discuss how to calculate the taxation effects of relevant cash flows, including the benefits of tax-allowable depreciation and the liabilities of taxable profit. Tax-allowable depreciation is a tax deduction that can be claimed for the decrease in the value of an asset over time. The amount of depreciation allowed for tax purposes depends on the tax regulations in a particular country. The tax deduction reduces the taxable profit, lowering the tax liability, which can increase the cash flows available for the investor.

For example, suppose a company invests in a machine that costs $10,000 and depreciates at a rate of $1,000 annually. In the first year, the taxable profit is $10,000, and applying a tax rate of 20%, the tax liability would be $2,000. However, if we apply the tax-allowable depreciation of $1,000, the taxable profit reduces to $9,000, reducing the tax liability to $1,800, an increase in cash flow of $200. In subsequent years, as the value of the machine decreases, the allowable depreciation decreases, leading to a smaller tax benefit.

On the other hand, taxable profits increase the tax liability and decrease the cash flows available from the investment. A taxable profit is the difference between the revenue generated and the costs associated with the investment. These costs include expenses like production costs, operating expenses, and financing costs. Determining the taxable profit requires a thorough evaluation of all the costs associated with the investment.

For example, suppose a company invests $100,000 in a project that generates revenues of $150,000 in the first year, and the costs associated with the investment amount to $70,000. The taxable profit would be $80,000, and applying a tax rate of 20%, the tax liability would be $16,000, leading to a decrease of $64,000 in cash flows.

In conclusion, understanding the taxation effects and benefits associated with an investment is crucial when evaluating the profitability of an investment project. Tax allowances such as depreciation can increase cash flows, while taxable profits can decrease available cash flows. To effectively calculate the tax implications, it is necessary to evaluate all costs associated with the investment, and it is recommended that an expert in tax laws be consulted with to better understand the applicable tax regulations.

Calculating and Applying Before- and After-Tax Discount Rates in Investment Appraisal

In an investment appraisal, the discount rate represents the opportunity cost of investing in a project. It is the minimum rate of return that an investor expects from an investment in order to compensate for the risks taken. The discount rate is usually expressed as a percentage and is used to calculate the present value of future cash flows. There are two types of discount rates: before-tax and after-tax discount rates.

The before-tax discount rate represents the rate of return that is required before accounting for the impact of taxes on the investment. It does not consider the tax implications of the investment, such as tax benefits from depreciation or tax liabilities from taxable profits. This type of discount rate is typically used to evaluate the profitability of investments in a tax-neutral environment.

The after-tax discount rate, on the other hand, considers the tax implications associated with the investment. It takes into account the tax benefits and liabilities that result from the investment, such as tax credits or tax expenses related to the investment. The after-tax discount rate is typically used to evaluate the profitability of investments after accounting for the impact of taxes.

To calculate the after-tax discount rate, the before-tax discount rate must first be determined. Then, the tax rate associated with the investment must be applied to the before-tax discount rate to determine the after-tax discount rate.

Here are five examples to illustrate the calculation and application of before- and after-tax discount rates:

Example 1: An investor requires a 10% before-tax return on a project that has a tax rate of 25%. What is the after-tax discount rate?

Solution:
The after-tax discount rate can be calculated as follows:
After-tax discount rate = Before-tax discount rate x (1 - Tax rate)
After-tax discount rate = 10% x (1 - 0.25)
After-tax discount rate = 7.5%

Example 2: An investor requires a 12% before-tax return on a project that has a tax rate of 30%. What is the after-tax discount rate?

Solution:
The after-tax discount rate can be calculated as follows:
After-tax discount rate = Before-tax discount rate x (1 - Tax rate)
After-tax discount rate = 12% x (1 - 0.30)
After-tax discount rate = 8.4%

Example 3: An investor requires a 15% before-tax return on a project that has a tax rate of 20%. What is the after-tax discount rate?

Solution:

The after-tax discount rate can be calculated as follows:
After-tax discount rate = Before-tax discount rate x (1 - Tax rate)
After-tax discount rate = 15% x (1 - 0.20)
After-tax discount rate = 12%

Example 4: An investor requires a 8% before-tax return on a project that has a tax rate of 35%. What is the after-tax discount rate?

Solution:
The after-tax discount rate can be calculated as follows:
After-tax discount rate = Before-tax discount rate x (1 - Tax rate)
After-tax discount rate = 8% x (1 - 0.35)
After-tax discount rate = 5.2%

Example 5: An investor requires a 9% before-tax return on a project that has a tax rate of 15%. What is the after-tax discount rate?

Solution:
The after-tax discount rate can be calculated as follows:
After-tax discount rate = Before-tax discount rate x (1 - Tax rate)
After-tax discount rate = 9% x (1 - 0.15)
After-tax discount rate = 7.65%

In conclusion, calculating and applying before- and after-tax discount rates is an essential aspect of the investment appraisal process. Understanding the tax implications of an investment project and adjusting the discount rate accordingly can provide a more accurate measure of the profitability and risks associated with the investment.

Adjusting for risk and uncertainty in investment appraisal

Distinguishing Between Risk and Uncertainty in Investment Appraisal: Probability and Project Life Considerations

When evaluating investment projects, it is essential to consider the concepts of risk and uncertainty. While often used interchangeably, these terms represent different concepts that can have a significant impact on investment decisions. Risk is a probabilistic concept that involves the estimation of the probability of an event occurring, while uncertainty is a non-probabilistic concept that involves unknown or ambiguous information surrounding an event.

Risk involves the estimation of the probability of a project's success or failure. The probability is based on available information and past experiences. The more information available, the lower the level of risk involved in making investment decisions. Risk can be measured by statistical methods that rely on probability distributions.

For example, suppose a company is considering investing in a new product line. Based on previous experience, the company estimates that the probability of success is 70%. The company can then use this probability to evaluate the risks associated with the investment decision.

Uncertainty, on the other hand, involves a lack of information or an ambiguous situation that makes it difficult to estimate the probability of an event. It is often difficult to quantify and measure, making it a more challenging concept to deal with when evaluating investment decisions.

For instance, suppose a company is considering investing in a new technology that has not yet been released to the market. There may be uncertainty surrounding the technology's eventual success, making it challenging to estimate the likelihood of success. In such cases, investment decision makers may need to rely on expert opinions or alternative scenarios to evaluate the investment's potential outcomes.

Project life is another factor that can impact the differences between risk and uncertainty. As the project's lifespan increases, the probability and impact of uncertainty also increase, making investment decisions more challenging. When evaluating long-term investments, decision-makers must also consider factors such as macroeconomic trends, regulatory changes, and technological advancements that may impact the project's success.

In conclusion, risk and uncertainty are two critical concepts that must be considered when evaluating investment projects. While risk can be measured probabilistically, uncertainty involves a lack of information or an ambiguous situation that makes measurement more challenging. As project life increases, the probability and impact of uncertainty also increase, making investment decisions more difficult. Decision-makers should carefully evaluate both risk and uncertainty when making investment decisions for long-term projects.

Sensitivity Analysis in Investment Appraisal: Benefits, Techniques, and Limitations

Sensitivity analysis is a technique used in investment appraisal to identify variables that have a significant impact on the project's profitability. It involves assessing the impact of changes in key variables on the overall outcome of the investment decision. By analyzing the sensitivity of these variables to changes in assumptions, decision-makers can make more informed decisions and better manage the risks associated with an investment opportunity.

The sensitivity analysis involves changing one variable at a time and measuring the impact on the financial outcome of the project. The variables can include factors such as price, costs, inflation rates, exchange rates, and interest rates. Using sensitivity analysis, decision-makers can identify the level of risk associated with a project and optimize the decision-making process.

For instance, suppose a company is considering investing in a new manufacturing plant that will cost $5 million, and it is expected to generate annual cash flows of $1.5 million for five years. The project's sensitivity may be analyzed by varying the key variables such as the cost of production, the selling price, and the discount rate.

If the selling price varies, the sensitivity analysis can help determine the level of price decline that must occur before the project's profitability is compromised. If the cost of production changes, sensitivity analysis can help determine the effect on profitability. If the discount rate used in the project evaluation changes, the sensitivity analysis can help determine the level of rate increase that would make the project unprofitable.

The usefulness of sensitivity analysis in assisting investment decisions is that it provides a range of possible outcomes based on varying assumptions. It also identifies the critical factors that have the most significant impact on the project's profitability. This information can help investment decision-makers to determine the risk level associated with the project and optimize investment decisions.

One of the shortcomings of sensitivity analysis is that it assumes that the variables being analyzed are independent of each other. It also assumes that the variables are either positively or negatively correlated. In reality, the variables are not always independent, and their relationships can be more complicated. As such, using sensitivity analysis alone may not provide a complete picture of the real-world scenarios.

In conclusion, sensitivity analysis is a useful tool in investment appraisal that enables decision-makers to identify critical factors that have the most significant impact on the profitability of an investment project. It is important to note, however, that sensitivity analysis assumes that the variables being analyzed are independent, and relies on past data to inform the analysis. Decision-makers should, therefore, also consider other qualitative factors and consider the limitations of the technique when using sensitivity analysis to assist in investment decisions.

Applications and Effectiveness of Sensitivity Analysis in Investment Projects

Sensitivity analysis is a powerful tool that is commonly used in investment appraisal to determine the extent to which a variation in a critical variable affects the project's overall profitability. This technique allows decision-makers to identify and manage the risks associated with an investment opportunity by analyzing the effect of changes in key variables. By using sensitivity analysis, the decision-makers can make informed decisions based on a range of possible outcomes derived from varying assumptions.

Here are five potential applications of sensitivity analysis in investment projects:

1. Real estate investment: Real estate investors can use sensitivity analysis to determine the impact of fluctuations in property values, rental rates, or taxes on their property's overall profitability.

2. Technology investment: Technology investors can use sensitivity analysis to assess the impact of factors such as R&D costs, production costs, and changes in demand for a product on the investment's profitability.

3. Agriculture investment: Farmers and agricultural investors can use sensitivity analysis to determine the impact of weather conditions, crop yields, and commodity prices on their investment's profitability.

4. Energy investment: Energy investors can use sensitivity analysis to assess the impact of fluctuations in input costs, demand, and

government regulations on the investment's profitability.

5. Manufacturing investment: Manufacturers can use sensitivity analysis to determine the impact of changes in raw material costs, transportation costs, or labor costs on their investment's profitability.

The usefulness of sensitivity analysis in investment decisions is that it helps the decision-makers to identify the critical factors that have the most significant impact on the investment's profitability. However, it is essential to note that it relies on external factors that are out of the investor's control, such as market trends and economic conditions. Moreover, sensitivity analysis assumes that the variables being analyzed are independent of each other and may not provide a complete picture of the real-world scenarios. Therefore, it is crucial to use sensitivity analysis in conjunction with other techniques and consider other qualitative factors when making investment decisions.

Simulation Technique: Applications, Techniques, and Effectiveness in Adjusting for Risk and Uncertainty in Investment Appraisal

Simulation technique is a method used to adjust for risk and uncertainty in investment appraisal. This technique involves creating a model that simulates the range of outcomes resulting from uncertainties and risks associated with an investment opportunity. By developing the simulation model, decision-makers can evaluate various possible outcomes, assess the level of risk and uncertainty associated with the investment opportunity, and make informed decisions.
Here are five potential applications of simulation technique in investment appraisal:

1. Stock Market Investment: Stock market investors use simulation technique to simulate various market situations, including market volatility, interest rates changes, and inflation rates, and determine the

impact of these changes on the stock price.

2. Oil and Gas Exploration: Oil and gas exploration companies use simulation technique to simulate and evaluate drilling outcomes, including production rates, costs, and the likelihood of hitting a specific reservoir.

3. Real Estate Investment: Real estate investors use simulation technique to simulate market trends in sales, rents, or property values, which can impact the overall profitability of their investment.

4. Aerospace Investment: Aerospace companies use simulation technique to evaluate the impact of the development of new technologies or changes in airplane models on the overall profitability of their investment.

5. Pharmaceutical Investment: Pharmaceutical companies use simulation technique to simulate possible outcomes for drug trials, including the likelihood of success, the number of patients required, and the potential return on investment.

Here are five examples of applied techniques used in simulation technique:

1. Monte Carlo Simulation: This technique simulates a range of possible outcomes and calculates the probability of each outcome.

2. Decision Tree Analysis: This technique helps analyze the possible outcomes of a decision by mapping out different scenarios and calculating the probability of each scenario.

3. Sensitivity Analysis: This technique identifies the critical variables that affect the investment's profitability and measures the impact of changes in these variables.

4. Hypothetical Risk Analysis: This technique involves creating a sophisticated simulation model that simulates complex market behaviors.

5. Discrete Event Simulation: This technique simulates a range of discrete events that can impact an investment's profitability, such as natural disasters, production cycles, or customer behaviors.

The effectiveness of simulation technique in adjusting for risk and uncertainty in investment appraisal is that it enables decision-makers to evaluate various possible outcomes, assess the level of risk associated with the investment opportunity, and make informed decisions based on the simulation model. However, developing a simulation model can be complex and require a high level of expertise. Moreover, the accuracy of the simulation model is dependent on the quality of the data input into the model. Therefore, decision-makers should be aware of the limitations of the simulation technique and use it in conjunction with other techniques when analyzing and evaluating investment opportunities.

Applications and Techniques of Adjusted Payback Method in Investment Appraisal

The adjusted payback technique is a method used to adjust for risk and uncertainty in investment appraisal. This technique involves estimating the time required to recover the initial investment, taking into account the expected cash flows and the risk of receiving those cash flows. By using the adjusted payback technique, decision-makers can determine whether an investment is feasible and how long it will take to recover the initial investment.

Here are five potential applications of the adjusted payback technique in investment appraisal:

1. Renewable Energy Investment: Renewable energy companies can use the adjusted payback technique to evaluate the profitability of an investment in a specific renewable energy project, taking into account the risks and uncertainties associated with obtaining income from renewable energy sources.

2. Entertainment Industry Investment: Investors in the entertainment industry can use the adjusted payback technique to estimate the time to recover costs, taking into account the uncertainties associated with success rates, audience responses, and potential licensing fees.

3. Mining Investment: Mining companies can use the adjusted payback technique to assess the time required to recover costs, taking into account the uncertainties associated with the discovery of minerals, the cost of extraction, and the fluctuation of commodity prices.

4. Technology Investment: Technology investors can use the adjusted payback technique to determine the time required to recover costs, taking into account the uncertainties associated with the development and marketing of new technologies, patent or licensing fees, and market acceptance.

5. Healthcare Investment: Healthcare companies or investors can use the adjusted payback technique to evaluate the profitability of a specific healthcare investment, taking into account the uncertainties associated with regulatory approval, trial costs, and healthcare insurance policy changes.

Here are five examples of applied techniques used in the adjusted payback technique:

1. Present Value Calculations: This technique factors in the time value of money when estimating the adjusted payback period.

2. Monte Carlo Simulation: This technique involves estimating the adjusted payback period by simulating a range of possible outcomes based on varying assumptions and probabilities.

3. Sensitivity Analysis: This technique helps in analyzing the impact of fluctuating cash flows on the adjusted payback period.

4. Internal Rate of Return (IRR): This technique determines the rate at which the cash flows are discounted to reach a net present value of zero.

5. Risk Adjusted Discount Rate (RADR): This technique involves adjusting the discount rate to factor in risk and uncertainty elements while estimating the adjusted payback period.

The effectiveness of the adjusted payback technique in adjusting for risk and uncertainty in investment appraisal is that it provides a simple and easy-to-understand method to determine whether the initial investment is feasible based on various scenarios. However, the adjusted payback technique may not be effective in evaluating projects that have a longer payback period or where the uncertainties are too complex to estimate accurately. Therefore, decision-makers should use this technique in conjunction with other techniques to evaluate complex investment opportunities.

Risk-Adjusted Discount Rates Technique in Investment Appraisal: Applications and Discussions

The Risk-Adjusted Discount Rates (RADR) technique is a method of adjusting for risk and uncertainty in investment appraisal by considering the expected rate of return from an investment, taking into account the level of risk associated with it. This technique compares the expected return on investment to the risk-free rate of return and adjusts it accordingly. In other words, the RADR technique involves calculating the expected cash flows of the investment and adjusting the discount rate used to calculate present value based on the risk involved in achieving those cash flows. Below are five potential applications of the RADR technique in investment appraisal:

1. Real Estate Investment: Real estate investors can use the RADR technique to adjust for risks related to market volatility, changes in zoning laws, availability of amenities, and the duration it takes to complete and sell construction projects.

2. Acquisition of a Business: Investors looking to buy existing businesses can use the RADR technique to adjust for the risks associated with acquiring businesses such as changes in market competition, customer retention, and regulatory compliance.

3. Stock Investment: Investors can use the RADR technique to adjust for the inherent risks associated with the stock market, including volatility in the economy, interest rates, and changing market trends.

4. Venture Capital Investment: Venture capitalists can use the RADR technique to adjust for risks associated with start-ups, including the unproven nature of the business model, high rates of failure, and uncertain future cash flows.

5. Infrastructure Investment: Investors in infrastructure projects such as highways and airports can use the RADR technique to adjust for risks related to cost overruns, regulatory delays, and changes in government policies.

However, there are some discussions of concerns related to the RADR technique. Below are five discussions of applied applications of the RADR technique:

1. The argument that the RADR technique increases the subjective nature of investment appraisal since it relies heavily on the judgment of the decision-maker in determining the level of risk.

2. The RADR technique may not capture all the risks associated with an investment, particularly risks that are unanticipated or where data is unavailable.

3. The RADR technique may also overlook the potential benefits of the investment, such as increased efficiency or market share, which could offset risks.

4. The RADR technique may lead to overestimating or underestimating the true value of an investment, particularly when the assumptions used to estimate the expected cash flows and discount rate may be inaccurate.

5. There is also the concern that the RADR technique may not be suitable for comparing investments with different levels of risk, as the technique assumes all the risks can be quantified in a single measure.

In conclusion, the RADR technique is a method used to adjust for risk and uncertainty in investment appraisal, and it can be applied in various investment opportunities. However, decision-makers should consider the limitations of the technique and incorporate it with other investment appraisal methods to arrive at a more comprehensive investment decision.

4. Specific investment decisions (Lease or buy, asset replacement, capital rationing)

Companies encounter numerous investment decisions that can impact their financial condition and long-term success. These investment decisions can range from deciding whether to lease or buy equipment to determining when to replace current assets with new ones. One critical issue that firms often encounter in regard to investment decisions is capital rationing, where they need to allocate limited funds to various investment alternatives. This can result from various internal constraints, such as cash flow or budget limitations, or external factors, such as regulatory requirements or environmental concerns. As such, it is essential for companies to evaluate their investment options carefully and make informed decisions to ensure they maximize their returns while minimizing potential risks.

Analyzing Leasing and Borrowing to Buy - Before- and After-Tax Costs of Debt

Leasing and borrowing are two options businesses have when they want to secure assets without paying upfront costs. Leasing involves renting an asset for a fixed period, whereas borrowing involves taking out a loan to purchase an asset. In evaluating leasing and borrowing to buy, it is essential to consider the before- and after-tax costs of debt. Before-tax cost of debt is the interest rate a company pays on its borrowing, whereas after-tax cost of debt is the net rate after considering tax benefits associated with interest paid on debt.

One application of leasing and borrowing to buy is purchasing company vehicles. Let us consider one example each and apply both the leasing and borrowing options to buy company vehicles.

Example 1: Company A needs five vehicles to expand its operations.

The cost of a new vehicle is $25,000, and they intend to keep them for five years.

Leasing Option: The leasing company offers a lease with a monthly payment of $500 per vehicle. The leasing contract lasts for five years, with the company having the option to buy the vehicles at the end of the lease.

Borrowing Option: Company A can secure a loan with a 5% interest rate per annum to purchase the vehicles upfront. The loan needs to be repaid over a five-year period, with monthly payments of $471 or a total of $28,260 after five years.

Example 2: Company B needs new office equipment, consisting of computers, printers, and phones. The total cost of the equipment is $100,000, and their useful life is also five years.

Leasing Option: The leasing company offers a lease with a monthly payment of $2,000, and the contract stipulates that the lease will last for five years. The leasing company owns the equipment, and the company has the option to purchase them at the end of the lease.

Borrowing Option: Company B can also obtain a loan with a 5% interest rate per annum to purchase the equipment. The loan will also have a five-year repayment plan with monthly payments of $1,609. The total amount repaid will be $96,540.

When evaluating leasing and borrowing options, it is essential to analyze the outcome. In these two examples, the borrowing option has a higher total cost than the leasing option. However, the tax benefits associated with borrowing should also be considered. In both examples, since the interest paid by the company on the loan is tax-deductible, the total cost after-tax is lower than the total leasing cost. A tax rate of 30% can be assumed; therefore, the after-tax cost for borrowing options in Example

1 will be $19,782, while that of Example 2 will be $67,578.

In conclusion, deciding between leasing and borrowing to buy assets depends on the needs of the company and the tax benefits associated with each option. Companies should evaluate the before-tax and after-tax costs of debt associated with each alternative and weigh the benefits of each. Factors such as the asset's expected useful life, the company's credit rating, and the availability of tax deductions should all be considered when making a final decision.

Analyzing Asset Replacement Decisions Using Equivalent Annual Cost and Equivalent Annual Benefit Methods: Five Sample Examples

When making decisions regarding the replacement of an asset, businesses use various methods. Two of such methods are equivalent annual cost and equivalent annual benefit. Equivalent annual cost involves analyzing the full cost of buying and operating an asset over a specific period, such as its useful life, and dividing that cost by the asset's annuity factor to determine the equivalent annual cost. Equivalent annual benefit, on the other hand, takes into account the expected returns, savings, or revenue streams from owning or operating an asset. Let us consider five sample examples and apply the equivalent annual cost and equivalent annual benefit methods to evaluate asset replacement decisions:

Example 1: Company A is considering replacing its old crane with a new one. The cost of purchasing the new crane is $120,000, and the old crane's resale value is $25,000 after twelve years of use. The new crane has a useful life of twelve years, and its operating costs (fuel, maintenance, insurance, and taxes) are $12,000 per year.

Equivalent Annual Cost: The total cost of owning and operating the old crane is $205,000, and the equivalent annual cost is $20,384. The equivalent annual cost of the new crane is $16,000, making it a suitable replacement decision.

Equivalent Annual Benefit: Owning and operating the new crane provides an equivalent annual benefit of $17,000, making it a suitable replacement decision.

Example 2: Company B is considering replacing its outdated software system, which has an annual cost of $30,000, with a newer system that costs $200,000 and has an annual operating cost of $15,000.

Equivalent Annual Cost: Over five years, the total cost of owning and operating the old software system is $150,000, and the equivalent annual cost is $30,000. The equivalent annual cost of the new system is $46,832, making it an unsuitable replacement decision.

Equivalent Annual Benefit: Owning and operating the new software system provides an equivalent annual benefit of $20,031, making it an unsuitable replacement decision.

Example 3: Company C is considering replacing its old delivery truck, which costs $5,000 per year to maintain and repair, with a new one that costs $20,000 and has a useful life of six years. The resale value of the old truck is $3,000.

Equivalent Annual Cost: The total cost of owning and operating the old truck over six years is $33,000, and the equivalent annual cost is $5,500. The equivalent annual cost of owning and operating the new truck is $4,424, making it a suitable replacement decision.

Equivalent Annual Benefit: Owning and operating the new truck provides an equivalent annual benefit of $4,630, making it a suitable replacement decision.

Example 4: Company D is considering replacing an old piece of equipment that costs $10,000 per year to operate and maintain, with a new and more efficient one that costs $50,000 and has a useful life of ten years. The old equipment has a resale value of $5,000.

Equivalent Annual Cost: The total cost of owning and operating the old equipment over ten years is $105,000, and the equivalent annual cost is $10,500. The equivalent annual cost of the new equipment is $6,137, making it a suitable replacement decision.

Equivalent Annual Benefit: Owning and operating the new equipment provides an equivalent annual benefit of $7,858, making it a suitable replacement decision.

Example 5: Company E is considering replacing a printing press with a newer model that is more efficient, which costs $60,000 and has an annual operating cost of $10,000. The old printer's resale value is $15,000, and its operating cost is $20,000 per year.

Equivalent Annual Cost: The total cost of owning and operating the old printer over six years is $155,000, and the equivalent annual cost is $25,833. The equivalent annual cost of the new printer is $15,942, making it a suitable replacement decision.

Equivalent Annual Benefit: Owning and operating the new printer provides an equivalent annual benefit of $18,417, making it a suitable replacement decision.

In conclusion, the equivalent annual cost and equivalent annual benefit methods are useful analytical tools for evaluating asset replacement decisions. Comparing the equivalent annual costs or benefits of owning and operating multiple assets over the same period can help determine the most cost-effective option. Companies should weigh the benefits of each option against their costs while taking depreciation, taxes, financing, and resale value into consideration.

Calculating Profitability Indexes for Divisible Investment Projects under Single-Period Capital Rationing: Examples and Evaluations

The Calculation of Profitability Indexes for Divisible Investment Projects under Single-Period Capital Rationing:

Profitability index is a financial metric used to assess the attractiveness of a project by comparing the present value of its cash inflows to the present value of its cash outflows. In the context of single-period capital rationing, where firms have limited funds to invest in multiple projects, profitability index is a useful tool to determine which investment projects should be selected.

The formula for profitability index is:

Profitability Index (PI) = Present value of cash inflows / Initial investment

A PI greater than one indicates that the investment is profitable, while a value less than one suggests that the investment should be rejected. In the case of divisible investment projects, calculating PI is slightly different. In divisible projects, the initial investment can be incrementally increased, and the present value of cash inflows will change accordingly.

To calculate the PI for divisible investment projects, it is necessary to use incremental present value (IPV) which is the present value of an additional investment. The formula for this is:

IPV = (Present Value of Incremental Cash inflows) / (Incremental investment)

The PI formula for divisible investment projects is then:

PI = (PV of Cash inflows + IPV) / Initial investment

Now let's consider 5 sample investment projects and calculate their respective Profitability Indexes for Divisible Investment Projects:

Example 1: A company is considering investing $100,000 in a project that generates cash inflows of $30,000 per year for 5 years. The net present value of the project is $130,000, and the incremental investment required for each additional year is $20,000.

IPV = ($30,000 / (1 + 0.10)^1) / $20,000 = $13,636
PI = ($130,000 + $13,636) / $100,000 = 1.44

Example 2: Company B is considering investing $50,000 in a project that generates cash inflows of $15,000 per year for 4 years. The net present value of the project is $55,000, and the incremental investment required for each additional year is $12,000.

IPV = ($15,000 / (1 + 0.08)^1) / $12,000 = $14,034
PI = ($55,000 + $14,034) / $50,000 = 1.38

Example 3: Company C is considering investing $200,000 in a project that generates cash inflows of $80,000 per year for 3 years. The net present value of the project is $250,000, and the incremental investment required for each additional year is $30,000.

IPV = ($80,000 / (1 + 0.12)^1) / $30,000 = $18,594
PI = ($250,000 + $18,594) / $200,000 = 1.34

Example 4: Company D is considering investing $75,000 in a project that generates cash inflows of $25,000 per year for 4 years. The net present value of the project is $90,000, and the incremental investment required for each additional year is $10,000.

IPV = ($25,000 / (1 + 0.05)^1) / $10,000 = $23,810
PI = ($90,000 + $23,810) / $75,000 = 1.45

Example 5: Company E is considering investing $150,000 in a project that generates cash inflows of $60,000 per year for 2 years. The net present value of the project is $180,000, and the incremental investment required for each additional year is $40,000.

IPV = ($60,000 / (1 + 0.15)^1) / $40,000 = $12,000
PI = ($180,000 + $12,000) / $150,000 = 1.20

In conclusion, analyzing the Profitability Indexes for Divisible Investment Projects can help companies make better investment decisions under single-period capital rationing. A higher PI indicates a more attractive investment and should be selected, while a lower PI may be rejected. Companies must determine their hurdle rate which represents the minimum PI value needed for a project to be accepted. Only those projects that meet or exceed the hurdle rate should be selected to maximize the return on investment.

The Calculation of the NPV of Combinations of Non-Divisible Investment Projects under Single-Period Capital Rationing

In single-period capital rationing, companies have limited funds to invest in multiple projects, and therefore they must carefully evaluate the returns and risks of investment combinations. The Net Present Value (NPV) method is a popular tool to evaluate the profitability of investment projects by comparing the present value of expected cash inflows to the present value of expected cash outflows.

The formula for calculating the net present value of a project is:

$$NPV = \sum (\text{Cash inflow}_t / (1+r)^t) - \text{Initial investment}$$

Where t = the year of the cash inflow, r = the discount rate, which represents the hurdle rate of the project, and the sum is taken from t=0 to t=n, where n= the number of years of the project.

For combinations of non-divisible investment projects, the NPV is calculated by grouping two or more projects together and analyzing their combined cash inflows and outflows. The NPV of the combination is determined by summing the NPV of each individual project.

Now, let's consider 5 sample non-divisible investment projects and calculate their respective NPV:

Example 1: A company is considering investing in 3 projects: Project A with an initial investment of $50,000 and an NPV of $20,000, Project B with an initial investment of $100,000 and an NPV of $80,000, and Project C with an initial investment of $70,000 and an NPV of $40,000.

NPV of Combination Projects ABC = $20,000 + $80,000 + $40,000 - $50,000 - $100,000 - $70,000 = $20,000

Example 2: Company B is considering investing in 2 projects: Project D with an initial investment of $120,000 and an NPV of $60,000, and Project E with an initial investment of $80,000 and an NPV of $30,000.

NPV of Combination Projects DE = $60,000 + $30,000 - $120,000 - $80,000 = -$110,000

Example 3: Company C is considering investing in 4 projects: Project F with an initial investment of $60,000 and an NPV of $20,000, Project G with an initial investment of $80,000 and an NPV of $30,000, Project H with an initial investment of $100,000 and an NPV of $50,000, and Project I with an initial investment of $200,000 and an NPV of $110,000.

NPV of Combination Projects FGHI = $20,000 + $30,000 + $50,000 + $110,000 - $60,000 - $80,000 - $100,000 - $200,000 = -$30,000

Example 4: Company D is considering investing in 3 projects: Project J with an initial investment of $60,000 and an NPV of $30,000, Project K with an initial investment of $110,000 and an NPV of $50,000, and Project L with an initial investment of $80,000 and an NPV of $20,000.

NPV of Combination Projects JKL = $30,000 + $50,000 + $20,000 - $60,000 - $110,000 - $80,000 = -$50,000

Example 5: Company E is considering investing in 2 projects: Project M with an initial investment of $150,000 and an NPV of $60,000, and Project N with an initial investment of $100,000 and an NPV of $40,000.

NPV of Combination Projects MN = $60,000 + $40,000 - $150,000 -

$100,000 = -$150,000

In conclusion, analyzing the NPV of combinations of non-divisible investment projects is essential to determine the most profitable combination of investment projects under single-period capital rationing. A positive net present value indicates that the project generates value for the company, while a negative net present value suggests that the project is likely to lead to losses. Therefore, companies must calculate the NPV of each investment project, consider their combination, and select the most profitable projects to maximize the return on investment.

Reasons for Capital Rationing: Internal and External Factors

Capital rationing is one of the most critical financial management strategies used by companies to allocate their limited funds to different investment options. Capital rationing occurs when a company has a limited amount of capital to invest in several investment alternatives but cannot choose all of them because of constraints, such as financial limitations or project size. Below are the ten reasons for capital rationing based on common internal company considerations:

1. Cash Flow Constraints: Insufficient cash flow can cause capital rationing even if profitable investment opportunities are available.

2. Budget Constraints: Constraints arise when a company sets aside specified funds for specific allocations such as R&D or expansion.

3. Soft Capital Constraints: A non-binding lending structure in which the company is capable of borrowing only a limited quantity for a particular term.

4. **Regulatory Constraints:** The government sets certain restrictions such as environmental or location-specific regulations that limit the company's investment options.

5. **Financial Distress:** Troubled companies struggling with debt repayment and recovering losses predictably impose capital rationing on firms focusing on operations and reorganization.

6. **Project Size:** Large projects can put pressure on the capacity avoidance of capital rationing, resulting in the company's inability to choose projects that require large capital investments.

7. **Risk Management:** Controlling the overall risk implications of investments and balancing risk can limit a firm's decision-making flexibility.

8. **Competitive Pressures:** The competitive environment can create additional constraints as rivals attempt to out-compete each other or mark their position in the market.

9. **Priority Investment:** Priority projects often demand a substantial amount of capital, and then the capital is rationed to other projects.

10. **Strategic Planning:** Parallel to priority investment, strategic planning often guides management to reallocate funds across projects more closely aligned with long-term business goals.

In conclusion, capital rationing may be implemented for various reasons. Internal company consideration such as the need to balance cash flows and manage risks, as well as external factors such as regulatory constraints, may cause companies to invest in new projects while limiting others. To maximize the return on investment, firms are advised to determine investment priorities, determine NPV on each investment project and pursue a project combination to maximize cash flows. Through careful analysis and organization, the financial resources of a company can be used to maximize returns.

Business finance

Sources of, and raising, business finance

Business finance is the process of managing financial resources to meet business needs. It involves allocating limited resources to maximize the profits of the business. There are two categories of sources for raising business finance: internal and external.

Internal sources of financing come from funds generated within the business such as retained earnings. External sources refer to raising funds from outside sources such as bank loans or investors. Choosing the right sources of finance depends on factors such as the nature of the business, type of financing needed, and the cost of capital.

Businesses can raise funds through debt financing, equity financing, crowdfunding, or government grants. Debt financing involves taking on debt such as loans or issuing bonds. Equity financing involves raising funds through the sale of company shares. Crowdfunding involves raising funds from a large number of individuals through online platforms. Government grants are offered to businesses that meet specific criteria or are involved in certain industries.

Exploring Overdraft as a Short-Term Financing Option for Businesses

Short-term sources of finance refer to the methods that businesses use to acquire funds to meet operational needs, such as paying suppliers or managing day-to-day expenses. Some common sources of short-term finance include bank overdrafts, trade credit, factoring, and commercial paper. One such method of financing short-term needs is through an overdraft facility.

Overdraft is a type of short-term financing typically offered by banks to help businesses manage their temporary cash shortages. It allows companies to withdraw more funds than their current account balance, up to a predetermined limit, without requiring prior approval from the bank. Overdrafts are useful because businesses can access the funds they need quickly and easily, without having to go through a lengthy loan application process. It can offer flexibility in managing cash flow, especially when companies have uneven cash inflows and outflows, and it can help them avoid potential late payment penalties or running out of cash entirely.

Although overdrafts are a trusted option, they do come with a few pros and cons. One advantage is that they typically have relatively low-interest rates compared to other short-term financing options. Moreover, overdraft facilities are highly flexible and can be used to finance any business needs, from paying salaries to covering unexpected expenses, as long as they remain within the agreed overdraft limit. It is worth noting that overdrafts can provide businesses with a sense of financial security, knowing that they can access funds if needed.

However, there are also some potential downsides to overdrafts. One disadvantage is that it can be quite expensive if not managed well. Overdrafts carry interest rates, and additional fees may be charged if businesses exceed their limit or fail to repay the debt within the agreed timeframe. Moreover, they provide a temporary solution to cash flow issues, and businesses may become too reliant on overdrafts, leading to a situation where they are continually in debt. Furthermore, banks may request additional financial security, such as collaterals, before granting overdraft facilities, which may be problematic for small or new businesses.

In conclusion, overdrafts are a fast and efficient way for businesses to overcome their short-term cash flow difficulties. They offer the flexibility that firms need to manage their finances correctly, but they should also be approached with caution to avoid high costs and prevent reliance on them over the long term. Companies should carefully weigh the pros and cons of overdrafts and seek expert advice to determine if it is the right option for their particular needs.

Exploring Short-Term Loans as a Financing Option for Businesses

Short-term sources of finance refer to the methods that businesses use to acquire funding to meet short-term operational needs. Some common sources of short-term finance include bank overdrafts, trade credit, factoring, commercial paper, and short-term loans.

Short-term loans are another popular method of financing short-term needs. It is a form of credit that businesses can use to finance their operations, expand their businesses, or cover expenses during periods of cash flow shortfalls. Short-term loans usually have a repayment term of fewer than 12 months and carry a higher interest rate than long-term loans, making them useful for short-term purposes.

Short-term loans are useful for businesses because they offer a quick solution to their financial needs. The application process for a short-term loan is faster and less cumbersome than that of long-term loans. Businesses can obtain the funds they need more rapidly, enabling them to tackle any short-term financial needs, such as managing cash flow, purchasing inventory, or covering unexpected expenses promptly.

There are several pros and cons to short-term loans that businesses should consider. One of the advantages is that it offers a fixed interest rate, which enables businesses to forecast their expenses and set up a repayment plan. Additionally, short-term loans do not require collateral, which means businesses can use them without risking their assets. Finally, the loans enable businesses to build or restore their credit score if they do not default on the loan.

On the other hand, short-term loans come with some disadvantages. One of the most obvious ones is that the borrowing costs, including interest rates and fees, can be higher than with other forms of credit.

Furthermore, businesses must have a reliable source of revenue to repay the loan promptly; otherwise, they could end up in a worse financial situation. Finally, the strict repayment time frame can put pressure on businesses to repay the loan promptly, which is fine when they have the cash flow to do so, but can be a risk if they do not.

In conclusion, short-term loans are an excellent source of finance for businesses to manage their short-term financial needs. They offer a quick solution to businesses that require cash infusion immediately. However, the high interest rates and strict repayment time frames imply that businesses should choose short-term loans cautiously and ensure that they have a strategy in place to pay them back promptly.

Understanding Trade Credit as a Financing Option for Businesses

Trade credit is a common form of short-term financing in which one company extends credit to another company to purchase goods or services, allowing them to pay for the acquired items later. In essence, trade credit functions as a deferred payment facility.

Trade credit is useful for businesses because it allows them to acquire the goods or services they need without upfront payment. This enables them to keep their cash flow healthy and devote the funds they have on hand elsewhere in their businesses. Additionally, it is typically less expensive than other forms of financing, such as bank loans or overdrafts, as it often comes with no interest charges or lower fees, depending on the terms of the arrangement.

One of the significant benefits of trade credit is that it allows businesses to build a good reputation with their suppliers. By paying invoices on time, businesses can boost their supplier relationships, negotiating better deals and more favorable payment terms in the future, such as accessing discounts or longer payment terms. Additionally, trade credit allows companies to manage their cash flow, ensuring they can meet their financial obligations promptly while also keeping sufficient funding available to pay for other expenses.

However, there are some drawbacks to trade credit that businesses should consider. One of the most significant concerns is that it can be difficult to access for small and new businesses without track records or established credit histories, making it challenging for them to obtain favorable terms. Additionally, if payments are not made promptly or in full, the relationship between the supplier and the buyer may be damaged, which can have negative consequences for future business dealings. Moreover, companies might end up overspending or over-relying on trade credit, which is problematic when they are unable to honor the agreements, potentially leading to legal disputes or damaged credit ratings.

In conclusion, trade credit is an essential funding option for businesses to consider for their short-term financing needs. The flexibility and convenience it offers businesses with established relationships can help them sustain their operations and keep their cash flow healthy. However, it is vital to approach trade credit with caution, ensuring that the agreed-upon terms can be honored and balanced with other financial obligations to avoid falling into debt.

Exploring Lease Financing as a Financing Option for Businesses

Lease finance is a form of financing offered by financial institutions that allow businesses to lease equipment, such as machinery, vehicles, or computer equipment, for a predetermined period in exchange for regular payments, which are generally less than the cost of buying the equipment outright.
Lease financing can be useful to businesses looking to acquire expensive equipment that they cannot afford to purchase or when they wish to

avoid the risk and cost of equipment ownership, such as maintenance, repairs, and depreciation. Moreover, lease payments are usually tax-deductible, providing tax benefits for businesses.

One of the key benefits of lease financing is that it enables businesses to obtain the latest equipment without tying up their capital. This is because lease agreements often include low upfront deposits and lower monthly payments when compared to outright purchases, helping minimize the impact of the equipment cost on the business' cash flow. Also, businesses can negotiate flexible terms, such as lease periods and buyout options, to match their specific needs.

However, there are several downsides to lease financing that businesses should be aware of. For example, leasing over long periods may result in higher overall costs compared to purchasing the equipment. Moreover, lease agreements are often rigid and require businesses to have excellent credit ratings or provide security to secure the lease agreement, which small or new businesses may struggle to do. Furthermore, businesses typically cannot capitalize on the equipment's residual value, which means that they may not benefit from appreciation in the asset's value.

In conclusion, lease financing is an excellent financing solution for businesses that require expensive equipment but cannot afford the upfront payment or, alternatively, are unwilling to own the equipment due to other concerns such as maintenance or depreciation. While there are pros and cons to leasing, businesses should carefully evaluate their options before signing on to a lease agreement, ensuring that they fully understand the terms and have a solid plan to meet payments to get the most benefit from it.

Equity Finance for Businesses

Equity finance is a type of long-term financing in which a business raises funds by selling shares of ownership to investors. It is different from debt finance, whereby companies borrow money and pay back the principal amount plus interest, while equity finance has no repayment obligation.

Equity finance can be useful for businesses that require significant funding to support long-term investment projects. One of the significant advantages of equity finance is that businesses can obtain the funds they need without incurring debt. This helps to minimize their financial risk while also providing them with a long-term capital base that can enable them to take advantage of growth opportunities.

Another advantage of equity finance is that equity holders share the risks and returns of the company with the owners, meaning they are compensated with dividends or a share of net profits. Equity investors, such as venture capitalists, can also offer valuable support and guidance to new or growing businesses, including access to industry networks, expertise, and business advice.

However, equity finance also comes with some potential drawbacks. For example, selling shares means that the investors become owners and consequently have a say in how the business is run, which may lead to disagreements and divergent opinions on the best decisions for the company. Giving up the ownership also restricts the control of the owners, which some owners may view as an issue. Moreover, equity finance often requires businesses to give up a percentage of equity, potentially limiting their financial flexibility and restricting their decision-making autonomy.

In conclusion, equity finance can be an attractive financing option for businesses that require significant capital investment to support strategic growth initiatives. By selling ownership shares, businesses can obtain the funds they need without incurring debt and can access dividends and additional support from equity investors. However, it is important for businesses to weigh the pros and cons of equity finance carefully and to ensure that investors are aligned with their overall business goals before moving forward with any equity finance arrangements.

Debt Finance for Businesses

Debt finance is a type of long-term financing where a company borrows money from lenders or investors, which must be repaid over time with interest. Debt finance is an essential source of funding for many companies, particularly for those that might not have access to other financing options. Businesses can use debt financing to raise capital to start a new project, expand their operations, or fund other activities. One of the main advantages of debt finance is that it allows businesses to acquire the funding they need without diluting the ownership of the company. Unlike equity finance, where investors purchase a share of ownership, the investors in debt finance only lend money and do not gain equity in the business. This means that business owners can maintain full control over the operations and direction of their company.

Additionally, debt finance can be advantageous due to the potential tax benefits. The interest paid on business loans is typically tax-deductible, effectively lowering the total cost of borrowing. This can make it an attractive option for businesses looking to minimize their overall tax burden.

However, there are several drawbacks to consider when weighing the pros and cons of debt finance. One major limitation is the cost associated with borrowing money. Interest payments can add up quickly, particularly for loans with high-interest rates or long repayment terms. This can be particularly challenging for small businesses or startup ventures, which may struggle to meet these financial obligations over time.

Another potential disadvantage of debt finance is the risk of default. If a business is unable to repay the loan, it may face serious consequences, such as forced liquidation or bankruptcy. This can lead to significant financial losses for business owners and investors alike, making it critical to carefully consider the risks and benefits of any debt financing arrangement.

Overall, debt finance is a common and often necessary form of long-term financing for many businesses. While it can be an effective way to raise capital and fund growth, it is important to carefully consider the costs and risks associated with borrowing money and ensure that your business can meet its financial obligations over time.

Lease Finance for Businesses

Lease finance is a type of long-term financing where businesses can rent or lease assets rather than purchasing them outright. This form of financing allows companies to access the assets they require for their operations without having to pay the full purchase price upfront. Instead, the business will make regular payments to the leasing company over the term of the lease agreement.

One of the main advantages of lease finance is that it allows companies to acquire the assets they need without having to pay the full purchase price upfront. This can be particularly beneficial for businesses that may not have the capital available to make a significant upfront investment in assets. Lease agreements may also come with customizable terms, such as repayment periods and payment schedules, which can make them more flexible than other types of financing arrangements.

Another potential advantage of lease finance is that it can provide businesses with access to a wider range of assets that may otherwise be difficult or impossible to obtain. For example, businesses may lease specialized machinery or other equipment that would be prohibitively expensive to purchase outright.

However, there are also some potential drawbacks to consider when evaluating the pros and cons of lease finance. One is that leasing assets can be more expensive over the long term than purchasing them outright. This is because interest and other fees may be applied to the regular lease payments, which can add up over time.

Another potential downside is that leased assets do not offer the same long-term value as those that are purchased outright. At the end of the lease agreement, the business will typically have to return the asset to the leasing company or renew the lease agreement. This can result in ongoing costs associated with using the assets, rather than building equity in assets that the business owns outright.

Overall, lease finance can be a useful long-term financing option for businesses that need to acquire assets but do not have the capital available for an outright purchase. However, it is essential to carefully evaluate the costs and the long-term benefits of leasing versus purchasing assets before making any financing decisions.

The Role and Limitations of Rights Issues in Raising Equity Finance

A rights issue is a method used by companies to raise additional equity finance. In a rights issue, existing shareholders of the company are offered the opportunity to purchase new shares of stock at a discounted price. By purchasing these new shares, shareholders can increase their ownership stake in the company and provide additional funding to support the company's growth initiatives.

Rights issues are a common way for companies to raise capital from existing shareholders as they allow the company to raise funds without going through the costly and time-consuming process of finding new investors. The discounted price of the shares can also make it an attractive investment opportunity for existing shareholders looking to increase their investment in the company.

However, there are also some potential drawbacks to consider when evaluating a rights issue as a method of raising equity finance. One potential limitation is that the discount offered to existing shareholders can dilute the value of the company's shares in the market. This can lower overall investor confidence in the company and negatively impact the company's long-term value.

Another potential downside is that rights issues may not always be successful in raising the required amount of funds. This can be particularly challenging for smaller or less-established companies that may lack the investor base and support needed to make a rights issue a viable financing option.

Overall, rights issues can be a useful method for companies to raise additional equity finance from existing shareholders. However, it is essential to carefully weigh the potential benefits and drawbacks of this financing method before making any decisions. Companies should also consider other financing options, such as debt finance or private equity, to ensure they have access to the capital they need to fund their growth initiatives.

Placing as a Method of Raising Equity Finance for Companies

Placing is a method used by companies to raise equity finance by selling shares of stock to a select group of investors, such as institutional investors or high net worth individuals. The company identifies a group of potential investors and offers them the opportunity to purchase shares of the company at a set price. Placing is a popular way for more established companies to raise capital since it can be quicker and easier than other methods of equity finance.

Placing can be an attractive option for companies that are looking for a large amount of funding in a relatively short period since the investors that they approach are often willing to invest significant sums of money. This can be beneficial for the company since it allows them to raise the capital they need without going through a more extended, and potentially more expensive, process of finding new investors.

However, there are also some potential drawbacks to consider when evaluating the use of placing as a method of equity finance. One potential downside is that it can be a more expensive option when compared to other forms of financing since the company may have to pay fees or commissions to the investment banks or brokers involved in the placing.

Another potential disadvantage of placing is that it may dilute the ownership of existing shareholders since the new shares of stock are sold to a select group of investors rather than being offered more widely to the public or existing shareholders.

Overall, placing can be an effective method of raising equity finance for established companies, particularly those looking to raise a large amount of capital in a short amount of time. However, it is important for companies to carefully consider the potential drawbacks of placing before making any decisions and to tailor their financing approach to their specific business needs and growth objectives.

Public Offers (IPOs) for Companies Looking to Raise Equity Finance

A public offer, also known as an initial public offering (IPO), is a method of raising equity finance by offering shares of stock in a company to the general public. It is a significant milestone for a company, marking the first time that it has listed its shares on a public stock exchange.

Public offers can be a popular method for companies to raise capital since they offer access to a wide pool of potential investors. The company and its underwriters will promote the public offering through advertisements and other means, building interest and excitement for the upcoming offering.

Once the offering is complete, the company will receive the funds from the sale of its shares. These can then be used to finance expansion projects, pay off existing debts, research and development initiatives, among other expenses.

However, there are also several potential drawbacks to consider when evaluating the use of a public offer as a method of raising equity finance. One potential drawback is that the costs associated with an IPO can be high, between legal fees and underwriting fees, which can often result in a significant amount of money being used up in the process.

Another potential disadvantage of a public offer is that the company will have to meet regulatory requirements and adhere to financial reporting requirements once it has listed its shares on a public exchange. This can increase the amount of paperwork, financial auditing, ongoing regulatory compliance, and legal costs which can be both time-consuming and expensive.

Overall, public offers can be an effective way for companies to raise significant amounts of equity finance by opening up their shares to a wide pool of potential investors. However, it is important for companies to weigh the costs and benefits of this strategy carefully, taking into account their specific needs and long-term growth objectives before making any decisions.

Differences Between Islamic Finance and Conventional Finance: Principles, Practices, and Funding

Islamic finance differs from other forms of business finance in several major ways, particularly in terms of its principles, practices, and sources of funding.

1. Interest-based Financing: Conventional finance, such as traditional bank loans, rely on interest-based financing, which involves levying interest on the amount borrowed by an individual or business. Islamic finance forbids this practice and instead utilizes mudarabah, a partnership-based financing structure where the investor provides the funding and the entrepreneur provides the expertise.

2. Risk and Profit Sharing: Islamic finance is based on the principle of risk and profit sharing, which means that lenders or investors share in both the risks and rewards of a business venture. Under conventional finance, the borrower assumes all the risks and the lender receives a fixed interest rate as compensation.

3. Prohibition on Speculation: Islamic finance prohibits speculation, which involves investing in assets based on expected price changes. Instead, Islamic finance favors tangible assets such as real estate, commodities, and other physical investments.

4. Long-Term Financing: Islamic finance is geared towards long-term

financing. This means businesses that seek to take out an Islamic thikr are typically required to provide a detailed plan of their long-term goals and operations to ensure that investments align with the goals of the financier.

5. Sharia Law Compliance: Islamic finance is governed by Islamic Sharia law. Therefore, all financial products and services must comply with Sharia legislations and regulations.

Overall, Islamic finance is characterized by its adherence to religious principles, profit sharing, partnership-based financing, and long term financing. While conventional finance focuses on interest-based lending, short-term financing, speculation, and individual gain over collective growth.

The Concept of Riba in Islamic Finance and Examples of How Returns are Generated through Shari'ah-Compliant Financing Methods

In Islamic finance, riba (i.e., interest) is prohibited as it goes against the religious law and belief of exploiting others' financial weakness.
Therefore, Islamic financial institutions use Shari'ah-compliant investment methodologies to generate returns for its investors. Different techniques are utilized to provide financing options that are based on equity and profit-sharing methods instead of conventional interest-based loans.
While conventional finance focuses predominantly on interest-bearing instruments, Islamic banking comprises various investment vehicles that exclude riba.

Here are five sample application examples to explain how returns can be generated by the use of ruba in Islamic finance:

1. Conventional bank account: An example of conventional interest-based finance. The bank offers a fixed interest rate on the funds deposited into the account. The deposit is wrapped for a specific period, longer-term deposits earning a higher interest percentage.

2. Fixed return deposit account: In Islamic fixed-term deposits, the financial institution promises to give the client a fixed rate of return at maturity. The financial institution determines that profit rate based on the earning of their assets.

3. Staggered return deposit account: In Islamic staggered return deposit accounts, the financial institution offers varying rates of return based on the deposit's term. A long-term deposit earns a higher rate of return than a short-term deposit.

4. Deferred payment sale: A deferred payment sale involves the sale of a specific asset with a pre-determined payment schedule. The financial institution claims remittance against the agreed deferred payment and is allowed to include a specified profit margin as part of the deferred payment schedule.

5. Lease-based financing: The financial product is used for big-ticket items such as real estate, cars, or other significant assets where the bank purchases the item and leases it out, allowing the lessee to acquire the property through eventual ownership.

Overall, these ethical Islamic financing methods aim to raise customers' short-term and long-term Islamic finance while placing a mindful priority on the equitable and socially responsible distribution of returns. Shari'ah-compliant finance provides different ethical alternatives that are not only sustainable from a religious perspective, but a true and substantial method of financing significant projects.

Understanding Murabaha

Murabaha is an Islamic financial instrument used by businesses, which is based on the sale of goods with an agreed-upon profit margin. It involves the purchase of goods by a financial institution and the subsequent sale to customers at an agreed price, which includes a defined profit margin. Murabaha is often used by businesses to finance their working capital needs, making it a popular method for short-term Islamic financing.

Here are five sample examples to explain how Murabaha works:

1. Purchasing inventory: Suppose a business requires additional inventory to meet customer demand. In this case, the business can approach an Islamic financial institution for Murabaha financing, whereby the financial institution purchases the inventory and sells it to the business, including a previously agreed-upon profit margin.

2. Purchasing machinery: A company that requires machinery or heavy equipment can use Murabaha financing to acquire the equipment. The financial institution purchases the machinery and sells it to the company with a specific profit margin included in the sale price.

3. Purchasing raw material: A business that needs raw materials can seek out Murabaha financing from a financial institution. The institution will purchase the required raw materials with an added profit margin and sell them to the business.

4. Financing a project: Suppose a business requires funds to complete a project. It can approach an Islamic financial institution for Murabaha financing, where the financial institution will purchase the required products or material and sell them to the business at an agreed-upon price.

5. Purchasing a vehicle: A business in need of vehicles can use Murabaha financing to acquire them. The financial institution will

purchase the vehicle and sell it to the business for a profit margin that has been agreed upon previously.

Overall, Murabaha financing is a popular type of Islamic financing because it is simple, transparent, and provides an alternative method to traditional interest-based financing. Murabaha facilitates the purchase of goods without breaking Islamic law, and it provides businesses with the working capital they need to grow and expand. It is a flexible and beneficial Islamic financial tool for businesses of all kinds, including start-ups and established companies.

Understanding Ijara

Ijara is an Islamic financial instrument that is based on leasing arrangements. It is widely used by businesses operating under Islamic law to finance their operations. Ijara is a contract between two parties, whereby one party – the lessor – owns an asset and rents it out to another party – the lessee – for a specific period. Here are five sample examples to explain how Ijara works in business financing:

1. Leasing of equipment: A business requiring equipment for its operations can approach an Islamic financial institution for Ijara financing. The institution purchases the equipment and leases it out to the business for a fixed period, typically with the option to purchase the equipment at the end of the Ijara contract.

2. Leasing of property: An individual or business in need of property can use Ijara financing to lease it. The financial institution purchases the property and enters into an Ijara contract with the individual or business, renting out the property for a specific period.

3. Leasing of vehicles: A business in need of vehicles can use Ijara financing to lease them. The financial institution purchases the vehicles and leases them out to the business for a specific period with the option

to purchase the vehicles at the end of the Ijara contract.

4. Leasing of machinery: A company that requires machinery for its operations can use Ijara financing to lease it. The financial institution purchases the machinery and leases it to the company for a specific period, typically with the option to purchase the machinery at the end of the Ijara contract.

5. Leasing of office equipment: A business in need of office equipment can use Ijara financing to lease it. The financial institution purchases the equipment and leases it out to the business for a fixed period, typically with the option to purchase the equipment at the end of the Ijara contract.

Overall, Ijara financing is a popular type of Islamic financing because it is simple and provides an alternative method to traditional interest-based financing. Ijara allows businesses to acquire the assets they need for their operations without breaking Islamic law, providing them with the flexibility and working capital to grow and expand.

Understanding Mudaraba

Mudaraba is an Islamic financial instrument based on equity finance. It is widely used by businesses operating under Islamic law to finance their operations. Mudaraba is a contract between two parties, where one party – the investor (Rab-ul-Mal) – provides the capital while the other party – the entrepreneur (Mudarib) – provides the expertise to manage and operate the business. Here are five sample examples to explain how Mudaraba works in business financing:
1. Investment in real estate development: An investor seeking to invest in real estate development can use Mudaraba financing. The entrepreneur will use the investor's capital to acquire land and develop it, while the investor provides the capital and receives a share of the profits generated.

2. Investment in a start-up: An investor seeking to invest in a start-up can

use Mudaraba financing. The entrepreneur will use the investor's capital to start the business, while the investor provides the capital and receives a share of the profits generated.

3. Investment in a restaurant: An investor seeking to invest in a restaurant can use Mudaraba financing. The entrepreneur will use the investor's capital to start the restaurant, while the investor provides the capital and receives a share of the profits generated.

4. Investment in a manufacturing plant: An investor seeking to invest in a manufacturing plant can use Mudaraba financing. The entrepreneur will use the investor's capital to build the plant and produce goods, while the investor provides the capital and receives a share of the profits generated.

5. Investment in a technology start-up: An investor seeking to invest in a technology start-up can use Mudaraba financing. The entrepreneur will use the investor's capital to develop and market the technology while the investor provides the capital and receives a share of the profits generated.

Overall, Mudaraba financing is a popular type of Islamic financing because it provides an alternative to traditional interest-based financing. It allows investors to invest in businesses without having to manage the day-to-day operations while giving entrepreneurs access to the capital they need to grow and expand their businesses. Mudaraba financing is a flexible and beneficial Islamic financial tool for all kinds of businesses, from start-ups to established companies.

Understanding Sukuk

Sukuk is a type of Islamic financial instrument used in Islamic finance that is based on debt finance. It is widely used by businesses operating under Islamic law to finance their operations. Sukuk is a type of bond where investors provide the capital and receive regular payments based on the profitability of the underlying assets. Here are five sample examples to explain how Sukuk works in business financing:

1. Financing a project: A business seeking financing for a specific project such as real estate development or infrastructure construction can use Sukuk financing. The investors provide the capital, and the business pays regular payments based on the profitability of the underlying assets. Once the project is complete, the investors receive payment from the proceeds of the sale of the completed project.

2. Refinancing debt: A business seeking to refinance its debt can use Sukuk financing. The investors provide the capital, and the business pays regular payments based on the profitability of the underlying assets. The business can use the proceeds to pay off its previous debt obligations.

3. Financing working capital: A business requiring working capital financing can use Sukuk financing. The investors provide the capital, and the business pays regular payments based on the profitability of the underlying assets. The business can use the proceeds to finance its day-to-day operations.

4. Sukuk issuance for a specific high-value asset: A business can issue Sukuk if it has a specific high-value asset that it wishes to finance. The investors provide the capital, and the business pays regular payments based on the profitability of the underlying assets. This type of Sukuk issuance is known as an asset-backed Sukuk.

5. Sukuk issuance for a specific short-term project: A business can issue Sukuk for a specific short-term project with a defined repayment date. The investors provide the capital, and the business repays the debt by a specific date.

Overall, Sukuk financing is a popular type of Islamic financing because it provides an alternative to traditional interest-based financing. It allows businesses to raise capital without breaking Islamic law, giving them the flexibility and working capital to grow and expand. Sukuk is a flexible and beneficial Islamic financial tool for all kinds of businesses, from start-ups to established companies.

Understanding Musharaka

Musharaka is an Islamic financial instrument based on venture capital. It is widely used by businesses operating under Islamic law to finance their operations. Musharaka is a partnership agreement between two or more parties, where each partner contributes capital, expertise and shares profits and losses in the proportion of their contribution. Here are five sample examples to explain how Musharaka works in business financing:

1. Investing in a start-up: An investor seeking to invest in a start-up can use Musharaka financing. The entrepreneur will provide expertise, while the investor provides the capital, and they will share the profits and losses in the proportion of their contribution.

2. Joint-venture: Two companies can enter a Musharaka contract to undertake a joint venture in a new business. They will contribute capital, expertise and share profits and losses in the proportion of their contribution.

3. Investing in real estate: A business seeking to acquire real estate can use Musharaka financing. An Islamic financial institution would provide the capital, and the business would provide the expertise. The parties would jointly purchase and manage the asset, sharing the profits and losses in the proportion of their contribution.

4. Financing a construction project: A business can seek Musharaka financing for a specific construction project. The investor provides the capital, while the business manages the construction and provides the

expertise. The parties would jointly manage the project, sharing the profits and losses in the proportion of their contribution.

5. Investing in a high-growth business: An investor seeking to invest in a high-growth business may provide capital through Musharaka financing. The entrepreneur would provide the expertise, and both parties would share profits and losses according to their contribution.

Overall, Musharaka financing is a popular type of Islamic financing because it provides a flexible method of raising capital without breaking Islamic law. Musharaka allows investors to participate in the management and decision-making of the business, giving entrepreneurs access to the capital they need to grow and expand their businesses while sharing profits and losses. It is a flexible and beneficial Islamic financial tool for all kinds of businesses, from start-ups to established companies.

Understanding Retained Earnings

Retained earnings refer to the portion of a company's net income that is retained by the business to reinvest back into the company, rather than being distributed as dividends to shareholders. Retained earnings can be used to finance a variety of activities, from research and development to capital expenditures. Here are five sample examples to explain how retained earnings work in business financing:
1. Investing in research and development: A company may retain its earnings to invest in research and development for new products or services. This investment in R&D may lead to new revenue streams for the company in the future.

2. Funding expansion into new markets: A business looking to expand into new markets may use its retained earnings to finance this expansion. Retained earnings can be used to cover the costs of opening new locations, hiring additional staff, or establishing a new distribution network.

3. Financing capital expenditures: A business may retain its earnings to finance capital expenditures, such as purchasing new equipment, upgrading facilities, or investing in technology. This investment in the company's infrastructure may help to increase efficiency and productivity.

4. Reducing debt: A company may use its retained earnings to pay off debt, reducing interest payments and improving the company's financial position.

5. Providing a cushion during tough times: Retained earnings can provide a cushion for businesses during tough times, such as economic downturns or unexpected events. Having retained earnings on hand can help companies weather these challenges without having to cut back on operations or reduce employees.

Overall, retained earnings are a crucial internal source of financing for businesses. Retaining earnings can help to fund growth opportunities, reduce debt, and provide a buffer during challenging times. Retained earnings represent a long-term investment in the company, rather than a short-term benefit for shareholders.

Internal Sources of Finance to Increase Working Capital Management Efficiency

Increasing working capital management efficiency means improving the management of a business's current assets and liabilities in order to optimize cash flow and profitability. Internal sources of finance are the funds generated by a business's own operations or assets, without the need to take on external debt or equity financing. Here are 5 examples of internal sources of finance:

Delaying payment to suppliers: A business can communicate with its suppliers to extend payment terms, thereby freeing up cash that can be used for other needs.

2. Reducing inventory levels: A business can optimize inventory levels to prevent excess stockpiling, which frees up cash that might otherwise be

tied up in stagnant or slow-moving items.

3. Accelerating accounts receivable collection: A business can design and implement more effective strategies to collect owed payments from clients, thus increasing cash flow.

4. Reinvesting profits: A business can reinvest earnings back into the company to develop new products, markets, and services, or to enhance the business's financial position.

5. Selling fixed assets: A business can sell assets such as land, equipment, or vehicles that are no longer needed or are underutilized, and use the proceeds for other business purposes.

For example, if a retail store wants to increase its working capital management efficiency, it can streamline its inventory management system to ensure that product is moving efficiently through the supply chain. Other examples might include the negotiation of longer payment terms with suppliers to improve cash flow or selling off poorly performing assets to focus on core business strengths. In each case, the goal is to find ways to maximize cash flow from internal sources while minimizing the need for external financing.

The Relationship between Dividend Policy and Financing Decision

The dividend policy of a company determines how much of its earnings are distributed to shareholders in the form of dividends, versus how much is retained for reinvestment in the business. The financing decision, on the other hand, is the choice a company makes about how to raise funds for new investments or operations.

Here are 5 specific examples of the relationship between dividend policy and the financing decision:

1. If a company has a high dividend payout ratio, it may need to rely more heavily on external financing to fund new investments or growth. This is because it is retaining less earnings for internal reinvestment.

2. Conversely, if a company has a low dividend payout ratio, it may have more cash on hand to fund new investments, reducing the need for external financing.

3. If a company begins paying dividends for the first time, it may impact its ability to raise external financing. Investors may see dividends as an indication that the company is not putting enough money back into the business for growth.

4. If a company has a history of consistently increasing its dividend payouts, it may be seen as a stable and reliable investment. This could lead to increased interest from investors, which could make it easier to raise external financing as needed.

5. The decision to pay dividends versus retaining earnings for internal reinvestment can affect a company's cost of capital. If investors expect dividends and the company fails to deliver, their perception of the company's stability and performance may decrease, leading to higher financing costs.

Overall, the dividend policy choices a company makes can have a significant impact on its need for external financing, its reputation among investors, and its cost of capital.

Theoretical Approaches and Practical Influences on Dividend Decisions

Dividend decision refers to the decision made by a board of directors regarding the payment of dividends to shareholders of a company. There are different theoretical approaches to making dividend decisions, as well as practical influences that can impact these decisions. Here are some detailed explanations of these approaches and influences:

1. Theoretical Approaches to Dividend Decisions: There are several different approaches to dividend decisions, including:

- Residual Theory: This theory suggests that dividends should be paid only after all necessary investments have been made in the company's positive NPV projects. This ensures that the company maintains an optimal capital structure while also providing returns to shareholders.

- Bird-In-The-Hand Theory: This theory argues that investors prefer current dividends over future capital gains because future capital gains are uncertain. Therefore, companies should pay out as much of their earnings as possible as current dividends rather than retaining earnings for reinvestment.

- Tax Preference Theory: This theory states that investors prefer stocks that pay higher dividends because they are taxed less than capital gains.

2. Practical Influences on Dividend Decisions: Several practical factors can also impact dividend decisions, including:

- Legal Constraints: Companies may be subject to legal constraints that limit their ability to pay dividends, such as debt covenants that prevent them from distributing more than a certain percentage of earnings.

- Liquidity: Companies may need to hold back earnings for liquidity purposes in order to maintain financial stability in the short term.

- Shareholder Expectations: Companies may consider shareholder expectations when deciding whether to pay dividends, as investors may become dissatisfied if dividends are lower than expected.

- Alternatives to Cash Dividends: Companies may also consider alternative methods of returning value to shareholders, such as stock buybacks or special dividends.

Overall, dividend decisions are influenced by both theoretical approaches to determining optimal capital structure and practical factors such as legal constraints, liquidity, shareholder expectations, and alternative methods of capital allocation. Companies must balance these factors to make optimal dividend decisions.

Cost of Capital

Cost of capital refers to the rate of return that a company must earn on its investments to satisfy the demands of its investors. It represents the minimum rate of return that a company must generate to create value for its shareholders.

The cost of capital can be calculated using the following formula:

Cost of capital = (cost of debt x weight of debt) + (cost of equity x weight of equity)

The cost of debt is the interest rate a company must pay on its debt, while the cost of equity represents the expected returns demanded by equity investors.

The weight of debt and equity refers to their proportional contribution to the company's capital structure.

In practical terms, the cost of capital is used by companies in evaluating investment opportunities. A company will compare the expected returns on a potential investment against the cost of capital to determine whether the investment would be profitable or not. For example, a company may need to decide whether to invest in new equipment, research and development, or new markets. They would then consider the expected returns on each potential investment relative to the cost of capital. If the expected returns are higher than the cost of capital, the investment is considered viable.

The cost of capital can also play a role in financial decision-making, such as choosing between debt and equity financing. A company would calculate the cost of each financing option and select the one with the lower cost of capital.

In a real-life scenario, a company will use its cost of capital to evaluate potential acquisition targets. If the cost of capital is higher than the expected returns of the acquisition that they are considering, the acquisition will not go ahead.

Estimate the Cost of Equity

The cost of equity is a financial metric used to determine the required rate of return on a company's common stock. It is the return that equity investors, such as shareholders, expect to receive on their investment in the company. The cost of equity is a critical factor in determining a company's overall cost of capital and overall profitability. Estimating the cost of equity is important for companies to make informed decisions regarding capital investment, financial strategy, and valuation. The cost of equity can be estimated through various methods, including the capital asset pricing model (CAPM), dividend discount model (DDM), and the earnings capitalization model (ECM). Depending on the method used, the cost of equity can vary depending on different factors such as stock market conditions, interest rates, and the company's risk profile.

Dividend Growth Model

The dividend growth model is a valuation approach used to estimate the intrinsic value of a stock based on the present value of expected future dividends. It assumes that the expected future dividends of a stock grow at a constant rate indefinitely and discounts these future expected dividends to their present value.

Assumptions:
- The dividends paid are constant and growing at a constant rate indefinitely.
- The cost of capital is constant and exceeds the constant growth rate of dividends.

Advantages:
- Provides a simple and straightforward approach to valuing stocks.
- Based on the expected future dividends rather than accounting measures like book value or earnings.
- Appropriate for companies with a consistent history of dividends and stable growth.

Disadvantages:
- May not be suitable for companies with an unpredictable dividend policy or where the dividend-growth rate is volatile.
- Assumes constant growth, which may not be realistic for many companies in practice.
- Relies on the prediction of future dividend growth, which can be difficult to accurately forecast.

Application:
1. Assume a stock pays a starting dividend of $2 per share that is expected to increase by 5% annually. With a cost of capital of 8%, the dividend growth model calculates a fair value of $50 per share.
2. If a company starts paying dividends for the first time, shareholders may use the dividend growth model to estimate potential future earnings and value of the stock.
3. An investor may use the dividend growth model when deciding whether to invest in a new stock or to buy additional shares of an existing one.
4. During a period of market volatility, investors may use the dividend growth model to estimate the intrinsic value of their holdings and decide whether to hold or sell.
5. An analyst may use the dividend growth model to compare a company's value with that of its industry competitors, and to identify overvalued or undervalued stocks.

Systematic and Unsystematic Risk

Systematic risk and unsystematic risk are two types of financial risk that investors face when investing in the stock market.
Systematic risk, also known as market risk, is the overall risk inherent in the entire market. This type of risk affects every company and industry within the market and is largely due to macroeconomic events and government policies. Examples of systematic risk include changes in interest rates, political instability, and recessions.

Here are five detailed reasons why systematic risk is important to consider:

1. It is uncontrollable: Systematic risk cannot be controlled or avoided by individual investors. It is inherent in the market and affects all companies and industries equally.

2. It is long-term: Since systematic risk is driven by macroeconomic events, it can have a long-lasting impact on the stock market. This can make it difficult for investors to predict market changes.

3. It is unavoidable: Even investors who diversify their portfolio cannot avoid systematic risk. This is because the entire market is affected by systematic risk factors.

4. It affects all stocks: Systematic risk affects all stocks that make up the market. As a result, an investor's portfolio can be significantly impacted by events such as a recession or political crisis.

5. It can lead to significant losses: Systematic risk can sometimes cause sudden or rapid shifts in the market, which can lead to significant losses for investors.

Unsystematic risk, on the other hand, is risk that is specific to a particular company or industry. This type of risk is caused by company-specific events, such as management changes or legal issues.

Here are five detailed reasons why unsystematic risk is important to consider:

1. It can be controlled: Unlike systematic risk, unsystematic risk can be controlled or avoided. Investors can mitigate unsystematic risk by diversifying their portfolio and investing in a variety of companies and industries.

2. It is specific to certain stocks: Unsystematic risk only affects certain stocks or industries, rather than the entire market.

3. It can be predicted: Since unsystematic risk is driven by company-specific events, it can be predicted and assessed more easily. This makes it easier for investors to manage and mitigate the risk.

4. It can lead to significant gains: Although unsystematic risk can lead to significant losses for investors, it can also lead to significant gains for those who invest wisely in the right companies.

5. It is variable: Unsystematic risk can vary greatly between different companies and industries. This makes it important for investors to research and analyze individual stocks before making investment decisions.

Portfolio Theory and CAPM

Portfolio theory and the Capital Asset Pricing Model (CAPM) are both concepts that are widely used in finance to help investors make informed decisions about their investment portfolios.

Portfolio theory is a concept developed by Harry Markowitz that provides a framework for investors to manage their risk by diversifying their investments. The theory holds that an investor can reduce his or her portfolio's risk by holding a mix of assets, rather than investing in a single company or industry. Portfolio theory considers the risk and return of different assets, as well as the correlations between them.

The Capital Asset Pricing Model (CAPM) is a financial model that relates the expected return of an asset to its risk. The model assumes that investors are rational and risk-averse, and therefore require compensation for bearing risk. The CAPM calculates an expected return based on a risk-free rate, the market portfolio's expected return, and the asset's beta (a measure of its sensitivity to market risk).

The relationship between portfolio theory and CAPM is that portfolio theory provides a framework for understanding how to diversify a portfolio to reduce risk, while CAPM provides a method to calculate expected returns based on risk. Portfolio theory suggests that investors should hold a mix of assets to diversify risk, while CAPM provides a way to measure an asset's risk and expected return.

Specifically, portfolio theory proposes that investors should construct a portfolio of assets that have a low correlation with one another, so that if one asset performs poorly, the others will likely perform well. By holding a mix of assets, investors are able to achieve a higher return for a given level of risk than they would by investing in just a few securities.

CAPM, on the other hand, suggests that the expected return of an asset should be commensurate with its risk. The model proposes that an investor's required return on an asset should be equal to the risk-free rate plus a premium that is proportional to the asset's beta. The beta measures the asset's exposure to market risk, and is used to adjust the asset's expected return for its level of risk.

The Capital Asset Pricing Model (CAPM)

The Capital Asset Pricing Model (CAPM) is a financial model used to calculate the expected returns of a security or a portfolio of securities. Here's a detailed look at the application of the CAPM, its assumptions, advantages, and disadvantages:

The formula for CAPM (Capital Asset Pricing Model) is:

$$r = Rf + \beta * (Rm - Rf)$$

In this formula:
- r is the expected return on the investment
- Rf is the risk-free rate of return
- β is the beta coefficient, which measures the risk of the investment
- Rm is the expected return of the stock market

The formula shows that the expected return on an investment is equal to the risk-free rate plus a premium for the risk of the investment relative to the market. The premium is calculated by multiplying the investment's beta coefficient by the expected return of the market minus the risk-free rate, and then adding the risk-free rate to the result.

Application of the CAPM:

The CAPM is applied to determine the expected returns of an asset or a portfolio of assets. This is achieved by calculating the expected return required by investors, given the asset's risk as measured by beta, the risk-free rate, and the market risk premium. The CAPM is useful in deciding the appropriate return on investment for an asset and is widely used by financial analysts, portfolio managers, and investors.

Assumptions of the CAPM:

The CAPM relies heavily on certain assumptions that may not always hold true in the real world. The model is based on the following assumptions:

1. Investors are rational and risk-averse.
2. Investors have homogenous expectations about the future cash flows of the asset.
3. Securities are all traded in an efficient market where risk-free rates are constant and publicly available.

Advantages of the CAPM:

The CAPM has several advantages for investors and analysts. These include:

1. Straightforward model: The CAPM is a relatively simple model to use, making it easily accessible to financial analysts and investors with no advanced statistical knowledge.

2. Risk measurement: CAPM is an effective risk measurement tool that can help investors better understand the risks associated with their investments.

3. Reliable basis for investment decisions: The CAPM is a widely accepted model that is used by investors to make informed investment decisions.

Disadvantages of the CAPM:

Despite its advantages, the CAPM has certain disadvantages, including:

1. Unrealistic assumptions: The CAPM's underlying assumptions are not always realistic, which can limit its accuracy in the real world.

2. Cannot be applied to all investments: The CAPM is best suited for investments that are sensitive to market risk or systematic risk. However, it may not be appropriate for investments with significant unsystematic or company-specific risks.

3. Dependency on market indices: The CAPM depends on the salient characteristics of the market, such as the risk-free interest rates, which can be volatile and unpredictable over time.

Estimating the cost of debt

When a company requires funds to support its operations, one of the ways to finance the business is through debt. The cost of debt refers to the cost that a company incurs in borrowing money to finance its operations. It is an important financial metric used to evaluate the company's overall cost of capital and profitability. The cost of debt is the interest rate that a company must pay on its outstanding debt, and it can vary depending on the type of debt, the interest rate environment, and the company's creditworthiness. Estimating the cost of debt is important for companies to accurately determine their cost of capital as well as to make informed decisions regarding financing options.

Irredeemable Debt

Irredeemable debt refers to a type of bond or loan, which has no predefined maturity date or repayment schedule. In simpler words, this type of debt or bond cannot be paid off by the borrower until the lender agrees to it or until it is redeemed by the borrower. Here's a detailed explanation of irredeemable debt, its application, and its pros and cons.

Explanation:

Irredeemable debt is a type of debt or bond usually issued by companies or government entities. Unlike most other types of debt, this type of debt has no fixed maturity date or repayment schedule. This means that the borrower can hold on to the debt indefinitely, without any obligation to repay the principal amount. The only way an irredeemable debt can be paid off is if the lender agrees to it or if the borrower redeems it.

Examples:
1. Preferred stock in a company that does not have a fixed maturity date and pays dividends indefinitely.
2. Perpetual debentures or bonds, which are issued by companies without any maturity date.
3. Zero-coupon bonds with no redemption date.
4. Infrastructure investments with indefinite life spans.
5. Government loans or bonds that contain a "perpetual debt" clause.

Application:
Irredeemable debt is typically used by large organizations or governments that require funds for long-term projects. By issuing this type of debt, borrowers can avoid the need to pay off the entire amount of debt at once, which can be a significant burden on their cash flow. Instead, the borrower can pay only the interest on the debt, which makes it easier for them to manage their finances.

Pros:
1. Irredeemable debt allows companies and governments to finance long-term projects.
2. This type of debt is attractive to investors because it offers a relatively stable and predictable income stream.
3. The issuer does not have to worry about refinancing or rolling over their debt, which can save them money and reduce the cost of borrowing.
4. Irredeemable debt can be a useful tool for investors who want to generate a predictable income stream.

Cons:

1. Irredeemable debt carries a higher degree of risk than other types of debt because it has no maturity date or redemption schedule.
2. There is a risk that the issuer may not be able to repay or redeem the debt, which can lead to a default.
3. Irredeemable debt may not be suitable for investors who require more liquidity in their investments.
4. Due to its inherent risk, investors demand a higher yield on irredeemable debt, which can make the cost of borrowing more expensive.

Usage:

Businesses and governments can use irredeemable debt to raise long-term capital without having to worry about repayment schedules, which can be an attractive option if they have long-term projects, such as infrastructure development or research and development, that require sustained investment. In general, irredeemable debt is also more attractive to investors who are looking for a relatively stable and predictable income stream, although the risk associated with the debt may make it less attractive to some investors.

Redeemable Debt

Redeemable debt is a type of debt or bond that has a fixed maturity date or repayment schedule, and which must be repaid by the borrower to the lender on or before the maturity date. Here's a detailed explanation of redeemable debt, its application, and its pros and cons.

Explanation:

Redeemable debt is a type of debt or bond that is issued by companies or governments and has a fixed maturity date or redemption schedule. This means that the borrower is obligated to repay the principal and interest to the lender on or before the maturity date. The borrower has the option to buy back or redeem the bond before the maturity date by paying back a certain percentage of the principal amount to the lender.

Examples:
1. Corporate bonds with a fixed maturity date and repayment schedule.
2. Treasury bills with a fixed maturity date and discount rate.
3. Certificates of deposit (CDs) with a fixed maturity date and rate of interest.
4. Residential mortgage-backed securities (RMBS) with a fixed maturity date and payment schedule.
5. Municipal bonds with a fixed maturity date and coupon rate.

Application:
Redeemable debt is usually used by companies or governments to raise funds for a short-term or medium-term project. This type of debt provides borrowers with an initial source of capital, which can be repaid over time. Redeemable debt is also attractive to investors because it offers a fixed income stream, which can be predictable.

Pros:
1. Redeemable debt offers a predictable income stream, which is attractive to investors who want a fixed return on their investment.
2. This type of debt can be easily traded in the secondary market, which provides investors with liquidity.
3. Redeemable debt can be used by companies or governments to finance short-term or medium-term projects.
4. This type of debt is generally less risky than irredeemable debt because there is a fixed repayment schedule.

Cons:
1. Redeemable debt carries a risk of default if the borrower is unable to repay the principal amount or interest on the debt.
2. The cost of borrowing for redeemable debt can be higher than other types of debt, due to the fixed maturity date and repayment schedule.

3. There is a risk that market interest rates will rise, which can make the issuer's debt less attractive to investors.
4. Redeemable debt can limit the issuer's ability to take on additional debt in the future.

Usage:

Businesses and governments can use redeemable debt to raise short-term or medium-term capital without having to worry about refinancing or rolling over their debt. This type of debt is also attractive to investors who are looking for a predictable and fixed income stream. In general, redeemable debt is less risky than irredeemable debt and can be a useful tool for borrowers who need more certainty around their financing needs.

Convertible Debt

Convertible debt is a type of bond or loan that can be converted into equity (such as stocks) at a later date, usually at the option of the holder of the bond or loan. Here's a detailed explanation of convertible debt, its application, and its pros and cons.

Explanation:

Convertible debt is a hybrid financial instrument that contains both debt and equity characteristics. It is typically issued by companies that need to raise capital but may not qualify for a traditional loan or bond. The key feature of convertible debt is that it can be converted into equity at the option of the holder. This means that the holder can receive a fixed income stream from the debt, or alternatively, convert the debt into equity and participate in any potential upside in the company's stock price.

Examples:

1. A start-up company wants to raise capital from investors but does not want to give up ownership or control of the company. The company issues convertible debt to investors that can be converted into equity in

the future.

2. A mid-sized company is planning to IPO soon. To attract investors who are interested in the potential upside of the IPO, the company issues convertible bonds that can be converted into shares of the company at the IPO price.

3. A company with a high debt load wants to raise more capital to pay off its debt. The company issues convertible bonds that can be converted into equity if the company's financial performance improves.

4. A company has a project with high long-term potential but requires significant upfront investment. The company issues convertible debt to fund the upfront investment, with the option for investors to convert their debt into equity if the project succeeds.

5. A company wants to diversify its funding sources and reduce its dependence on traditional debt. The company issues convertible debt to a group of investors who are interested in both the fixed income stream and the potential for equity participation.

Application:

Convertible debt is commonly used by start-ups and early-stage companies that need to raise capital but may not qualify for traditional loans or bonds. It allows companies to raise capital at a lower cost than equity financing and gives the option for investors to convert the debt into equity if the company's financial performance improves or if investors see potential for high returns.

Pros:

1. Convertible debt provides an avenue for companies to raise capital without giving up control of their company or diluting existing equity holders.

2. This type of debt offers investors the potential for both an income stream and equity participation.

3. Convertible debt is a useful tool for start-ups and early-stage

companies that may not qualify for traditional financing.
4. Investors are attracted to convertible debt because it offers a relatively low-risk investment that can also provide high returns if the company's performance improves.

Cons:
1. Companies carrying a high debt load may find that issuing convertible debt increases their leverage, which may increase financial risk.
2. The conversion rate of convertible debt may not be favorable to investors if the company's stock price declines or underperforms.
3. Companies may find that the fixed income stream of convertible debt becomes burdensome when their financial performance is poor.
4. Investors may be hesitant to invest in convertible debt if they are not confident in the company's financial performance.

Usage:
Businesses use convertible debt as a way to raise capital while minimizing dilution and maintaining control of the company. It is particularly popular among start-ups and early-stage companies that may not be able to secure traditional financing. Investors are attracted to convertible debt because it offers a relatively low-risk investment that can provide high returns if the company's performance improves or if there is potential for equity participation.

Preference Shares

Preference shares are a type of equity security that gives shareholders certain preferences and rights over common shareholders, such as priority in the payment of dividends and/or assets in case of liquidation. Here's a detailed explanation of preference shares, its application, and its pros and cons.

Explanation:

Preference shares are a type of equity security that contains both equity and debt characteristics. They are often used by companies that want to raise capital but may not want to issue traditional debt or dilute their existing equity. Preference shareholders are entitled to a fixed dividend and may have additional rights such as priority in the payment of dividends or redemption rights.

Examples:

1. A utility company issues preference shares with the right to a fixed dividend and preference in the payment of dividends over common shareholders.
2. A real estate investment trust (REIT) issues preference shares that provide a fixed dividend rate and the right to convert the shares into common stock at a later date.
3. A technology company issues preference shares that include a liquidation preference, providing a preference for the repayment of capital in case of company liquidation.
4. An oil and gas exploration company issues preference shares with a cumulative dividend that accrues if it is not paid in full.
5. A company with a high risk profile issues preference shares to investors who want a fixed return but are willing to take on more risk than traditional debt holders.

Application:

Preference shares are commonly used by companies that want to raise capital without issuing traditional debt or diluting their existing equity holders. They are also popular with investors who want a fixed return and some degree of preference and security over common shareholders.

Pros:
1. Preference shares provide a fixed dividend rate or preference in the payment of dividends, which is attractive to investors who want a predictable return on their investment.
2. This type of equity security allows companies to raise capital without issuing traditional debt or diluting their existing equity.
3. Preference shares may offer additional rights such as priority in the payment of dividends or redemption rights, which provides some degree of security to investors.
4. Companies can customize the terms of preference shares to suit their specific financing needs and requirements.
5. Investor demand for preference shares can be strong, particularly during periods of low interest rates or economic uncertainty.

Cons:
1. Preference shares can be more expensive for companies to issue than traditional debt or common equity.
2. The rights and preferences of preference shareholders can be complicated and may require specialized knowledge to fully understand.
3. Companies may find that the fixed dividend or preference rights become burdensome in times of financial difficulty, particularly if they have also issued traditional debt.
4. Investors may be hesitant to invest in preference shares if they are not confident in the company's ability to pay the fixed dividend or honor the preference rights.

Usage:
Businesses use preference shares as a way to raise capital while minimizing dilution and maintaining control of the company. They are particularly popular among companies that want to attract investors who are seeking a fixed income stream or have a higher risk tolerance than

traditional debt holders. Preference shares also allow companies to customize the terms to suit their specific financing needs and requirements.

Bank Debt

Bank debt means the loans and credit facilities provided by banks to businesses, organizations, or individuals. Here's a detailed explanation of bank debt, its application, and its pros and cons.

Explanation:

Bank debt is a term that refers to any type of loan or credit facility provided by banks to borrowers. This type of debt is issued as a form of lending, where the borrower pays interest on the amount borrowed. Bank debt usually involves a set repayment schedule and may be secured or unsecured.

Examples:
1. An auto manufacturing company borrows from a bank to finance a new production plant.
2. A homeowner takes out a mortgage loan from a bank to purchase a new house.
3. A small business owner uses a line of credit from a bank to finance short-term expenses.
4. A construction company borrows from a bank to purchase new equipment.
5. A large corporation issues commercial paper to finance its operations.

Application:
Bank debt is widely used by businesses, organizations, or individuals who need access to funds to finance their operations, invest in new assets, or purchase new equipment. It's usually more accessible compared to other forms of debt, such as bonds or convertible debt, and offers a relatively low cost of borrowing.

Pros:
1. Bank debt is a flexible form of financing that can be tailored to meet the specific needs of the borrower.
2. This type of debt is usually less expensive than other types of unsecured debt.
3. Bank debt can be secured against assets, which can reduce the risk for the lender and minimize borrowing costs for the borrower.
4. Bank debt offers borrowers a set repayment schedule, which can help with budgeting and financial planning.
5. Bank debt usually comes with a fixed interest rate, which means the borrower knows exactly how much they need to repay.

Cons:
1. Bank debt can be difficult to obtain for businesses or individuals with poor credit histories.
2. The terms of bank debt can be restrictive, with the lender requiring the borrower to meet specific conditions or covenants.
3. Borrowers who default on bank debt can face consequences such as increased interest rates or foreclosure.
4. Banks may require collateral, and if the borrower fails to repay the loan, the collateral can be repossessed by the bank.
5. Bank debt can have a negative impact on the borrower's credit score if they do not make payments on time.

Usage:
Businesses and individuals use bank debt for a variety of reasons, such as short-term working capital, funding longer-term projects, or to purchase assets. Bank debt is usually the most accessible and affordable form of financing, particularly for small businesses or those without a solid credit rating.

Estimating the Overall Cost of Capital

As businesses seek to finance their operations and initiatives, one of the foremost considerations is the cost of capital. The cost of capital refers to the expenses incurred in obtaining financing from various sources, such as equity or debt, and is a critical aspect of determining a business's returns on investment. Estimating the overall cost of capital is essential for organizations attempting to make sound financial decisions and considering the feasibility of potential investments. By understanding the concept of the cost of capital, businesses can make informed decisions about their financing strategies and optimize their returns on investment while minimizing costs. In this essay, we will examine the concept of the overall cost of capital and the various factors that contribute to it.

Distinguishing between Average and Marginal Cost of Capital

The cost of capital is an essential consideration for businesses when seeking to finance their operations and initiatives. Two primary concepts that businesses should be aware of when evaluating their cost of capital are the average cost of capital and the marginal cost of capital. Average cost of capital refers to the total cost of financing a business, including both equity and debt financing, divided by the total amount of capital raised. It takes into account the costs associated with all sources of financing and represents the average rate of return that the business must earn on all of its investments to break even. This means that if a business earns less than its average cost of capital, it is not generating enough returns to compensate for the cost of financing and losing money.

On the other hand, the marginal cost of capital refers to the cost of raising additional funds for a business. This means that it is the cost of each additional dollar of financing, as opposed to the average cost of all financing. For example, if a business were to raise an additional dollar of financing through debt, the marginal cost of capital would be the interest rate on the new debt. Marginal cost of capital is important because it helps businesses make decisions about obtaining additional financing by evaluating the return on investment they expect to receive and whether it is greater than the cost of financing.

Calculating Weighted Average Cost of Capital (WACC) Using Book Value and Market Value Weightings

Example 1: XYZ Co.
Book Value of Equity: $500,000
Market Value of Equity: $700,000
Book Value of Debt: $300,000
Market Value of Debt: $350,000
Cost of Equity: 10%
Cost of Debt: 6%

Using Book Value Weighting:
The weight of equity = (Book value of equity / Total capital) = (500,000 / 1,300,000) = 0.38461538
The weight of debt = (Book value of debt / Total capital) = (300,000 / 1,300,000) = 0.23076923
WACC = (Cost of equity x Weight of equity) + (Cost of debt x Weight of debt) x (1 - Tax rate)
WACC = (0.10 x 0.38461538) + (0.06 x 0.23076923) x (1 - 0) = 8.12%

Using Market Value Weighting:
The weight of equity = (Market value of equity / Total capital) = (700,000 / 1,050,000) = 0.66666667
The weight of debt = (Market value of debt / Total capital) = (350,000 / 1,050,000) = 0.33333333
WACC = (Cost of equity x Weight of equity) + (Cost of debt x Weight of debt) x (1 - Tax rate)

WACC = (0.10 x 0.66666667) + (0.06 x 0.33333333) x (1 - 0) = 8.67%

Example 2: ABC Co.
Book Value of Equity: $400,000
Market Value of Equity: $600,000
Book Value of Debt: $250,000
Market Value of Debt: $300,000
Cost of Equity: 9%
Cost of Debt: 5%

Using Book Value Weighting:
The weight of equity = (Book value of equity / Total capital) = (400,000 / 950,000) = 0.42105263
The weight of debt = (Book value of debt / Total capital) = (250,000 / 950,000) = 0.26315789
WACC = (Cost of equity x Weight of equity) + (Cost of debt x Weight of debt) x (1 - Tax rate)
WACC = (0.09 x 0.42105263) + (0.05 x 0.26315789) x (1 - 0) = 7.63%

Using Market Value Weighting:
The weight of equity = (Market value of equity / Total capital) = (600,000 / 900,000) = 0.66666667
The weight of debt = (Market value of debt / Total capital) = (300,000 / 900,000) = 0.33333333
WACC = (Cost of equity x Weight of equity) + (Cost of debt x Weight of debt) x (1 - Tax rate)
WACC = (0.09 x 0.66666667) + (0.05 x 0.33333333) x (1 - 0) = 8.00%

Example 3: DEF Co.
Book Value of Equity: $800,000
Market Value of Equity: $1,200,000
Book Value of Debt: $500,000
Market Value of Debt: $550,000
Cost of Equity: 12%

Cost of Debt: 7%

Using Book Value Weighting:

The weight of equity = (Book value of equity / Total capital) = (800,000 / 1,300,000) = 0.61538462

The weight of debt = (Book value of debt / Total capital) = (500,000 / 1,300,000) = 0.38461538

WACC = (Cost of equity x Weight of equity) + (Cost of debt x Weight of debt) x (1 - Tax rate)

WACC = (0.12 x 0.61538462) + (0.07 x 0.38461538) x (1 - 0) = 10.97%

Using Market Value Weighting:

The weight of equity = (Market value of equity / Total capital) = (1,200,000 / 1,750,000) = 0.68571429

The weight of debt = (Market value of debt / Total capital) = (550,000 / 1,750,000) = 0.31428571

WACC = (Cost of equity x Weight of equity) + (Cost of debt x Weight of debt) x (1 - Tax rate)

WACC = (0.12 x 0.68571429) + (0.07 x 0.31428571) x (1 - 0) = 11.02%

Example 4: GHI Co.

Book Value of Equity: $2,000,000
Market Value of Equity: $3,000,000
Book Value of Debt: $1,500,000
Market Value of Debt: $1,800,000
Cost of Equity: 8%
Cost of Debt: 4%

Using Book Value Weighting:

The weight of equity = (Book value of equity / Total capital) = (2,000,000 / 3,500,000) = 0.57142857

The weight of debt = (Book value of debt / Total capital) = (1,500,000 / 3,500,000) = 0.42857143

WACC = (Cost of equity x Weight of equity) + (Cost of debt x Weight

of debt) x (1 - Tax rate)
WACC = (0.08 x 0.57142857) + (0.04 x 0.42857143) x (1 - 0) = 6.86%

Using Market Value Weighting:

The weight of equity = (Market value of equity / Total capital) = (3,000,000 / 4,800,000) = 0.625

The weight of debt = (Market value of debt / Total capital) = (1,800,000 / 4,800,000) = 0.375

WACC = (Cost of equity x Weight of equity) + (Cost of debt x Weight of debt) x (1 - Tax rate)

WACC = (0.08 x 0.625) + (0.04 x 0.375) x (1 - 0) = 6.88%

Example 5: JKL Co.

Book Value of Equity: $3,500,000
Market Value of Equity: $5,000,000
Book Value of Debt: $2,000,000
Market Value of Debt: $2,200,000
Cost of Equity: 11%
Cost of Debt: 6.5%

Using Book Value Weighting:

The weight of equity = (Book value of equity / Total capital) = (3,500,000 / 5,500,000) = 0.63636364

The weight of debt = (Book value of debt / Total capital) = (2,000,000 / 5,500,000) = 0.36363636

WACC = (Cost of equity x Weight of equity) + (Cost of debt x Weight of debt) x (1 - Tax rate)

WACC = (0.11 x 0.63636364) + (0.065 x 0.36363636) x (1 - 0) = 9.09%

Using Market Value Weighting:

The weight of equity = (Market value of equity / Total capital) = (5,000,000 / 7,200,000) = 0.69444444

The weight of debt = (Market value of debt / Total capital) = (2,200,000 / 7,200,000) = 0.30555556

WACC = (Cost of equity x Weight of equity) + (Cost of debt x Weight of debt) x (1 - Tax rate)
WACC = (0.11 x 0.69444444) + (0.065 x 0.30555556) x (1 - 0) = 9.50%

Sources of finance and their relative costs

Sources of finance refer to the various ways in which businesses obtain the funds they need to operate, invest in new projects, and expand their operations. These sources of finance can be categorized into internal and external sources, based on whether the funds come from the company's own resources or from external sources. Companies often rely on a combination of these sources to obtain the necessary funds, and each source has its unique characteristics, advantages, and disadvantages. Understanding the various sources of finance and their relative costs is crucial for businesses to make informed decisions regarding their financing strategies. In this section, we will discuss the different sources of finance available to businesses and the relative costs associated with each option.

Relative Risk-Return Relationship and Costs of Equity and Debt

The relative risk-return relationship and the relative costs of equity and debt are important considerations for businesses when choosing their financing strategies.
The risk-return relationship refers to the principle that investments with higher expected returns must also carry a higher level of risk. This principle applies to both equity and debt financing. Equity financing involves selling stocks to investors, and the returns are not fixed;

meaning that they can fluctuate over time depending on the performance of the company. On the other hand, debt financing involves borrowing money from lenders, and the returns are fixed in the form of interest payments.

The relative costs of equity and debt also differ because of their risk-return relationship. Equity financing is generally more expensive than debt financing because equity investors demand a higher expected return due to the higher risk associated with equity financing. This is because equity investors own a portion of the company and have a claim on its assets and profits. For this reason, equity financing carries a higher cost of capital.

In contrast, debt financing carries a lower cost of capital relative to equity financing. This is because the lenders do not own a portion of the company and have no claim to its profits. Instead, they receive a fixed rate of return in the form of interest payments. Because debt financing has a lower level of risk, it carries a lower cost of capital.

However, it is important to note that debt financing also comes with risks, such as the risk of default on the loan. If a company is unable to make its interest payments, it can lead to financial distress and even bankruptcy. Additionally, lenders may impose restrictions on the company's operations or require collateral to secure the loan.

Creditor Hierarchy and Its Connection with Relative Costs of Sources of Finance

The creditor hierarchy refers to the order in which creditors are paid back in the case of a borrower's default. It is a critical consideration for lenders when evaluating the risk of loaning funds to a business. Generally, the first creditor to be paid back is the senior debt, followed by subordinated debt, and then equity holders.
Senior debt refers to loans that have priority over other types of debt in

the case of default. The lenders of senior debt are the first to receive payments from a borrower's assets and revenue. Hence senior debt has a lower level of risk compared to subordinated debt and equity. As a result, senior debt carries a lower cost of capital.

Subordinated debt, on the other hand, is considered junior to senior debt in repayment priority in the event of default. Therefore, subordinated debt carries a higher level of risk compared to senior debt, and this increases its cost of financing.

Equity holders are last in line in the creditor hierarchy, and they receive payment only after other creditors have been repaid. Equity financing carries the highest risk and, therefore, the highest cost of financing.

The relative costs of sources of finance are affected by the risk-return relationship and the creditor hierarchy. The higher the rank of a lender in the creditor hierarchy, the lower the risk associated with its investment, and hence lower the cost of financing.

For example, secured loans are considered senior because they are backed by collateral, such as equipment or real estate, and therefore carry a lower risk compared to unsecured loans. Similarly, bonds are considered senior to stocks because they carry less risk.

In contrast, unsecured loans and equity financing are considered junior to secured loans and bonds, respectively, and carry a higher level of risk. Therefore, their cost of financing is higher.

The Problem of High Levels of Gearing: Risks and Challenges

High levels of gearing can be a problem for any organization that relies heavily on debt financing to operate its business. Here are some problems that may arise from high levels of gearing:

1. Financial Risk: When a company takes on high levels of debt, it increases its financial risk because it becomes more sensitive to changes in interest rates, economic conditions, and cash flow. This can result in the company being unable to make debt payments, which can lead to bankruptcy.

2. Limited flexibility: Another problem with high levels of gearing is that it can limit a company's flexibility to invest in growth opportunities, such as new projects or acquisitions. If a company is servicing a large amount of debt, it may not have the financial resources to take advantage of these opportunities.

3. Higher interest expense: A company that has a high level of gearing will typically have higher interest expenses, which can reduce its profitability. This, in turn, can make it more difficult for the company to pay off its debt, as well as to attract new investors.

4. Reduced creditworthiness: A company that has high levels of gearing may be viewed as having a higher risk of default by lenders and investors. This can make it more difficult for the company to obtain additional financing in the future, as well as to negotiate favorable terms on its existing debt.

Overall, high levels of gearing can be a significant problem for any company, as it increases financial risk, limits flexibility, increases interest expense, and reduces creditworthiness. It's important for companies to strike a balance between debt and equity financing to ensure that they can operate their business effectively while minimizing financial risk.

Assessing the Impact of Sources of Finance on Financial Position, Financial Risk, and Shareholder Wealth Using Appropriate Measures

Understanding how various sources of finance impact financial position, financial risk, and shareholder wealth is essential for anyone interested in finance or investing. The financial position of a company is a measure of its ability to meet its financial obligations, while financial risk is the level of uncertainty or variability of a company's expected future returns from its investments. Shareholder wealth is the value of a company to its investors, measured by the price of its shares, dividends, and other assets.

Different sources of finance can have a significant impact on a company's financial position, risk, and shareholder wealth. Debt financing, for example, enables companies to raise funds by borrowing money from financial institutions and investors, which can increase financial risk if not properly managed. On the other hand, equity financing allows companies to raise money by selling shares of ownership in the business, which can dilute shareholder wealth but may also reduce financial risk.

To assess the impact of various sources of finance on financial position, financial risk, and shareholder wealth, appropriate measures must be used. These measures could include ratios such as debt-to-equity, return on equity, earnings per share, and price-to-earnings ratio. By analyzing these measures, investors and financial analysts can gain insight into the impact of different sources of finance on a company's financial position, risk, and shareholder wealth, which can help inform investment decisions and financial strategies.

Ratio Analysis Using Statement of Financial Position: Exploring Gearing, Operational and Financial Gearing, Interest Coverage Ratio and Other Relevant Ratios

1. Gearing Ratio: The gearing ratio is a measure of the proportion of total capital that is financed by debt. The formula for the gearing ratio is:

Gearing Ratio = (Total Debt / Total Equity + Total Debt) x 100%

Let's say that Company A has total debt of $500,000 and total equity of $1,000,000. The gearing ratio would be:

Gearing Ratio = ($500,000 / $1,500,000) x 100% = 33.33%

2. Operational Gearing: Operational gearing is the degree to which a company's costs are fixed rather than variable. It is measured by the ratio of fixed costs to variable costs. The formula for operational gearing is:

Operational Gearing = (Fixed Costs / Variable Costs)

For example, if Company B has fixed costs of $1,000,000 and variable costs of $2,000,000, the operational gearing would be:

Operational Gearing = $1,000,000 / $2,000,000 = 0.5

3. Financial Gearing: Financial gearing is the degree to which a company's earnings are leveraged by the use of debt. It is measured by the ratio of fixed interest charges to operating profit. The formula for financial gearing is:

Financial Gearing = (Fixed Interest Charges / Operating Profit)

For example, if Company C has fixed interest charges of $50,000 and operating profit of $200,000, the financial gearing would be:

Financial Gearing = $50,000 / $200,000 = 0.25

4. Interest Coverage Ratio: The interest coverage ratio is a measure of the ability of a company to meet its interest payments on outstanding debt. It is calculated as follows:

Interest Coverage Ratio = (Operating Profit / Interest Expense)

Suppose that Company D has an operating profit of $500,000 and an interest expense of $50,000. The interest coverage ratio would be:

Interest Coverage Ratio = $500,000 / $50,000 = 10

These ratios can help investors and analysts understand a company's financial position, risk, and potential for growth. For instance, a high gearing ratio may indicate that a company is overly reliant on debt financing, which can increase financial risk. A low interest coverage ratio may signify that a company is struggling to meet its debt obligations. In contrast, a low operational gearing may indicate that a company is more vulnerable to fluctuations in sales, while a high financial gearing may suggest that a company's earnings are more sensitive to changes in interest rates.

Assessing the Impact of Sources of Finance on Financial Position, Financial Risk, and Shareholder Wealth Using Appropriate Measures ii) Cash Flow Forecasting

Cash flow forecasting is a financial tool that helps businesses analyze their expected inflows and outflows of cash over a defined period. It's a crucial tool for assessing the impact of various sources of financing on an organization's financial position, financial risk, and shareholder wealth. With a cash flow forecast, businesses can plan strategically, identify potential cash shortfalls, and respond proactively to changing financial circumstances.

Sources of finance can have a significant impact on a company's cash flow. For example, taking on debt financing can lead to increased cash inflow, but may also increase financial risk if the debt servicing costs become a burden. In contrast, equity financing may not have immediate cash inflow, but can provide a solid financial foundation, increased confidence on the part of investors, and potentially lower financial risk.

Through cash flow forecasting, businesses can assess the impact of different financing options on their financial position, financial risk, and shareholder wealth. By analyzing the expected inflows and outflows of cash, businesses can determine their ability to repay debt, invest in growth opportunities, and meet other financial obligations.

Here are two examples that illustrate the benefits of cash flow forecasting:

Example 1:
A small manufacturing business is considering taking on a significant amount of debt to expand its operations. To assess the potential impact of debt financing on its cash flow, the company produces a cash flow forecast over the next five years. The forecast reveals that while the initial cash inflow from the debt financing will allow the company to expand, the increased debt servicing costs will result in significant outflows of cash, ultimately leading to a potential cash shortfall if growth is slower than expected.

Example 2:
A startup technology firm is considering accepting venture capital financing to help fund its research and development efforts. The company produces a cash flow forecast based on potential revenue and expenses over the next two years to determine if the proposed funding is a suitable source of finance. The forecast reveals that while the initial cash inflow from the venture capital will allow the company to fund its R&D efforts, the level of risk associated with the investment is high, and there is a potential for a cash shortfall in the third year.

In addition to helping businesses assess the impact of sources of finance on financial position, financial risk, and shareholder wealth, cash flow forecasting provides a range of benefits. These include helping businesses to:

- Plan and budget effectively
- Identify potential cash shortfalls
- Respond proactively to changes in financial circumstances
- Anticipate opportunities for growth
- Monitor and optimize cash flow over time

As a result, cash flow forecasting is an essential tool for any business seeking a clear picture of its financial position and cash flow situation, and wanting to make informed decisions about future growth and investment opportunities.

Assessing the Impact of Sources of Finance on Financial Position, Financial Risk, and Shareholder Wealth Using Appropriate Measures iii) Leasing or Borrowing to Buy

Leasing or borrowing to buy are two common sources of finance that businesses can use to obtain the assets they need to operate. Both leasing and borrowing to buy have their advantages and disadvantages that can impact a company's financial position, financial risk, and shareholder wealth.

When a business decides to lease assets, it makes regular payments to the leasing company in exchange for the use of the asset. At the end of the lease term, the business may have the option to purchase the asset or return it to the leasing company. On the other hand, when a business borrows to buy assets, it takes out a loan to purchase the asset outright and then makes regular loan payments to pay off the principal and interest.

Here are two examples that illustrate the impact of leasing and borrowing to buy on a company's financial position, financial risk, and shareholder wealth:

Example 1:

A small printing company wants to purchase a new piece of equipment for its operations. The company could either lease the equipment or borrow to buy it. If the company chooses to lease the equipment, it will make regular lease payments and avoid making a significant upfront payment, which can be beneficial for its cash flow. However, since the company does not own the equipment, it does not add value to its assets. On the other hand, if the company chooses to borrow to buy the equipment, it will take on a significant financial burden upfront, but will own the equipment outright and have the ability to extract more value from it over time.

Example 2:

A growing wholesale bakery wants to expand its operations by purchasing a new property. It could either lease the property or borrow to buy it. If the company leases the property, it will avoid the upfront costs of a down payment, and make regular lease payments, which can free up cash for other investments. However, if the business does not buy the property, they will not have any equity in the property, limiting its ability to use it as collateral for borrowing in the future. On the other hand, if the company borrows to buy the property, it will have to take on significant debt, but will own the property and potentially extract more long-term value.

In terms of the impact of leasing and borrowing to buy on financial position, financial risk, and shareholder wealth, businesses need to consider a range of factors. These include the total cost of ownership, the potential impact on cash flow and profit, and the ability to use the asset once the lease or loan term ends.

Impact of cost of capital on investments

Investments are a crucial aspect of any business, and their success depends on a variety of factors. One such factor is the cost of capital, which refers to the cost of obtaining funds for investment purposes. The cost of capital is influenced by a range of factors such as interest rates, inflation, and the level of risk associated with the investment. Understanding the impact of the cost of capital on investments is essential for businesses to make informed strategic decisions and maximize their profits. In this paper, we will explore the impact of the cost of capital on investments and how businesses can overcome challenges associated with it.

The Relationship between Company Value and Cost of Capital

The relationship between a company's value and the cost of capital is a complex and important concept that can greatly impact a business's bottom line. Let's explore this relationship by applying it to three sample examples.

Example 1: Company A has a low-cost capital and high company value. Company A is able to invest more in its growth and expansion, ultimately leading to higher profitability, as they can take on more projects and have access to cheaper capital.

Example 2: Company B has a high cost of capital and low company value. As a result, Company B is unable to access cheaper funds to invest in projects that would increase their profitability. Consequently, they are forced to cut costs and reduce their overall value.

Example 3: Company C has a moderate cost of capital and modest company value. While they may not have access to cheaper funds like Company A, they are still able to invest in projects that would benefit their profitability without breaking the bank on interest payments. As a result, Company C is able to maintain its value and growth path.

In analyzing these examples, we can see that the relationship between a company's value and cost of capital is quite evident. In example 1, where Company A has a low-cost capital, they are able to invest more in their growth and expansion leading to increased profitability and hence value. While in example 2, the high cost of capital hinders Company B's ability to access funds for investment, ultimately leading to reduced value. Finally, Company C's moderate cost of capital still allows them to invest in projects without having to sacrifice their value, unlike Company B. Hence, businesses need to understand the impact of cost of capital on the company's value and growth potential and manage it effectively to maximize their profitability.

Circumstances Under Which WACC Can Be Used in Investment Appraisal

WACC (Weighted Average Cost of Capital) is a critical component in making investment decisions for businesses. It is the weighted average cost of debt and equity capital a company uses to finance its investments. In real-time business cases, here are five circumstances under which WACC can be used in investment appraisal:

1. Evaluating New Investment Opportunities: When a company is considering investment opportunities, evaluating the investment's potential return against the WACC can help to establish whether the investment will generate a return greater than the cost of capital required.

2. Comparing Alternative Investments: By using WACC, a company can compare alternative projects and investments based on their net present value relative to their respective costs of capital. This ensures that businesses invest only in projects generating positive net present value.

3. Setting the Firm's Capital Structure: WACC can be used to define the optimal capital structure for a company by analyzing how changes in capital mix will impact the overall cost of capital. As a result, businesses can determine the proportion of debt and equity that will maximize their value.

4. Acquisitions and Mergers: WACC can be used in determining the value of company acquisitions as it can be used to calculate expected cash flows resulting from the acquisition and compared against the current market value. It can also be used to establish the cost of refinancing that may be required.

5. Estimating the ROI: When a company is investing in long-term projects such as infrastructure or research and development, WACC can be used as a benchmark for estimating the project's return on investment (ROI).

Advantages of Using CAPM Over WACC in Determining Project-Specific Cost of Capital

The Capital Asset Pricing Model (CAPM) and Weighted Average Cost of Capital (WACC) are two methods commonly used to determine the cost of capital for a project or investment. Although WACC is the most widely used method, there are various advantages of using CAPM over WACC. Here are ten advantages of using the CAPM over WACC in determining a project-specific cost of capital, and examples of how these advantages can be applied in real-time business cases:
1. Flexibility: CAPM is more flexible than WACC as it accounts for the risks of individual investments rather than the overall business. For example, in the hotel industry, different hotels may have varying risks, and CAPM can calculate the cost of capital for each hotel, accounting for its unique risks.

2. Specific Asset Pricing: CAPM allows investors to price assets based

on their specific risk level rather than their overall business risk. For example, if a new factory is being built, CAPM can calculate the cost of capital for it, accounting for its unique risks, rather than using the overall WACC of a company.

3. Clearer Risk-Return Relationship: CAPM provides a clearer understanding of the risk-return relationship between an investment and the overall market. For example, for an investment in a technology startup, CAPM can calculate the cost of capital based on the expected returns and risks of the startup and its position in the market.

4. Systematic Risk: CAPM better calculates systematic risk than WACC. For example, in the airline industry, CAPM can evaluate the cost of capital for individual planes compared to the company's overall WACC.

5. Personalization: CAPM allows personalization of returns for investors. For example, in financial services, CAPM can personalize the cost of capital for individual investor portfolios, with unique expected returns and risks.

6. Mainstream Method: CAPM is the mainstream method for calculating the cost of capital in many industries. For example, in the tech industry, CAPM is used to analyze the cost of capital for individual tech products.

7. Single Factor Risk: CAPM contributes to single-factor risk assessment. Risk assessment can be based on a single factor such as a product line, part of a company, or a specific industry in specific periods of time.

8. Forward-Looking: CAPM is forward-looking and factors in the future potential of investments. For example, in the pharmaceutical industry, CAPM can calculate the cost of capital based on the potential value,

development time, and risk of new drugs, rather than assessing the industry in general.

9. Accounting for Market Conditions: CAPM accounts for market conditions and situations that may impact the investment. For example, in the real estate industry, CAPM can account for interest rates, local government policy, and construction costs when calculating the cost of capital for a new property.

10. More Accurate: CAPM provides a more accurate calculation of the cost of capital for an investment than WACC as it accounts for the specific risks of the investment. For example, a utility company can use CAPM to calculate the cost of capital for a renewable energy project, accounting for tax incentives and the volatility of energy prices.

In conclusion, CAPM offers numerous advantages over WACC for calculating the cost of capital for a project or investment, such as flexibility, specific asset pricing, clearer risk-return relationship, accounting for market conditions, which make it the better choice in many business cases.

The Application of the CAPM in Calculating a Project-Specific Discount Rate

The Capital Asset Pricing Model (CAPM) is a financial model used to determine the expected return on an investment based on the risk-free rate, market risk premium, and beta of individual stocks. In calculating a project-specific discount rate, CAPM can be used to determine the expected return on an investment based on both systematic and unsystematic risks. Here are five examples of how CAPM can be applied to calculate a project-specific discount rate:

1. Real Estate Development: In real estate, CAPM can be used to calculate a project-specific discount rate to help determine the cost of capital required for a development project. CAPM would consider the

specific risks of the project, such as market demand, rental rates, and cost of construction, to determine the required rate of return.

2. Manufacturing Expansion: CAPM can also be applied to calculating the discount rate for a manufacturing expansion project. CAPM would evaluate the project's expected cash flows, risks of the expansion, market conditions, and competition to determine the required rate of return.

3. Software Development: In the technology sector, CAPM can be used in software development projects to determine the project-specific discount rate, which considers the risks of the project, such as project timelines, market competition, and development costs.

4. Mining Operations: CAPM can be applied to determine the discount rate for mining projects by evaluating the project's resource, risks, capital costs, and revenue forecasts. With CAPM, mining companies can evaluate investments specifically and determine the rate of return specific to the project.

5. Energy Project: In the energy sector, CAPM can be used to determine the discount rate for a specific energy project that considers the project's expected cash flows, risks, and market conditions. For example, a solar company could use CAPM to evaluate the cost of capital associated with developing a new solar farm or energy storage system.

In conclusion, CAPM can be applied to various industries to determine a project-specific discount rate by evaluating the risk and expected returns of the project, which is an essential tool for businesses to evaluate investments and make crucial decisions.

Capital structure theories and practical considerations

The Traditional View of Capital Structure and its Assumptions

The traditional view of capital structure suggests that firms should have a target capital structure mix of debt versus equity that minimizes the cost of capital and maximizes shareholder value. It is based on several assumptions, including the following:

1. Capital Markets are Efficient: The traditional view assumes that capital markets are efficient and that relevant information is reflected in stock prices. Therefore, firms can raise capital at the lowest possible cost.

2. No Taxes: The traditional view assumes that there are no tax benefits associated with debt financing.

3. Fixed Investment Policy: The traditional view assumes that firms have a fixed investment policy and that investment opportunities are independent of financing decisions.

4. Symmetric Information: The traditional view assumes that shareholders and investors have equal access to information about the company's operations, projects, financial health, and cash flows.

5. No Bankruptcy Costs: The traditional view assumes that there are no bankruptcy costs associated with the use of debt financing.

6. Unchanging Risk: The traditional view assumes that a firm's risk level does not change with the use of debt financing.

7. Homogeneous Expectations: The traditional view assumes that

investors have homogeneous expectations concerning the future earnings of the firms.

8. No Agency Issues: The traditional view assumes no agency issues between the firm's management and its shareholders and creditors.

In conclusion, the traditional view of capital structure suggests that firms should aim to have a target debt-equity mix that maximizes their value by minimizing the cost of capital. The assumptions of the traditional view help provide guidance for businesses to determine their optimal capital structure mix. However, recent research suggests that these assumptions are not always valid in real-world situations, which has led to the emergence of alternative views on capital structure.

Miller-Modigliani Theory of Capital Structure Under Different Tax Regimes

Miller and Modigliani (M&M) proposed a theory on capital structure that challenged the traditional view by suggesting that the capital structure of a firm does not affect its value under certain conditions. These were the conditions of perfect capital markets, no taxes, and no agency costs. The M&M propositions were then extended to incorporate corporate taxation.

Miller and Modigliani's Propositions without Corporate Taxation:
1. Irrelevance Proposition: M&M's first proposition without corporate taxation suggests that the capital structure of a firm does not affect its value. M&M assumes that in perfect markets, investors have access to the same information and same risk appetite, thus there is no advantage of one financing source over another.

2. Homemade Leverage Proposition: M&M's second proposition without corporate taxation suggests that investors can create leverage themselves by borrowing or lending on their accounts. M&M assumes

that DIY leverage is possible in the absence of taxes or transaction costs, as investors can replicate the capital structure of the firm.

Miller and Modigliani's Propositions with Corporate Taxation:

1. Tradeoff Proposition: M&M's first proposition with corporate taxation suggests that firms have optimal capital structures that balance the value of tax shields offered by debt against the costs of bankruptcy. Debt capital is valued for tax shields, while equity capital is valued for its low bankruptcy costs.

2. Signaling Proposition: M&M's second proposition with corporate taxation suggests that it becomes rational for firms to use higher levels of debt to signal to the market that the firm is of high quality. M&M assumes that potential investors infer a positive signal from the firm's decision to use high levels of debt, interpreting the firm as financially strong and able to meet its obligations.

Assumptions:

Miller and Modigliani made several assumptions in proposing their theory of capital structure, including:

1. Capital markets are frictionless and efficient.

2. Information about investments is freely available to all market participants.

3. There are no bankruptcy costs or transaction costs.

4. The real-world is realistic, and investors make rational decisions.

5. Taxes and agency costs are the only reasons firms may choose to adjust their capital structures.

In conclusion, Miller and Modigliani's theories propose that the capital structure of a firm is irrelevant in perfect capital markets. However, corporate taxation changes the analysis entirely, and firms must consider achieving an optimal balance between the benefits of leverage to obtain tax shields and the costs of bankruptcy. The M&M propositions have since been challenged by empirical research, particularly in the real world.

Impact of Capital Market Imperfections on Miller-Modigliani Theory of Capital Structure

Capital market imperfections refer to various factors that deviate from the ideal assumptions of perfect financial markets. The following are some common capital market imperfections that impact the views of Miller and Modigliani on capital structure:

1. Taxes: Corporate taxes can reduce the value of the firm, making debt financing less expensive than equity financing. This implies that a higher debt-to-equity ratio could lead to a lower cost of capital.

2. Bankruptcy costs: Bankruptcy costs are the expenses incurred by a company when it goes out of business. These costs can be significant and tend to increase with debt levels. Therefore, there is an optimal debt-to-equity ratio that minimizes the bankruptcy costs.

3. Information asymmetry: Information asymmetry occurs when one party has access to more information than the other party. In the context of capital structure, it means that shareholders and management may have more information than creditors about the true risk level of the firm. As a result, creditors may require higher interest rates to compensate for the risk of default, which can increase the cost of debt financing.

4. Agency costs: Agency costs refer to the costs associated with aligning the interests of shareholders and managers. If managers are not incentivized to maximize shareholder value, they may engage in activities that benefit themselves over the shareholders. This can lead to a suboptimal capital structure.

5. Market timing: Market timing refers to the ability of firms to issue securities when the market conditions are favorable. If a firm chooses to issue equity when the market is high, it could lead to dilution of existing shareholders. Similarly, if a firm chooses to issue debt when interest rates are high, it could increase the cost of capital.

These capital market imperfections challenge the validity of the Miller-Modigliani theory of capital structure. The theory assumes perfect capital markets, which do not exist in reality. Therefore, the optimal capital structure depends on the specific circumstances of the firm and its environment.

The Pecking Order Theory and Its Relevance to the Selection of Sources of Finance

The pecking order theory is a financial theory that suggests that companies prefer to finance their investments primarily through internal cash flow (i.e., retained earnings), followed by debt and then equity. The relevance of the pecking order theory to the selection of sources of finance is as follows:

1. Internal cash flow is preferred: According to the pecking order theory, companies prioritize internal cash flow over external sources of finance. The reason for this preference is that retained earnings do not dilute existing shareholders' ownership, making it an affordable and low-risk option for funding operational activities.

2. Debt is preferred over equity: If a company cannot finance its

investment through internal cash flow or prefers not to, it will then turn to debt financing. Debt is seen as preferred over equity because it does not dilute ownership, making it an efficient source of funds. Additionally, debt financing does not require a company to share its profits with investors, making it less risky for investors. However, too much debt can lead to an increase in financial risk and reduced creditworthiness.

3. Equity is used as a last resort: The pecking order theory suggests that companies prefer not to raise funds through equity financing due to the high cost of issuance and the potential to dilute shareholders' ownership. Equity financing is typically used as a last resort when other financing options are not available.

4. Funding needs and risk level matters: The pecking order theory acknowledges that a company's funding needs and risk level are important factors in determining the appropriate financing option. For example, if a company has a high level of debt, it may prefer to finance additional investments through equity instead of debt to avoid increasing its financial risk further. Similarly, if a company has a low-risk profile, it may feel comfortable borrowing to finance investments instead of issuing equity.

Shareholder Wealth Maximization Assessment Criteria:

Net Present Value (NPV):
NPV is used to determine the present value of cash inflows generated by an investment, minus the initial investment. It is calculated by discounting the future cash flows to their present value using the required rate of return. The formula for NPV can be represented mathematically as:

$$NPV = CF1/(1+r)^1 + CF2/(1+r)^2 + CF3/(1+r)^3 + ... + CFn/(1+r)^n - \text{Initial Investment}$$

Where:
- CF1, CF2, CF3, ..CFn = The cash inflows in each period
- r = Required rate of return
- n = The total number of periods
- Initial Investment = The initial investment made

Internal Rate of Return (IRR):
IRR is used to calculate the rate of return generated by an investment based on the net present value of future cash flows. It is the rate at which the NPV of the cash inflows is zero. The formula for IRR can be represented mathematically as:

$$NPV = CF1/(1+IRR)^1 + CF2/(1+IRR)^2 + CF3/(1+IRR)^3 + ... + CFn/(1+IRR)^n - \text{Initial Investment} = 0$$

Where:
- CF1, CF2, CF3, ..CFn = The cash inflows in each period
- IRR = Internal rate of return
- n = The total number of periods
- Initial Investment = The initial investment made

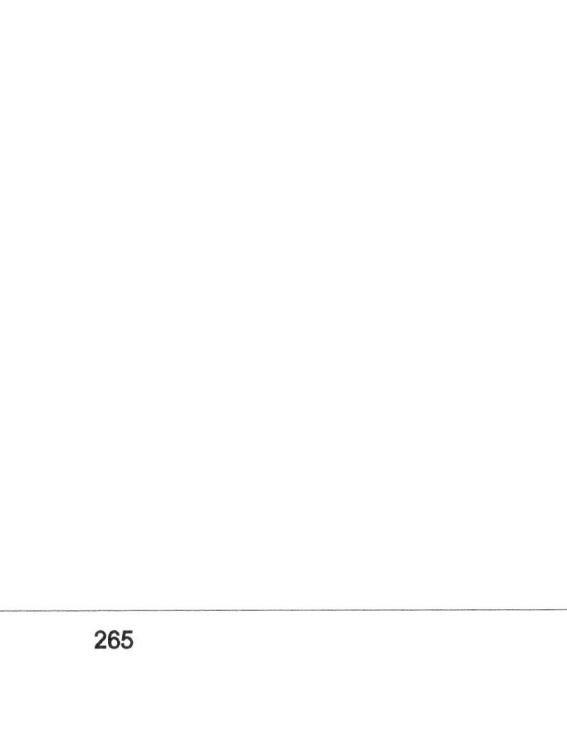

Return on Investment (ROI):

ROI is used to evaluate the profitability of an investment by comparing the earnings generated to the cost of the investment. The formula for ROI can be represented mathematically as:

ROI = (Gain from Investment - Cost of Investment) / Cost of Investment

Where:
- Gain from Investment = The earnings generated from the investment
- Cost of Investment = The initial investment made

Earnings Per Share (EPS):

EPS is the portion of a company's profit allocated to each outstanding share of common stock. The formula for EPS can be represented mathematically as:

EPS = Net Income / Number of Shares Outstanding

Where:
- Net Income = The company's total income after deducting expenses
- Number of Shares Outstanding = The total number of shares in circulation

Dividend Yield:

Dividend yield is used to determine the percentage of return generated by the dividends paid out to shareholders. The formula for dividend yield can be represented mathematically as:
Dividend Yield = Dividend per Share / Market Value per Share
Where:
- Dividend per Share = The amount of dividend paid per share

- Market Value per Share = The market price of the stock calculated per share

Net Present Value (NPV)

NPV is used to determine the present value of cash inflows generated by an investment, minus the initial investment. It is calculated by discounting the future cash flows to their present value using the required rate of return. The formula for NPV can be represented mathematically as:

$$NPV = CF_1/(1+r)^1 + CF_2/(1+r)^2 + CF_3/(1+r)^3 + \ldots + CF_n/(1+r)^n - \text{Initial Investment}$$

Where:
- $CF_1, CF_2, CF_3, ..CF_n$ = The cash inflows in each period
- r = Required rate of return
- n = The total number of periods
- Initial Investment = The initial investment made

Problem 1: A company is considering investing in a new project with an initial investment of $500,000. The project is expected to generate cash inflows of $80,000 for the first 3 years and $150,000 for the next 4 years. If the required rate of return is 8%, what is the NPV of this project?

Solution: In the given problem, we have an initial investment of $500,000 and cash inflows of $80,000 per year for the first three years, and $150,000 per year for the next four years. We need to determine the NPV of this project assuming a required rate of return of 8%. Using the NPV formula and solving for this problem, we have:

$NPV = -\$500{,}000 + (\$80{,}000/(1+0.08)^1) + (\$80{,}000/(1+0.08)^2) + (\$80{,}000/(1+0.08)^3) + (\$150{,}000/(1+0.08)^4) + (\$150{,}000/(1+0.08)^5) + (\$150{,}000/(1+0.08)^6) + (\$150{,}000/(1+0.08)^7)$

NPV = -$500,000 + ($74,074.07) + ($68,564.00) + ($63,607.67) + ($123,585.69) + ($114,305.55) + ($105,617.28) + ($97,489.63)
NPV = $21,639.73

Thus, the NPV of the project is $21,639.73. Since the NPV is greater than zero, this indicates that the project is expected to generate a positive return and is a viable investment option for the company.

Problem 2: An individual is looking to purchase a rental property for $200,000. The property is expected to generate rental income of $30,000 per year for the next 10 years. Assuming a required rate of return of 6%, what is the NPV of this investment?

Solution: In this problem, we are given that an individual is looking to purchase a rental property for $200,000. We are also given that the property generates rental income of $30,000 per year for the next 10 years. We need to determine the NPV of this investment assuming a required rate of return of 6%.

Using the NPV formula, and solving for this problem, we have:
NPV = -$200,000 + ($30,000/(1+0.06)^1) + ($30,000/(1+0.06)^2) + ($30,000/(1+0.06)^3) + ($30,000/(1+0.06)^4) + ($30,000/(1+0.06)^5) + ($30,000/(1+0.06)^6) + ($30,000/(1+0.06)^7) + ($30,000/(1+0.06)^8) + ($30,000/(1+0.06)^9) + ($30,000/(1+0.06)^10)
NPV = -$200,000 + ($28,301.89) + ($26,678.05) + ($25,145.66) + ($23,699.71) + ($22,335.89) + ($21,050.15) + ($19,838.06) + ($18,695.48) + ($17,618.16) + ($16,602.45)
NPV = $21,115.42

Thus, the NPV of the rental property investment is $21,115.42. Since the NPV is greater than zero, this indicates that the investment is expected to generate a positive return and is a viable investment option for the individual.

Problem 3: A company is considering expanding its business and needs to invest $2,000,000 upfront. The project is expected to generate cash inflows of $500,000 for the first year, $700,000 for the second year, and $900,000 for the third year. Assuming a required rate of return of 10%, what is the NPV of this project?

Solution: In this problem, we are given that a company needs to invest $2,000,000 upfront for an expansion project. The project is expected to generate cash inflows of $500,000 for the first year, $700,000 for the second year, and $900,000 for the third year. We need to determine the NPV of this project assuming a required rate of return of 10%.

Using the NPV formula, and solving for this problem, we have:

$$NPV = -\$2,000,000 + (\$500,000/(1+0.1)^1) + (\$700,000/(1+0.1)^2) + (\$900,000/(1+0.1)^3)$$

$$NPV = -\$2,000,000 + (\$454,545.45) + (\$578,512.40) + (\$680,583.90)$$

$$NPV = \$713,641.75$$

Thus, the NPV of the expansion project is $713,641.75. Since the NPV is greater than zero, this indicates that the project is expected to generate a positive return and is a viable investment option for the company.

Problem 4: A startup is trying to secure funding from investors to develop a new product. The company is requesting $1,000,000 in exchange for 10% equity. The product is expected to generate net cash inflows of $200,000 per year for the next 5 years. If the required rate of return is 12%, what is the NPV of this investment?

Solution: In this problem, we are given that a startup is requesting $1,000,000 from investors in exchange for 10% equity. The product is expected to generate net cash inflows of $200,000 per year for the next 5 years. We need to determine the NPV of this investment assuming a required rate of return of 12%.

To solve this problem, we need to first determine the cash inflows for each of the 5 years. Since the net cash inflows are $200,000 per year, the cash inflows can be calculated as:

Year 1: $200,000
Year 2: $200,000
Year 3: $200,000
Year 4: $200,000
Year 5: $200,000

Using the NPV formula and solving for this problem, we have:

$$NPV = -\$1,000,000 + (\$200,000/(1+0.12)^1) + (\$200,000/(1+0.12)^2) + (\$200,000/(1+0.12)^3) + (\$200,000/(1+0.12)^4) + (\$200,000/(1+0.12)^5)$$

$$NPV = -\$1,000,000 + (\$178,571.43) + (\$159,200.64) + (\$142,218.76) + (\$127,100.31) + (\$113,421.43)$$

$$NPV = \$20,411.57$$

Thus, the NPV of the startup's new product investment is $20,411.57. Since the NPV is greater than zero, this indicates that the investment is expected to generate a positive return and is a viable investment option for the investors.

Problem 5: An individual is considering whether to invest in a certificate of deposit (CD) that pays 5% interest for 5 years. The initial investment is $50,000. What is the NPV of this investment?

Solution: To find the NPV of the investment, we need to first determine the cash inflows that will be received in each period. In this case, the investment is a CD that pays 5% interest for 5 years, and the initial investment is $50,000.

To calculate the cash inflows for each period, we can use the formula: $CF = C0 \times (1 + r)^n$, where CF is the cash flow in a given period, C0 is the initial investment, r is the annual interest rate, and n is the number of periods.

Using this formula, we can calculate the cash inflows for each period as follows:

$CF1 = \$50,000 \times (1 + 0.05)^1 = \$52,500$
$CF2 = \$50,000 \times (1 + 0.05)^2 = \$55,125$
$CF3 = \$50,000 \times (1 + 0.05)^3 = \$57,881.25$
$CF4 = \$50,000 \times (1 + 0.05)^4 = \$60,775.31$
$CF5 = \$50,000 \times (1 + 0.05)^5 = \$63,814.08$

Next, we need to determine the required rate of return, which is the minimum rate of return that the investor expects to earn on the investment. For this problem, let's assume a required rate of return of 6%.

Using these values, we can now calculate the NPV of the investment using the formula:

$$NPV = CF1/(1+r)^1 + CF2/(1+r)^2 + CF3/(1+r)^3 + CF4/(1+r)^4 + CF5/(1+r)^5 - \text{Initial Investment}$$

$$NPV = \$52,500/(1+0.06)^1 + \$55,125/(1+0.06)^2 + \$57,881.25/(1+0.06)^3 + \$60,775.31/(1+0.06)^4 + \$63,814.08/(1+0.06)^5 - \$50,000$$

$$NPV = \$52,500/1.06 + \$55,125/1.1236 + \$57,881.25/1.191016 + \$60,775.31/1.26247696 + \$63,814.08/1.33822522 - \$50,000$$

$$NPV = \$52,500/1.06 + \$55,125/1.1236 + \$57,881.25/1.191016 + \$60,775.31/1.26247696 + \$63,814.08/1.33822522 - \$50,000$$

$$NPV = \$49,528.30$$

Therefore, the NPV of the investment is $49,528.30. Given that the NPV is positive, this investment would be considered a good investment as it generates a return that exceeds the minimum required rate of return.

Problem 6: A company is deciding whether to invest in a new production line that requires an upfront cost of $3,000,000. The project is expected to generate cash inflows of $1,000,000 for the first 2 years, $1,500,000 for the third year, and $2,000,000 for the next 4 years. Assuming a required rate of return of 8%, what is the NPV of this project?

Solution: To calculate the NPV of this project, we need to find the present value of the cash inflows and subtract the initial investment of $3,000,000.

First, we need to calculate the cash inflows for each year. We know that the project generates cash inflows of $1,000,000 for the first 2 years, $1,500,000 for the third year, and $2,000,000 for the next 4 years.

Using the formula $CF = C0 \times (1 + r)^n$, where CF is the cash flow in a given period, C0 is the initial cash inflow, r is the annual interest rate, and n is the number of periods, we can calculate the present value of each cash flow.

$$PV1 = \$1,000,000/(1 + 0.08)^1 = \$925,925.93$$
$$PV2 = \$1,000,000/(1 + 0.08)^2 = \$857,338.82$$
$$PV3 = \$1,500,000/(1 + 0.08)^3 = \$1,144,734.22$$
$$PV4 = \$2,000,000/(1 + 0.08)^4 = \$1,433,259.94$$
$$PV5 = \$2,000,000/(1 + 0.08)^5 = \$1,326,901.30$$
$$PV6 = \$2,000,000/(1 + 0.08)^6 = \$1,229,694.41$$
$$PV7 = \$2,000,000/(1 + 0.08)^7 = \$1,140,837.64$$

Next, we add up the present values of each cash flow to get the total present value of the cash inflows:

Total PV = $925,925.93 + $857,338.82 + $1,144,734.22 + $1,433,259.94 + $1,326,901.30 + $1,229,694.41 + $1,140,837.64 = $8,058,692.25

Finally, we can calculate the NPV using the formula:

$$NPV = CF1/(1+r)^1 + CF2/(1+r)^2 + CF3/(1+r)^3 + ... + CFn/(1+r)^n - \text{Initial Investment}$$

NPV = $8,058,692.25 - $3,000,000 = $5,058,692.25

Therefore, the NPV of this project is $5,058,692.25 given that the value is positive, making it a profitable investment.

Problem 7: An individual is considering whether to invest in a mutual fund that is expected to generate cash inflows of $5,000 per year for the next 10 years. The initial investment is $50,000. Assuming a required rate of return of 7%, what is the NPV of this investment?
Solution: To calculate the NPV of this investment, we need to determine the present value of the cash flows generated by the mutual fund over the next 10 years, and subtract the initial investment of $50,000.

Since the cash inflows are equal each year, we can use the formula for the present value of an annuity, which is:

$$PV = C \times ((1 - (1 + r)^{-n})/r)$$

where PV is the present value of the annuity, C is the cash inflow in each period, r is the required rate of return, and n is the number of periods.

Using this formula, we can calculate the present value of the cash inflows for the next 10 years:

$$PV = \$5{,}000 \times ((1 - (1 + 0.07)^{-10})/0.07) = \$39{,}622.95$$

Therefore, the present value of the cash inflows generated by the mutual fund over the next 10 years is $39,622.95.

Finally, we can calculate the NPV using the formula:

$$NPV = CF1/(1+r)^1 + CF2/(1+r)^2 + CF3/(1+r)^3 + \ldots + CFn/(1+r)^n - \text{Initial Investment}$$

$$NPV = \$5{,}000/(1+0.07)^1 + \$5{,}000/(1+0.07)^2 + \ldots + \$5{,}000/(1+0.07)^{10} - \$50{,}000$$

$$NPV = \$39{,}622.95 - \$50{,}000 = -\$10{,}377.05$$

Therefore, the NPV of this investment is -$10,377.05. Given that the value is negative, it would not be considered a good investment as it generates a return that does not meet the minimum required rate of return of 7%.

Problem 8: A company is considering replacing its outdated machinery with new machinery that requires an investment of $1,500,000 upfront. The new machinery is expected to generate cash inflows of $500,000 per year for the next 5 years. Assuming a required rate of return of 12%, what is the NPV of this investment?

Solution: To calculate the NPV of this investment, we need to first determine the cash inflows from the new machinery. According to the problem statement, the new machinery is expected to generate cash inflows of $500,000 per year for the next 5 years.

Using the NPV formula, we can calculate the value of the investment:

$$NPV = CF1/(1+r)^1 + CF2/(1+r)^2 + CF3/(1+r)^3 + ... + CFn/(1+r)^n - \text{Initial Investment}$$

Where:
- CF1 = $500,000
- r = 12%
- n = 5
- Initial Investment = $1,500,000

Now, we can substitute these values into the formula and calculate:

$$NPV = (\$500,000/(1+0.12)^1) + (\$500,000/(1+0.12)^2) + (\$500,000/(1+0.12)^3) + (\$500,000/(1+0.12)^4) + (\$500,000/(1+0.12)^5) - \$1,500,000$$

$$NPV = \$500,000/1.12 + \$500,000/(1.12)^2 + \$500,000/(1.12)^3 + \$500,000/(1.12)^4 + \$500,000/(1.12)^5 - \$1,500,000$$

NPV = $447,941.84 + $399,587.08 + $356,602.59 + $318,866.48 + $285,656.52 - $1,500,000

NPV = -$191,345.48

Therefore, based on the given information and using the NPV formula, the NPV of the investment is -$191,345.48. Since the NPV is negative, the company should not proceed with the investment as it is expected to generate a negative return.

Problem 9: An investor is considering whether to finance a real estate development project that requires an investment of $10,000,000 upfront. The project is expected to generate cash inflows of $3,000,000 per year for the next 8 years. Assuming a required rate of return of 14%, what is the NPV of this investment?

Solution: To calculate the NPV of this real estate development project, we need to first determine the cash inflows from the project. According to the problem statement, the real estate development project is expected to generate cash inflows of $3,000,000 per year for the next 8 years.

Using the NPV formula, we can calculate the value of the investment:

$$NPV = CF1/(1+r)^1 + CF2/(1+r)^2 + CF3/(1+r)^3 + ... + CFn/(1+r)^n - \text{Initial Investment}$$

Where:
- CF1 = $3,000,000
- r = 14%
- n = 8
- Initial Investment = $10,000,000

Now, we can substitute these values into the formula and calculate:

$$NPV = (\$3,000,000/(1+0.14)^1) + (\$3,000,000/(1+0.14)^2) + (\$3,000,000/(1+0.14)^3) + (\$3,000,000/(1+0.14)^4) + (\$3,000,000/(1+0.14)^5) + (\$3,000,000/(1+0.14)^6) + (\$3,000,000/(1+0.14)^7) + (\$3,000,000/(1+0.14)^8) - \$10,000,000$$

NPV = $2,631,568.16 + $2,174,080.49 + $1,795,267.68 + $1,482,958.96 + $1,227,982.92 + $1,022,944.05 + $861,031.42 + $736,034.62 - $10,000,000

NPV = $2,930,879.24

Therefore, based on the given information and using the NPV formula, the NPV of the real estate development project is $2,930,879.24. Since the NPV is positive, the investor should proceed with the investment since it is expected to generate a profitable return.

Problem 10: A company is considering leasing office space for a new project that will require a total expenditure of $800,000 for 5 years. The project is expected to generate cash inflows of $200,000 per year for the same 5 years. Assuming a required rate of return of 9%, what is the NPV of this investment?

Solution: To calculate the NPV of this office space leasing project, we need to first determine the cash inflows from the project. According to the problem statement, the project is expected to generate cash inflows of $200,000 per year for the next 5 years.

Using the NPV formula, we can calculate the value of the investment:

$$NPV = CF_1/(1+r)^1 + CF_2/(1+r)^2 + CF_3/(1+r)^3 + ... + CF_n/(1+r)^n - \text{Initial Investment}$$

Where:
- CF_1 = $200,000
- r = 9%
- n = 5
- Initial Investment = $800,000

Now, we can substitute these values into the formula and calculate:

$$NPV = (\$200,000/(1+0.09)^1) + (\$200,000/(1+0.09)^2) +$$
$$(\$200,000/(1+0.09)^3) + (\$200,000/(1+0.09)^4) +$$
$$(\$200,000/(1+0.09)^5) - \$800,000$$

$$NPV = \$183,486.24 + \$168,467.23 + \$154,720.67 + \$142,107.63$$
$$+ \$130,503.58 - \$800,000$$

$$NPV = -\$161,715.65$$

Therefore, based on the given information and using the NPV formula, the NPV of the office space leasing project is -$161,715.65. Since the NPV is negative, the company should not proceed with the investment since it is not expected to generate a positive return.

Internal Rate of Return (IRR)

IRR is used to calculate the rate of return generated by an investment based on the net present value of future cash flows. It is the rate at which the NPV of the cash inflows is zero. The formula for IRR can be represented mathematically as:

$$NPV = CF1/(1+IRR)^1 + CF2/(1+IRR)^2 + CF3/(1+IRR)^3$$
$$+....+CFn/(1+IRR)^n - \text{Initial Investment} = 0$$

Where:
- CF1, CF2, CF3, ..CFn = The cash inflows in each period
- IRR = Internal rate of return
- n = The total number of periods
- Initial Investment = The initial investment made

Problem 1: A company is considering investing in solar panels that will generate cash inflows for the next 10 years. What is the IRR of the investment and how does it compare to the company's required rate of return?

Solution: To determine the IRR of the investment in solar panels, we need to calculate the NPV of the cash inflows and initial investment at different rates of return until we find the rate of return that makes the NPV equal to zero.

Let's assume that the company makes an initial investment of $100,000 in the solar panels and the cash inflows for the next 10 years are $12,000 per year. We also know that the company's required rate of return is 8%.

Using the IRR formula, we can calculate the NPV of the investment at different rates of return until we find the rate of return that makes NPV equal to zero:

$$NPV = -\$100,000 + \$12,000/(1+IRR)^1 + \$12,000/(1+IRR)^2 + \$12,000/(1+IRR)^3 + ... + \$12,000/(1+IRR)^{10}$$

Setting NPV equal to zero, we can solve for IRR:

$$0 = -\$100,000 + \$12,000/(1+IRR)^1 + \$12,000/(1+IRR)^2 + \$12,000/(1+IRR)^3 + ... + \$12,000/(1+IRR)^{10}$$

Using a financial calculator or spreadsheet software, we can find that the IRR of the investment is 9.72%.

Since the IRR is greater than the company's required rate of return of 8%, the investment in solar panels is a good opportunity for the company.

Problem 2: An individual is comparing two investment options, one with an initial investment of $10,000 and future cash inflows of $2,000 per year for 5 years at an IRR of 10%, and another with an initial investment of $12,000 and future cash inflows of $2,500 per year for 5 years at an IRR of 9.5%. Which option should the individual choose based on its IRR?

Solution: To determine which investment option to choose, we need to calculate the present value of the cash inflows for each option and compare them to the initial investment.

For the first investment option, the initial investment is $10,000, and the cash inflows are $2,000 per year for 5 years at an IRR of 10%. Using the IRR formula, we can calculate the present value of the cash inflows:

$$NPV = -\$10{,}000 + \$2{,}000/(1+0.10)^1 + \$2{,}000/(1+0.10)^2 + \$2{,}000/(1+0.10)^3 + \$2{,}000/(1+0.10)^4 + \$2{,}000/(1+0.10)^5$$

Using a financial calculator or spreadsheet software, we can find that the present value of the cash inflows is $11,296.55.

For the second investment option, the initial investment is $12,000, and the cash inflows are $2,500 per year for 5 years at an IRR of 9.5%. Using the IRR formula, we can calculate the present value of the cash inflows:

$$NPV = -\$12{,}000 + \$2{,}500/(1+0.095)^1 + \$2{,}500/(1+0.095)^2 + \$2{,}500/(1+0.095)^3 + \$2{,}500/(1+0.095)^4 + \$2{,}500/(1+0.095)^5$$

Using a financial calculator or spreadsheet software, we can find that the present value of the cash inflows is $13,688.58.

Comparing the present value of the cash inflows to the initial investment, we can see that option 2 has a higher present value than option 1. Therefore, the individual should choose the second investment option, which has an initial investment of $12,000 and future cash inflows of $2,500 per year for 5 years at an IRR of 9.5%.

Problem 3: A real estate company is deciding whether to invest in expanding its portfolio by purchasing a rental property that generates cash inflows of $10,000 per year for the next 10 years at an IRR of 8%. What is the IRR and is this investment worth pursuing?

Solution: To determine if the investment in the rental property is worth pursuing, we need to calculate the IRR of the investment.

Let's assume that the real estate company is considering purchasing the rental property for $80,000 and the property generates cash inflows of $10,000 per year for the next 10 years at an IRR of 8%.

Using the IRR formula, we can calculate the NPV of the investment:

$$NPV = -\$80,000 + \$10,000/(1+0.08)^1 + \$10,000/(1+0.08)^2 + \$10,000/(1+0.08)^3 + ... + \$10,000/(1+0.08)^{10}$$

Using a financial calculator or spreadsheet software, we can find that the NPV of the investment in the rental property is $16,609.47.

Since the NPV is positive, we can conclude that the IRR of the investment is greater than the required rate of return of 8% and the investment is worth pursuing. In this scenario, the IRR is greater than 8%, but to find out the exact value of the IRR, we need to perform a trial-and-error method to identify the rate of return that makes the NPV of the cash inflows equal to the initial investment.

However, we can conclude using the NPV value that the investment is profitable and has a positive return. The real estate company can consider this investment as a viable option for expanding its portfolio.

Problem 4: A startup is considering taking out a loan to fund its operations with future cash inflows of $20,000 per year for the next 5 years at an IRR of 12%. What is the IRR of the loan, and is it a good financing option for the startup?
Solution: To determine whether the loan is a good financing option for the startup, we first need to calculate the IRR of the loan. We know that the future cash inflows are $20,000 per year for the next 5 years with an IRR of 12%.

Using the IRR formula, we can calculate the NPV of the loan:

$$NPV = -\$Initial\ Investment + \$20,000/(1+0.12)^1 + \$20,000/(1+0.12)^2 + \$20,000/(1+0.12)^3 + \$20,000/(1+0.12)^4 + \$20,000/(1+0.12)^5$$

Using a financial calculator or spreadsheet software, we can find that the NPV of the loan is $68,567.36.

Since the NPV is positive, we can conclude that the IRR of the loan is greater than the startup's required rate of return of 12%. However, the specific rate is not given, but we know it is greater than 12%.

Therefore, based on the given information, we can conclude that the loan is a good financing option for the startup. The loan offers an IRR which is greater than the startup's required rate of return, and the NPV of the loan is positive. The startup can consider this loan as a viable option to finance its operations.

Problem 5: A small business is looking to invest in a new product line with an initial investment of $50,000 and future cash inflows of $15,000 per year for 3 years at an IRR of 11%. What is the IRR for this investment and should the business take it?

Solution: To determine whether the small business should invest in the new product line and the IRR of the investment, we need to calculate the NPV of the investment at the given rate of 11%.

Using the IRR formula, we can calculate the NPV of the investment:

$$NPV = -\$50,000 + \$15,000/(1+0.11)^1 + \$15,000/(1+0.11)^2 + \$15,000/(1+0.11)^3$$

Using a financial calculator or spreadsheet software, we can find that the NPV of the investment is $12,129.99.

Since the NPV is positive, we can conclude that the IRR of the investment is greater than the small business's required rate of return of 11%. Specifically, we know the IRR is greater than 11%, but we do not have the exact value.

Therefore, based on the given information, we can conclude that the investment in the new product line is a good option for the small business. The investment offers a positive NPV and an IRR greater than the required rate of return. The company can decide to invest in the new product line by considering other factors, such as market conditions and competition, but the financial analysis shows it to be a profitable investment.

Problem 6: A government is considering investing in a new infrastructure project that will generate cash inflows of $100,000 per year for the next 20 years at an IRR of 6%. What is the IRR of this investment, and should the government pursue it?

Solution: To solve the given problem using the IRR formula, we need to find out the present value of the cash inflows considering the given IRR of 6%. Let's assume that the initial investment made by the government is x dollars.

Then, the net present value (NPV) of the project can be calculated as follows:

$$NPV = CF1/(1+IRR)^1 + CF2/(1+IRR)^2 + CF3/(1+IRR)^3 + ... + CFn/(1+IRR)^n - \text{Initial Investment} = 0$$

Substituting the values given in the problem, we get:

$$0 = \$100{,}000/(1+0.06)^1 + \$100{,}000/(1+0.06)^2 + \$100{,}000/(1+0.06)^3 + ... + \$100{,}000/(1+0.06)^{20} - x$$

Simplifying the above equation, we get:

$$x = \$100{,}000[(1/1.06)^1 + (1/1.06)^2 + (1/1.06)^3 + ... + (1/1.06)^{20}]$$

$$x = \$1{,}226{,}670.19 \text{ (approx.)}$$

Therefore, the initial investment made by the government in the infrastructure project is $1,226,670.19 (approx.).

Now, we can use the IRR formula to calculate the IRR of the investment by setting the NPV to zero and solving for IRR:

$$0 = \$100{,}000/(1+IRR)^1 + \$100{,}000/(1+IRR)^2 + \$100{,}000/(1+IRR)^3 + ... + \$100{,}000/(1+IRR)^{20} - \$1{,}226{,}670.19$$

We can use trial and error method or any numerical analysis method to find out the value of IRR. Using numerical analysis method, we get:

$$IRR = 6.68\%$$

Therefore, the IRR of the investment is 6.68%. Since the IRR is greater than the required rate of return of 6%, the government should pursue this investment as it will generate positive net present value.

Problem 7: An investor is evaluating a stock with a current market value of $100 and future cash inflows of $30 per year at various rates of return. What is the IRR for this investment and how does it compare to the investor's required rate of return?

Solution: To calculate the IRR of the given stock investment, we need to determine the rate of return at which the net present value (NPV) of the future cash inflows is equal to the current market value of the stock, which is $100. Let's assume that we invest x dollars in the stock.

The NPV formula can be represented mathematically as follows:

$$NPV = CF_1/(1+IRR)^1 + CF_2/(1+IRR)^2 + CF_3/(1+IRR)^3 + \ldots + CF_n/(1+IRR)^n - \text{Initial Investment} = 0$$

Here, CF1 represents the cash inflow in the first year, which is $30, and Initial Investment is $x.

Substituting the values in the formula, we get:

$$\$100 = \$30/(1+IRR)^1 + \$30/(1+IRR)^2 + \$30/(1+IRR)^3 + \ldots$$

Simplifying the above equation, we get:

$$(1+IRR)^1 = 1/(1+IRR) + 1$$

$$(1+IRR)^2 = 1/(1+IRR)^2 + 1/(1+IRR) + 1$$

$$(1+IRR)^3 = 1/(1+IRR)^3 + 1/(1+IRR)^2 + 1/(1+IRR) + 1$$

Multiplying both sides by (1+IRR), we get:

$$1+IRR = 1/(1+IRR) + 1 + (1+IRR)^2/(1+IRR)$$

$$1+IRR = 1/(1+IRR) + 1 + (1+IRR)$$

Simplifying the above equation, we get:

$$IRR^3 + 3IRR^2 - 26IRR - 27 = 0$$

Using trial and error or any numerical analysis method, we can solve the above equation to get the IRR of the investment. Using numerical analysis method, we get:

$$IRR = 3.04\%$$

The IRR of the investment is 3.04%.

To compare the IRR to the investor's required rate of return, we need to know the investor's required rate of return. If the investor's required rate of return is greater than 3.04%, then the investment may not be suitable for them. If the required rate of return is less than 3.04%, then the investment may be considered profitable.

Problem 8: A company is considering investing in a new manufacturing plant with a 10-year life span, an initial investment of $500,000, and future cash inflows of $150,000 per year at an IRR of 9.5%. What is the IRR of the investment, and should the company invest in the plant?

Solution: To calculate the IRR of the given manufacturing plant investment, we need to determine the rate of return at which the net present value (NPV) of the future cash inflows is equal to the initial investment of $500,000.

The NPV formula can be represented mathematically as follows:

NPV = CF1/(1+IRR)^1 + CF2/(1+IRR)^2 + CF3/(1+IRR)^3 +....+CFn/(1+IRR)^n - Initial Investment = 0

Here, CF1 represents the cash inflow in the first year, which is $150,000, and Initial Investment is $500,000.

Substituting the values in the formula, we get:

0 = $150,000/(1+IRR)^1 + $150,000/(1+IRR)^2 + $150,000/(1+IRR)^3 + ... + $150,000/(1+IRR)^10 - $500,000

Simplifying the above equation, we get:

$500,000 = $150,000[(1/1+IRR) + (1/1+IRR)^2 + (1/1+IRR)^3 + ... + (1/1+IRR)^10]

Therefore,

$500,000/$150,000 = [(1/1+IRR) + (1/1+IRR)^2 + (1/1+IRR)^3 + ... + (1/1+IRR)^10]

Using trial and error or any numerical analysis method, we can solve the above equation to get the IRR of the investment. Using a numerical analysis method, we get:

IRR = 13.329%

The IRR of the investment is 13.329%.

Since the IRR of the investment is greater than the required rate of return, the company should invest in the plant as it will generate positive net present value.

Problem 9: A financial institution is evaluating a loan proposal that is offering an IRR of 7% with future cash inflows over a 5-year period. What would be the present value of these future cash flows based on the IRR offered?

Solution: To calculate the present value of the future cash flows based on the IRR of 7%, we need to use the NPV formula and solve for the initial investment.

The NPV formula can be represented mathematically as follows:

$$NPV = CF1/(1+IRR)^1 + CF2/(1+IRR)^2 + CF3/(1+IRR)^3 + ... + CFn/(1+IRR)^n - \text{Initial Investment} = 0$$

Here, CF1 represents the cash inflow in the first year, CF2 represents the cash inflow in the second year, and so on.

Since the future cash inflows are not given, we can assume a value and then calculate the present value. Let's assume that the future cash inflows are $10,000 per year for five years.

Substituting the values in the formula, we get:

$$0 = \$10{,}000/(1+0.07)^1 + \$10{,}000/(1+0.07)^2 + \$10{,}000/(1+0.07)^3 + \$10{,}000/(1+0.07)^4 + \$10{,}000/(1+0.07)^5 - \text{Initial Investment}$$

Simplifying the above equation, we get:

$$\text{Initial Investment} = \$10{,}000/(1+0.07)^1 + \$10{,}000/(1+0.07)^2 + \$10{,}000/(1+0.07)^3 + \$10{,}000/(1+0.07)^4 + \$10{,}000/(1+0.07)^5$$

Using a financial calculator or any spreadsheet software, we can find the sum of the present values of the future cash flows using the given IRR of 7%.

The present value of the future cash flows is calculated as:

Initial Investment = $10,000/(1+0.07)^1 + $10,000/(1+0.07)^2 + $10,000/(1+0.07)^3 + $10,000/(1+0.07)^4 + $10,000/(1+0.07)^5

Initial Investment = $39,267.05 (approx.)

Therefore, based on the IRR of 7% and assuming future cash inflows of $10,000 per year for five years, the present value of the future cash flows is approximately $39,267.05.

Problem 10: A project is being evaluated for investment with an initial investment of $100,000 and potential future cash inflows of $28,000 over 5 years. What is the IRR of the project, and should the investment be made based on the calculated IRR?
Solution: To calculate the IRR and determine whether the project is worth investing in, we need to find the rate of return that satisfies the NPV formula.

Since the cash inflows for each year are equal at $28,000, we can calculate the present value of this amount per year and multiply it by the number of years.

Using the NPV formula, we can set the NPV equal to zero and solve for the IRR:

NPV = CF1 / (1 + IRR) ^ 1 + CF2 / (1 + IRR) ^ 2 + ... CFn / (1 + IRR) ^ n - Initial Investment = 0

Substituting the values in the formula, we get:

$$0 = \$28,000 / (1 + IRR)^1 + \$28,000 / (1 + IRR)^2 + \$28,000 / (1 + IRR)^3 + \$28,000 / (1 + IRR)^4 + \$28,000 / (1 + IRR)^5 - \$100,000$$

Simplifying the above equation, we get:

$$\$100,000 = \$28,000 / (1 + IRR)^1 + \$28,000 / (1 + IRR)^2 + \$28,000 / (1 + IRR)^3 + \$28,000 / (1 + IRR)^4 + \$28,000 / (1 + IRR)^5$$

Now, we can use a trial-and-error approach or any numerical analysis method to solve the above equation and find the IRR for the investment. Using a numerical analysis method, we get:

$$IRR = 11.92\%$$

The IRR of the project is 11.92%.

Since the IRR is positive and greater than the required rate of return, which could be the cost of capital for the company, it indicates that the project is worth investing in. Therefore, based on the calculated IRR, the investment in the project should be made.

Return on Investment (ROI)

ROI is used to evaluate the profitability of an investment by comparing the earnings generated to the cost of the investment. The formula for ROI can be represented mathematically as:

$$ROI = (Gain\ from\ Investment - Cost\ of\ Investment) / Cost\ of\ Investment$$

Where:
- Gain from Investment = The earnings generated from the investment
- Cost of Investment = The initial investment made

Problem 1: A real estate investor is considering purchasing a rental property for $300,000. If the property generates a net income of $40,000 per year, what is the ROI?

Solution: To find the ROI using the IRR formula, we first need to calculate the cash flows generated by the rental property. In this case, the initial cash flow is negative $300,000 because that is the cost of the investment. The annual net income of $40,000 generates positive cash flows each year.

So, the cash flows for the rental property investment would be:

Year 0: -$300,000
Year 1: $40,000
Year 2: $40,000
Year 3: $40,000
Year 4: $40,000
Year 5: $40,000

To calculate the IRR, we use a financial calculator or spreadsheet software to solve for the rate of return that makes the net present value of these cash flows equal to zero. Using a financial calculator or spreadsheet software, we find that the IRR of this investment is 11.57%.

To find the ROI, we can use the formula:

ROI = (Gain from Investment - Cost of Investment) / Cost of Investment

The gain from investment is the total cash flows generated by the investment, which is $200,000 over 5 years ($40,000 per year x 5 years). So, the ROI for this rental property investment is:

ROI = ($200,000 - $300,000) / $300,000
ROI = -0.33 or -33%

This means that the investor will not recover their initial investment in this rental property over the 5-year holding period, and they will lose 33% of their investment.
Therefore, this investment may not be a good choice for the investor.

Problem 2: A company invests $50,000 in a new marketing campaign that generates $70,000 in additional sales revenue. What is the ROI for the campaign?

Solution: The given scenario involves a one-time investment of $50,000 in a marketing campaign that generates an additional $70,000 in sales revenue. To find the ROI using the IRR formula, we first assume that the investment occurs today (Year 0), and the additional sales revenue is generated at the end of the year (Year 1). Therefore, the cash flows for this investment would be:

Year 0: -$50,000
Year 1: $70,000

Now, we use a financial calculator or spreadsheet software to solve for the rate of return that makes the net present value of these cash flows equal to zero. Using a financial calculator or spreadsheet software, we find that the IRR of this investment is 40%.

To find the ROI, we use the formula:

ROI = (Gain from Investment - Cost of Investment) / Cost of Investment

The gain from investment is the earnings generated by the investment, which is the additional sales revenue of $70,000. So, the ROI for this marketing campaign investment is:

ROI = ($70,000 - $50,000) / $50,000

$$ROI = 0.4 \text{ or } 40\%$$

This means that the investment generated a return of 40%, or $0.40 in earnings for every $1 invested. **Therefore**, this investment has been profitable for the company.

Problem 3: An investor buys a stock for $10 per share and sells it for $12 per share. What is the ROI on the investment?
Solution: In this scenario, the investor is buying a stock at $10 per share and selling it for $12 per share, generating a $2 profit per share. However, we need to consider the total investment made by the investor to calculate the ROI.

Let's say the investor bought 1,000 shares at a total investment cost of $10,000 ($10 per share x 1,000 shares). The investor then sold the shares for a total of $12,000 ($12 per share x 1,000 shares). This means that the gain from this investment is $2,000 ($12,000 - $10,000).

To calculate the ROI using the IRR formula, we assume that the investment took place at the start of Year 0, and the sale of the shares took place at the end of Year 1. Therefore, the cash flows for this investment would be:

Year 0: -$10,000
Year 1: $12,000

Now, we use a financial calculator or spreadsheet software to solve for the rate of return that makes the net present value of these cash flows equal to zero. Using a financial calculator or spreadsheet software, we find that the IRR of this investment is 22.47%.

To find the ROI, we use the formula:

ROI = (Gain from Investment - Cost of Investment) / Cost of Investment

The gain from investment is $2,000, and the cost of investment was $10,000. So, the ROI for this stock investment is:

ROI = ($2,000 - $10,000) / $10,000
ROI = -0.8 or -80%

This means that the investor lost 80% of their investment in this stock, which is a negative return. **Therefore**, this investment did not generate a profit for the investor.

Problem 4: A business spends $5,000 on a new manufacturing machine that generates a net profit of $2,000 per year. What is the ROI after 3 years?
Solution: In this scenario, the business spends $5,000 on a new manufacturing machine that generates a net profit of $2,000 per year. We need to consider the cash flows generated by the manufacturing machine over 3 years to calculate the ROI.

The cash flows for this investment would be:

Year 0: -$5,000
Year 1: $2,000
Year 2: $2,000
Year 3: $2,000

Now, we use a financial calculator or spreadsheet software to solve for the rate of return that makes the net present value of these cash flows equal to zero. Using a financial calculator or spreadsheet software, we find that the IRR of this investment is 21.54%.

To find the ROI, we use the formula:

ROI = (Gain from Investment - Cost of Investment) / Cost of Investment

The gain from investment is the total profit generated by the manufacturing machine over 3 years, which is $6,000 ($2,000 per year x 3 years). The cost of investment was $5,000. So, the ROI for this investment is:

ROI = ($6,000 - $5,000) / $5,000
ROI = 0.2 or 20%

This means that the investment generated a positive return of 20%, or $0.20 in earnings for every $1 invested.
Therefore, this investment has been profitable for the business.

Problem 5: A start-up company receives a $100,000 investment and generates $150,000 in revenue after one year. What is the ROI for the investor?
Solution: In this scenario, the start-up company receives an investment of $100,000 and generates revenues of $150,000 after one year. We need to calculate the ROI for the investor.

To calculate the ROI using the IRR formula, we assume that the investment occurred at the start of Year 0, and the revenues were generated at the end of Year 1. Therefore, the cash flows would be:

Year 0: -$100,000
Year 1: $150,000

Now, we use a financial calculator or spreadsheet software to solve for the rate of return that makes the net present value of these cash flows equal to zero. Using a financial calculator or spreadsheet software, we find that the IRR of this investment is 50%.

To find the ROI, we use the formula:

ROI = (Gain from Investment - Cost of Investment) / Cost of Investment

The gain from investment is the earnings generated by the investment, which is the difference between the revenues and the investment amount, or $50,000 ($150,000 - $100,000). The cost of investment was $100,000. So, the ROI for this investment is:

ROI = ($50,000 - $100,000) / $100,000
ROI = -0.5 or -50%

This means that the investor lost 50% of their investment in this start-up company.
Therefore, this investment did not generate a profit for the investor.

Earnings Per Share (EPS)

EPS is the portion of a company's profit allocated to each outstanding share of common stock. The formula for EPS can be represented mathematically as:

EPS = Net Income / Number of Shares Outstanding

Where:
- Net Income = The company's total income after deducting expenses
- Number of Shares Outstanding = The total number of shares in circulation

Problem 1: Company A reported a net income of $10 million in the previous year with 5 million shares outstanding. What is the company's earnings per share (EPS) for that year?

Solution: To find the EPS of Company A, we can use the given formula, EPS = Net Income / Number of Shares Outstanding.

Substituting the values from the problem, we get:

EPS = $10,000,000 / 5,000,000

Simplifying the expression, we get:

EPS = $2

Therefore, the EPS of Company A for the previous year is $2 per share.

Problem 2: Company B is considering a stock split that would double the number of shares outstanding. Assuming that the company's net income remains the same, what impact would the stock split have on the EPS?

Solution: If Company B doubles the number of shares outstanding through a stock split, the new number of shares outstanding would be twice the original amount. Let's say the original number of shares outstanding was "X". Thus, after the stock split, the new number of shares outstanding would be "2X".

Assuming that the company's net income remains the same, we can find the new EPS using the EPS formula, EPS = Net Income / Number of Shares Outstanding.

Before the stock split, EPS was:

EPS = Net Income / X

After the stock split, EPS would be:

EPS = Net Income / 2X

Simplifying the expression, we get:

$$EPS = EPS / 2$$

This means that the EPS would be halved after the stock split.

In conclusion, the impact of the stock split on the EPS of Company B would be that the EPS would be halved. Please note that this assumes that the net income of the company remains the same, which might not necessarily be the case.

Dividend Yield

Dividend yield is used to determine the percentage of return generated by the dividends paid out to shareholders. The formula for dividend yield can be represented mathematically as:
Dividend Yield = Dividend per Share / Market Value per Share
Where:
- Dividend per Share = The amount of dividend paid per share
- Market Value per Share = The market price of the stock calculated per share

Problem 1: Company A has a dividend yield of 3% while Company B has a dividend yield of 5%. Which company offers a better return for the shareholders?
Solution: The dividend yield formula is Dividend per Share divided by Market Value per Share. We are given that Company A offers a dividend yield of 3% and Company B offers a dividend yield of 5%. To determine which company offers a better return for the shareholders, we need to compare their dividend yields.

Let's assume that both companies have a market value of $100 per share. Using the dividend yield formula, we can calculate the dividend per share for each company.

For Company A:

Dividend per Share = (3/100) x 100 = $3

For Company B:

Dividend per Share = (5/100) x 100 = $5

Based on this calculation, Company B offers a better return for the shareholders as it pays a higher dividend per share than Company A. However, it's important to note that this calculation is based on the assumption that both companies have the same market value per share. In reality, market values can vary significantly, so it's important to consider other factors as well when comparing dividend yields.

Problem 2: An individual has invested $10,000 in a company's stock that currently trades at $50 per share. If the company pays out a dividend of $1.5 per share in the coming quarter, what will be the dividend yield for the investor's investment?
Solution: To determine the dividend yield for the investor's investment, we can use the dividend yield formula, which is Dividend per Share divided by Market Value per Share.

We are given that the investor has invested $10,000 in the company's stock that currently trades at $50 per share. This means that the investor owns 200 shares ($10,000 / $50 per share).

The company pays out a dividend of $1.5 per share in the coming quarter. This means that the total dividend paid out to the investor will be:

Dividend per Share = $1.5 x 200 = $300

Now we need to calculate the market value per share. We know that the stock currently trades at $50 per share, so we can use this value as the market value per share.

Substituting these values into the dividend yield formula:

Dividend Yield = Dividend per Share / Market Value per Share
Dividend Yield = $300 / ($50 x 200)
Dividend Yield = $300 / $10,000
Dividend Yield = 0.03 or 3%

Therefore, the dividend yield for the investor's investment is 3%. This means that the investor can expect to receive a return of 3% on their investment through the dividends paid out by the company.

Problem 3: An investor is trying to decide between two different stocks of equal value to invest in. Stock X currently offers a yield of 4% and the dividend per share is $2, while Stock Y currently offers a yield of 5% and the dividend per share is $1.5. Which stock should the investor choose to maximize their returns?

Solution: To determine which stock the investor should choose to maximize their returns, we need to compare the dividend yields of the two stocks.

Using the dividend yield formula, which is Dividend per Share divided by Market Value per Share, we can calculate the market value per share for each stock based on the given information.

For Stock X:
Dividend Yield = Dividend per Share / Market Value per Share
4% = $2 / Market Value per Share
Market Value per Share = $2 / 4%
Market Value per Share = $50

For Stock Y:
Dividend Yield = Dividend per Share / Market Value per Share
5% = $1.5 / Market Value per Share
Market Value per Share = $1.5 / 5%
Market Value per Share = $30

Based on these calculations, Stock X has a market value of $50 per share, while Stock Y has a market value of $30 per share.

To compare the dividend yield for the two stocks, we can use the dividend yield formula again:

For Stock X:
Dividend Yield = Dividend per Share / Market Value per Share
Dividend Yield = $2 / $50
Dividend Yield = 0.04 or 4%

For Stock Y:
Dividend Yield = Dividend per Share / Market Value per Share
Dividend Yield = $1.5 / $30
Dividend Yield = 0.05 or 5%

This calculation shows that Stock Y offers a higher dividend yield than Stock X, meaning that the investor can expect to receive a higher return on their investment through the dividends paid out by Stock Y.

Therefore, based on the given information, the investor should choose to invest in Stock Y to maximize their returns.

Profit Maximization Assessment Criteria:

Profit maximization is a common financial objective of companies where they aim to increase their profits to the highest possible level by determining the optimal level of output or sales. There are different formulas that can be used to find the profit maximization point for a company, including:

Approach One: Total Revenue - Total Cost Approach: In this approach, the profit maximization point can be found by calculating the total revenue and the total costs at different levels of output, and identifying the level of output where the difference between total revenue and total cost is the highest. The formula for this approach can be represented as:

$$\text{Profit } (\pi) = \text{Total Revenue (TR)} - \text{Total Cost (TC)}$$
$$\pi = TR - TC$$

Approach Two: Marginal Revenue - Marginal Cost Approach: This approach involves finding the level of output where marginal revenue (MR) equals marginal cost (MC) because at this point, the change in revenue from producing an additional unit of a product is equal to the change in cost. The formula for this approach can be represented as:

$$MR = MC$$

Approach Three: Average Revenue - Average Cost Approach: In this approach, the profit maximization point is determined by finding the level of output where the average revenue (AR) equals the average cost (AC). The formula for this approach can be represented as:

$$AR = AC$$

Approach Four: Elasticity Approach: In this approach, the profit maximization point is found by determining the level of output where the elasticity of demand is equal to one, because at this point, any adjustment in price will result in a proportional change in quantity demanded that does not affect total revenue. The formula for this approach can be represented as:

Elasticity of Demand (ED) = 1
Total Revenue - Total Cost Approach

The profit maximization point can be found by calculating the total revenue and the total costs at different levels of output, and identifying the level of output where the difference between total revenue and total cost is the highest. The formula for this approach can be represented as:

Profit (π) = Total Revenue (TR) - Total Cost (TC)
π = TR - TC

Problem 1: ABC Company is planning to launch a new product line, and they estimate the following production costs: fixed costs of $10,000 per month and variable costs of $5 per unit. If the company plans to sell each unit for $20, what is the monthly production level necessary to achieve the profit maximization point?

Solution:
Total Cost = Fixed Cost + Variable Cost
Total Cost = $10,000 + $5X
Total Revenue = Selling Price X Quantity
Total Revenue = $20X

Profit (π) = Total Revenue (TR) - Total Cost (TC)
π = TR - TC
π = ($20X) - [$10,000 + ($5X)]
π = 15X - $10,000

To ensure that we are earning the highest profits possible, we must determine at what level of production the slope of the total revenue and total cost curves are equivalent. In doing so, we will be able to pinpoint the optimal production level that generates the maximum profit. The optimal production level can be found by taking the derivative of the profit function with respect to X and setting it equal to zero:

$$d\pi/dX = 15 = 5$$
$$X = 1000$$

Therefore, to maximize profits, ABC Company should produce and sell 1000 units of the new product line each month.

Problem 2: An online retailer has fixed costs of $10,000 per month for maintaining their website, managing the warehouse and employees, etc. They sell one product with a variable cost of $3 per unit, and the selling price for each unit is $12. If they want to achieve the profit maximization point, what is the level of sales they need to generate each month?

Solution:
Total Cost = Fixed Cost + Variable Cost
Total Cost = $10,000 + $3X
Total Revenue = Selling Price X Quantity
Total Revenue = $12X

Profit (π) = Total Revenue (TR) - Total Cost (TC)
π = TR - TC
π = ($12X) - [$10,000 + ($3X)]
π = 9X - $10,000

To maximize profits, we need to find the level of sales that generates the highest profit. The optimal sales level can be found by taking the derivative of the profit function with respect to X and setting it equal to zero:

$$d\pi/dX = 9 - 3 = 0$$
$$X = 3333$$

Therefore, to maximize profits, the online retailer needs to generate sales of 3333 units of the product each month
Marginal Revenue - Marginal Cost Approach

This approach involves finding the level of output where marginal revenue (MR) equals marginal cost (MC) because at this point, the change in revenue from producing an additional unit of a product is equal to the change in cost. The formula for this approach can be represented as:

$$MR = MC$$

Problem 1: A construction company is currently producing 1,000 units of a particular building material, and their marginal cost per unit is $50. The company's management team wants to know if they should increase production to 1,100 units. The current marginal revenue per unit is $75. According to the Marginal Revenue - Marginal Cost Approach, should the company increase production?

Solution: The construction company wants to know if it is profitable to increase production from 1,000 units to 1,100 units. To determine this, we have to calculate the marginal revenue and marginal cost of producing one more unit. Given, the current marginal cost per unit is $50, and the current marginal revenue per unit is $75. Therefore, the marginal profit per unit produced is $25 ($75 - $50).

Now, we can compare the additional cost of producing 100 units more and the additional revenue generated from selling additional 100 units. 100 units will cost the company an additional $50 x 100 = $5,000. The additional revenue generated by producing 100 units at the current marginal revenue is $75 x 100 = $7,500. The change in profit is the difference between the additional revenue and the additional cost, which is $7,500 - $5,000 = $2,500. Since the change in profit is positive, it is profitable for the construction company to increase production to 1,100 units, according to the Marginal Revenue - Marginal Cost Approach.

Problem 2: A bakery is producing 500 loaves of bread per day, and their marginal cost per unit is $2.50. The bakery is considering reducing production to 400 loaves per day due to a decrease in demand. The current marginal revenue per unit is $3.50. According to the Marginal Revenue - Marginal Cost Approach, should the bakery reduce production?

Solution: The bakery wants to know if it is profitable to reduce production from 500 loaves per day to 400 loaves per day. To determine this, we have to calculate the marginal revenue and marginal cost of producing one less unit. Given, the current marginal cost per unit is $2.50 and the current marginal revenue per unit is $3.50. Therefore, the marginal profit per unit produced is $1 ($3.50 - $2.50). Now, we can compare the cost savings of producing 100 units less to the revenue loss from selling 100 units less. By reducing production to 400 loaves a day, the bakery can save $2.50 x 100 = $250 in marginal costs.

However, the bakery will also lose revenue by selling 100 fewer loaves per day, which would be ($3.50 x 100) = $350. The change in profit is the difference between the cost savings and the revenue loss, which is ($350 - $250) = $100. Since the change in profit is positive, it is not profitable for the bakery to reduce production to 400 loaves per day according to the Marginal Revenue - Marginal Cost Approach.

Average Revenue - Average Cost Approach

In this approach, the profit maximization point is determined by finding the level of output where the average revenue (AR) equals the average cost (AC). The formula for this approach can be represented as:

$$AR = AC$$

Problem 1: For a manufacturing company that produces and sells multiple products, how can the Average Revenue - Average Cost approach help determine which product line is generating the most profit?

Solution: Let's assume that a manufacturing company produces and sells three different products - product A, B, and C. The company's financial data for the year shows that they sold 10,000 units of product A for a total revenue of $100,000 and a total cost of $80,000. They sold 8,000 units of product B for a total revenue of $80,000 and a total cost of $70,000. Finally, they sold 5,000 units of product C for a total revenue of $50,000 and a total cost of $60,000.

Using the Average Revenue - Average Cost approach, we can calculate the average revenue and average cost for each product line:

- For product A, the average revenue per unit is $10 ($100,000 / 10,000 units) and the average cost per unit is $8 ($80,000 / 10,000 units).
- For product B, the average revenue per unit is $10 ($80,000 / 8,000 units) and the average cost per unit is $8.75 ($70,000 / 8,000 units).
- For product C, the average revenue per unit is $10 ($50,000 / 5,000 units) and the average cost per unit is $12 ($60,000 / 5,000 units).

Next, we can compare the profit margins of each product line by calculating the difference between the average revenue and average cost:

- For product A, the profit margin per unit is $2 ($10 - $8).
- For product B, the profit margin per unit is $1.25 ($10 - $8.75).
- For product C, the profit margin per unit is -$2 ($10 - $12).

To sum up, based on this analysis, we can conclude that product A has the highest profit margin and is generating the most profit for the manufacturing company. Conversely, product C has a negative profit margin and is running at a loss. This information can help the company make decisions about which product lines to focus more resources on and which ones may need improvement or be discontinued.

Problem 2: An owner of a coffee shop wants to analyze the profitability of their business. Using the Average Revenue - Average Cost approach, what would be the optimal level of output to ensure maximum profit?

Solution: Let's assume that the coffee shop owner has collected financial data for the year, showing that their shop sold 10,000 cups of coffee for a total revenue of $50,000 and a total cost of $30,000. Using the Average Revenue - Average Cost approach, we can calculate the average revenue and average cost per cup of coffee:

- The average revenue per cup of coffee is $5 ($50,000 / 10,000 cups).
- The average cost per cup of coffee is $3 ($30,000 / 10,000 cups).

To determine the optimal level of output to ensure maximum profit, we need to find the level of output where the average revenue equals the average cost, as per the formula represented as AR = AC. Thus, we need to equate $5 (AR) with $3 (AC):

$$AR = AC$$
$$\$5 = \$3$$
$$10{,}000 \text{ cups} = x$$

$$x = (10{,}000 \text{ cups} * \$3) / \$5$$
$$x = 6{,}000 \text{ cups}$$

Thus, 6,000 cups of coffee are the optimal level of output that will ensure maximum profit for the shop owner, assuming that the cost and revenue figures provided remain constant. Any output above or below this level will result in a decrease in profitability.

Elasticity Approach

In this approach, the profit maximization point is found by determining the level of output where the elasticity of demand is equal to one, because at this point, any adjustment in price will result in a proportional change in quantity demanded that does not affect total revenue. The formula for this approach can be represented as:

$$\text{Elasticity of Demand (ED)} = 1$$

Problem 1: A clothing store has noticed a decrease in sales over the past few months. Using the Elasticity Approach, how can they determine at what price point they should sell their clothing items to ensure maximum profitability?

Solution: To determine the price point at which the clothing store should sell their items to ensure maximum profitability, we can use the Elasticity Approach. The first step is to calculate the elasticity of demand for the clothing items. The elasticity of demand refers to the degree of responsiveness of the quantity demanded of a good or service in relation to changes in its price. If the demand is elastic, a change in price will result in a significant change in quantity demanded. A situation where the demand is considered inelastic means that a change in price would result in a relatively smaller change in the quantity demanded of a good or service.

Let's assume that the clothing store sells a particular type of shirt for $20 and they notice a decrease in sales from 1,000 units per month to 800 units per month. Using the formula for elasticity of demand, we can calculate the elasticity for this type of shirt:

Elasticity of Demand (ED) = percentage change in quantity demanded / percentage change in price

- Percentage change in quantity demanded = ((new quantity - old quantity) / old quantity) * 100% = ((800 - 1000) / 1000) * 100% = -20%
- Percentage change in price = ((new price - old price) / old price) * 100% = ((x - 20) / 20) * 100%

Substituting the values in the formula for ED and equating it with 1 (as per the Elasticity Approach formula), we get:

$$1 = (-20\% / ((x - 20) / 20))$$
$$20 = -((x - 20) / 20) / 0.2$$
$$x - 20 = -8$$
$$x = \$12$$

Thus, $12 is the optimal price point at which the clothing store should sell the shirts to ensure maximum profitability, assuming that the elasticity of demand remains constant. At this price point, a small price increase or decrease will not significantly affect the quantity demanded, leading to a stable total revenue. Consequently, any price below or above this point will lead to lower profits for the store. However, the store should also factor in other elements like costs, competition, etc. before determining the final selling price.

Problem 2: A ride-sharing company wants to analyze the price point for their service that would result in maximum profit. Using the Elasticity Approach, how can the company find the optimal price that would maximize their revenue?
Solution: To determine the optimal price point that would maximize their revenue, the ride-sharing company can use the Elasticity Approach. The first step is to calculate the elasticity of demand for their service, which measures the responsiveness of the quantity demanded to a change in price.

Let's assume that the ride-sharing company currently charges $10 for a ride and they want to determine the optimal price point that would maximize their profits. Using historical data, they find out that if the price is reduced to $8, the quantity demanded increases from 500 rides per day to 600 rides per day.

Using the formula for elasticity of demand, we can calculate the elasticity:

Elasticity of Demand (ED) = percentage change in quantity demanded / percentage change in price

- Percentage change in quantity demanded = ((new quantity - old quantity) / old quantity) * 100% = ((600 - 500) / 500) * 100% = 20%
- Percentage change in price = ((new price - old price) / old price) * 100% = ((8 - 10) / 10) * 100% = -20%

Substituting the calculated values into the formula of ED and equating it to 1, we get:

1 = (20% / -20%) * (10/y)

y = $12.50

Thus, the optimal price point that would maximize the ride-sharing company's profits is $12.50 per ride, assuming that the elasticity of demand remains constant. At this price point, a small price increase or decrease will not have a significant effect on the quantity demanded, leading to stable total revenue. Note that the ride-sharing company should also consider other factors such as costs, competitors, and budget constraints while determining the final price point for their service.

Current Ratio

Problem 1: What is the current ratio of our company, and how does it compare to the industry average?

Solution: Let's assume that our company has current assets of $200,000 and current liabilities of $100,000. What is the current ratio of our company, and how does it compare to the industry average, which is 1.5?

The current ratio is calculated by dividing current assets by current liabilities. In this case, the current ratio of our company is 2 (200,000/100,000). This means that our company has $2 worth of current assets to cover each dollar of current liabilities. When compared to the industry average of 1.5, our company's current ratio is higher, indicating that we have more liquidity and are better able to meet our short-term obligations. A higher current ratio is generally seen as favorable because it suggests that a company has a higher capacity to pay its debts and fund its operations with its current assets. It is essential to remember that industry averages can vary depending on the nature of the industry, which must be considered when interpreting the results.

Debt-to-Equity Ratio

Problem 2: Is our debt-to-equity ratio within acceptable limits for our industry, and how might we improve it?

Solution: Let's assume that our company has a total debt of $500,000 and total equity of $750,000. Is our debt-to-equity ratio within acceptable limits for our industry, and how might we improve it?

The debt-to-equity ratio measures the amount of debt that a company uses to finance its assets compared to the amount of equity. It is calculated by dividing total debt by total equity. In this case, the debt-to-equity ratio of our company is 0.67 (500,000/750,000). To determine whether this ratio is within acceptable limits for our industry, we need to consider industry averages and standards. Many industries have accepted thresholds for the debt-to-equity ratio, so it is important to compare our ratio to those standards. If our company's debt-to-equity ratio is higher than the industry average, we may need to consider ways to reduce our debt or increase our equity. This could include measures such as taking steps to increase profits, raising additional capital through equity financing instead of debt financing, or restructuring our debt. On the other hand, if our company's debt-to-equity ratio is lower than the industry average, it could indicate that we are not taking full advantage of the benefits of debt financing. In this case, we may want to consider taking on additional debt to fund strategic initiatives that could help grow our business. Ultimately, the debt-to-equity ratio is just one of many financial ratios that must be considered when evaluating a company's financial health, so it is important to analyze multiple ratios and factors to get a complete picture of our company's financial position.

Inventory Turnover Ratio

Problem 3: How has our inventory turnover ratio changed over the past three years, and what does this suggest about our inventory management?

Solution: Let's assume that our company's inventory turnover ratio for the past three years has been as follows:

- Year 1: 4.0
- Year 2: 3.5
- Year 3: 2.8

How has our inventory turnover ratio changed over the past three years, and what does this suggest about our inventory management?

Inventory turnover ratio is a measure of how quickly a company is able to sell its inventory and replace it with new inventory. It is calculated by dividing the cost of goods sold by the average inventory. Based on the given information, we can see that our inventory turnover ratio has declined over the past three years. This suggests that our inventory management has become less efficient over time, either due to an increase in inventory levels or a decrease in sales.

A decrease in the inventory turnover ratio could indicate that our company is experiencing slower sales or difficulty in managing inventory levels. It may also suggest that we are holding onto inventory for too long, which can be costly due to storage expenses, potential obsolescence, and lost opportunity costs. To improve our inventory turnover ratio, we could consider measures such as reducing inventory levels, developing more accurate sales forecasts, and implementing more efficient inventory management systems. By doing so, we would be able to improve our cash flow, reduce carrying costs associated with holding onto inventory, and ensure that we have the appropriate amount of inventory to meet customer demand.

Return on Assets

Problem 4: What is our return on assets, and is it competitive in comparison to our peers?

Solution: Let's assume that our company has a net income of $200,000 and total assets of $2,000,000. What is our return on assets, and is it competitive in comparison to our peers?

Return on assets (ROA) is a profitability ratio that measures how much profit a company generates for each dollar of assets it owns. It is calculated by dividing net income by total assets. In this case, our company's ROA is 0.1 (200,000/2,000,000), which means that we generate $0.10 in net income for each dollar of assets we own. To determine whether our company's ROA is competitive with our peers, we need to compare it to industry benchmarks and standards. If our company's ROA is higher than the industry average, it indicates that we are more efficient in generating profits from our assets than our competitors. Conversely, if our company's ROA is lower than the industry average, it may suggest that we need to find ways to improve profitability, reduce expenses or optimize asset utilization. It is important to consider industry-specific factors that may affect a company's ROA, such as the type of assets held and the nature of the industry. Additionally, we can also identify the strengths and weaknesses of our company compared to our competitors by analyzing multiple ratios and data points, in order to identify areas where we can improve our performance.

Gross Profit Margin

Problem 5: How does our gross profit margin compare to industry standards, and are there ways we can improve it?

Solution: Let's assume that our company has a gross profit of $400,000 and revenue of $1,000,000. How does our gross profit margin compare to industry standards, and are there ways we can improve it?

The gross profit margin is a measure of a company's profitability, which indicates the percentage of revenue that is left after deducting the cost of goods sold. It is calculated by dividing gross profit by revenue. In this case, the gross profit margin of our company is 40% (400,000/1,000,000). To assess whether this gross profit margin is competitive with the industry standards, we need to compare it against our competitors. It is essential to remember that industry standards and averages can vary depending on various factors such as the sector, industry trends, and competitive landscape.

If our gross profit margin is higher than the industry average, it indicates that we are more profitable and efficient in controlling our costs compared to our competitors. On the other hand, if our gross profit margin is lower than the industry average, it may suggest that we need to optimize our cost structure or pricing strategy to generate profit. To improve gross profit margin, businesses must focus on improving aspects such as reducing overheads costs, optimizing the procurement process, and adjusting the pricing policy while being mindful that competition might pose restrictions

In general, maintaining a healthy gross profit margin is extremely critical for any business not only in terms of financial stability but also it serves as a signal for investors, creditors, and potential partners.

Debt service coverage ratio

Problem 6: What is our debt service coverage ratio, and how does it impact our ability to service debt?

Solution: Let's assume that our company's operating income is $300,000, and our annual debt service is $100,000. What is our debt service coverage ratio, and how does it impact our ability to service debt?

The debt service coverage ratio (DSCR) is a measure of a company's ability to repay its debt obligations. It indicates how much cash flow is available to cover debt payments after considering other operating expenses. To calculate DSCR of our company, we can divide the operating income by the annual debt service. In this case, our company's DSCR is 3.0 (300,000/100,000), which means we generated three times the amount of cash required to repay our debts. A higher DSCR ratio suggests that we have enough cash flow to meet our debt obligations, making it an attractive option for lenders and creditors. This ratio provides companies with leverage to secure financing, often at more favorable rates.

On the other hand, if our company's DSCR ratio is lower, it can indicate that we faced challenges in generating sufficient cash to cover our debt payments. As a result, this creates the potential for the company to default on its debt obligations, making it harder for the firm to secure financing in the future. Therefore, it is always essential to evaluate the debt service coverage ratio alongside other important financial ratios when seeking external financing from creditors or lenders. If companies maintain a higher DSCR, it provides them with greater financial flexibility and resilience during economically challenging times.

Trend Analysis

Problem 7: How might we use trend analysis to identify potential issues with our earnings per share ratio?

Solution: Let's assume that our company has the following earnings per share (EPS) values for the past four years:
- Year 1: $2.50
- Year 2: $3.00
- Year 3: $2.70
- Year 4: $2.20

How might we use trend analysis to identify potential issues with our earnings per share ratio?

Trend analysis is a technique used to evaluate a company's financial performance over time by comparing current and historical data. In this case, we can monitor trends in the earnings per share ratio over the past few years. The declining trend of earnings per share from year 2 to year 4 could indicate that the company's profitability and ability to grow is decreasing over time. This could be symptomatic of underlying business problems, such as decreasing sales or increasing costs, which could diminish investor confidence and cause the stock price to decline. During times of declining EPS trends, companies must leverage strategic initiatives, such as cost-cutting measures, increasing sales revenue or diversifying product portfolios, to stabilize revenues and profitability. Furthermore, comparing our EPS trend with that of industry peers to assess the relative competitiveness of the company and to provide further insights into financial performance. If our company's EPS trend is declining at a more accelerated rate compared to those of our competitors over the same time period, it may indicate that our firm is not adapting with market demand as quickly or as effectively as our peers. Trend analysis can serve as a powerful tool for identifying performance issues and providing insights to make informed decisions about our company's financial status. By identifying and addressing issues preemptively, we can initiate strategies to mitigate risks, seize opportunities, and drive financial performance.

Working Capital Ratio

Problem 8: Is our working capital ratio within acceptable limits, and what risks do we face if it isn't?

Solution: Let's assume that our company has current assets of $500,000 and current liabilities of $400,000. Is our working capital ratio within acceptable limits, and what risks do we face if it isn't? Working capital ratio measures a company's ability to meet its short-term financial obligations. It indicates whether a company has sufficient current assets to cover its current liabilities. The formula to calculate the working capital ratio is current assets divided by current liabilities. In this case, our company's working capital ratio is 1.25 (500,000/400,000).

In order to determine whether our company's working capital ratio is within acceptable limits, we need to compare it against industry standards and norms. Generally, a ratio of 1.2 to 2.0 is considered acceptable. If our company's working capital ratio is lower than the industry average or below the acceptable threshold, it indicates that our company may have difficulty meeting our short-term obligations or paying off our creditors, which could lead to severe financial problems. This gap could also pose risks to the credibility and reputation of the company, leading to credit downgrades or reduced investor confidence, which could further exacerbate any pre-existing financial issues. In order to mitigate these risks and maintain an acceptable working capital ratio, companies may consider measures such as optimizing cash flow, streamlining procurement processes, and increasing inventory turnover. Companies could also explore financing options to decrease financial stress such as short-term loans or reduce the expenses by negotiating better terms with suppliers.

Overall, as one of the most critical measures of a company's financial health, it is essential to keep a close watch on the working capital ratio and make informed decisions to ensure long-term financial sustainability.

Quick Ratio

Problem 9: How does our quick ratio compare to industry standards, and what does this suggest about our ability to meet short-term obligations?

Solution: The management of the Firm B has asked for a quick ratio analysis to evaluate their ability to meet short-term obligations. The company's financial statements show:

- Current assets: $350,000
- Inventories: $100,000
- Accounts receivable: $75,000
- Cash and Marketable securities: $50,000
- Current liabilities: $150,000

1) Calculate the quick ratio for the Firm B

2) How does the quick ratio compare to industry standards?
3) What does this suggest about the company's ability to meet short-term obligations?

1) Calculation of the quick ratio for the Firm B:
Quick ratio = (Current assets - Inventories - Prepaid expenses) / Current liabilities
Prepaid expenses are not given in the problem, so we will assume they are negligible.
Quick ratio = ($350,000 - $100,000 - $0) / $150,000 = 1.33

2) Comparison of the quick ratio to industry standards:

Industry standards for the quick ratio vary depending on the sector and the type of business. However, in general, a quick ratio of 1 is considered acceptable, while a quick ratio above 1 indicates that the company can meet its short-term obligations more easily.

Firm B's quick ratio of 1.33 is above the industry standard of 1. This suggests that the company is in a relatively strong position to pay its short-term obligations and can do so more easily than other companies in the same industry.

3) What does this suggest about the company's ability to meet short-term obligations?

Firm B's quick ratio of 1.33 suggests that the company has a relatively strong ability to meet its short-term obligations. The company can easily cover its current liabilities with its quick assets, which include cash, marketable securities, and accounts receivable. This is a positive sign for the company's financial health and may indicate that the company has good control over its working capital management, such as inventory management and collections.

Interest Rate Impact on Interest Coverage Ratio

Problem 10: What is the impact of changes in interest rates on our interest coverage ratio, and how might we manage this risk?

Solution: Firm A is considering taking on additional debt to fund a new project. The management wants to know how changes in interest rates might affect the company's interest coverage ratio and what they can do to manage this risk.

The financial statements for the company show:

- Net income: $500,000
- Interest expense: $100,000
- Earnings before interest and taxes (EBIT): $800,000
- Total debt: $1,000,000
- Cash and cash equivalents: $200,000

1) Calculate the interest coverage ratio for Firm A.
2) What would happen to the interest coverage ratio if interest expenses increased by 1%?
3) How can Firm A manage the risk of changes in interest rates on its interest coverage ratio?

Solution:

1) Calculation of the interest coverage ratio for Firm A:
Interest coverage ratio = EBIT / Interest expense
Interest coverage ratio = $800,000 / $100,000 = 8

2) The impact of a 1% increase in interest expenses on the interest coverage ratio:

If interest expenses were to increase by 1%, the new interest expense would be $101,000, and the new interest coverage ratio would be:

Interest coverage ratio = $800,000 / $101,000 = 7.92

Therefore, a 1% increase in interest expenses would result in a decrease of 0.08 in the interest coverage ratio.

3) How to manage the risk of changes in interest rates on the interest coverage ratio:

To manage the risk of changes in interest rates, Firm A can consider the following strategies:

- Diversifying the sources of funding: The company can seek alternative sources of funding, such as equity financing or convertible debt, which are less sensitive to changes in interest rates.
- Refinancing the debt: The company can refinance its existing debt with new debt at a lower interest rate, thereby reducing the interest expense and improving the interest coverage ratio.
- Hedging against interest rate risks: The company can use financial instruments such as interest rate swaps or options to hedge against adverse interest rate movements. These instruments can provide protection against interest rate fluctuations but also involve risks and costs that must be considered.

By implementing one or more of these strategies, Firm A can manage the risk of changes in interest rates on its interest coverage ratio and ensure its long-term financial stability.

Price-to-Earnings Ratio

Problem 11: How might we use the price-to-earnings ratio to evaluate investment opportunities?

Solution: Firm T is considering investing in a publicly traded company and is examining the price-to-earnings (P/E) ratio as a measure of their potential investment opportunity. The financial statements of the company show:

- Current market price per share: $50
- Earnings per Share (EPS): $4

1) Calculate the P/E ratio for the company.

2) How can Firm A use the P/E ratio to evaluate the investment opportunity?

3) What factors should Firm T consider in addition to the P/E ratio when making investment decisions?

Solution:

1) Calculation of the P/E ratio for the company:

P/E ratio = Market Price per share / Earnings per share (EPS)

P/E ratio = $50 / $4 = 12.5

2) Using the P/E ratio to evaluate the investment opportunity:

The P/E ratio is a widely used valuation metric that relates the market price per share to the earnings per share. It can help investors assess whether a stock is overvalued, undervalued or fairly valued compared to the rest of the market.

In general, a higher P/E ratio indicates that investors are willing to pay a premium for a company's stock, which means they are expecting higher growth and profitability in the future. Conversely, a lower P/E ratio may suggest that a company is undervalued or that the market has limited expectations of future earnings growth.

In the case of Firm T, a P/E ratio of 12.5 suggests that the company has a relatively low P/E ratio compared to the industry average. This may indicate that the company is undervalued and has potential for future growth, which may make it a good investment opportunity for Firm T.

3) Factors to consider in addition to the P/E ratio:

While the P/E ratio is a useful tool to evaluate a company's investment opportunity, investors should consider additional factors when making their investment decisions. These factors may include:

- The industry and competitors' average P/E ratios: Investors should compare a company's P/E ratio with the industry standards and its competitors to put the ratio into perspective.
- Company's growth and profitability: Investors should evaluate a company's historical and projected growth rate and profitability to ensure that the company is positioned for long-term success.
- Market trends and conditions: Investors should consider macroeconomic factors such as inflation rates, interest rates, and political stability to ensure that the investment aligns with market trends.
- Financial health and management: Investors should examine a company's financial health by looking at the balance sheet, cash flow statement, and management team to evaluate its ability to execute its business plan effectively.

By examining these factors in addition to the P/E ratio, Firm T can make informed investment decisions that align with their investment objectives and risk tolerance.

Inventory Turnover Ratio

Problem 12: What is our inventory turnover ratio, and how does it relate to potential issues with obsolete inventory?

Solution: Firm X is concerned that they may have issues with obsolete inventory and wants to know how their inventory turnover ratio can help identify the problem. The financial statements of the company show:

- Cost of Goods Sold (COGS): $500,000
- Average Inventory: $50,000

1) Calculate the inventory turnover ratio for Firm X.

2) How can the inventory turnover ratio help identify potential issues with obsolete inventory?

3) What steps can Firm X take to manage the risk of obsolete inventory?

Solution:

1) Calculation of the inventory turnover ratio for Firm X:

Inventory turnover ratio = Cost of Goods Sold (COGS) / Average Inventory

Inventory turnover ratio = $500,000 / $50,000 = 10

2) The relationship between the inventory turnover ratio and the risk of obsolete inventory:

The inventory turnover ratio is a measure of how efficiently a company manages its inventory. A high inventory turnover ratio indicates that the company is selling its inventory quickly, which minimizes the risk of obsolete inventory. Conversely, a low inventory turnover ratio may suggest that the company is struggling to sell its inventory, which increases the risk of obsolete inventory.

In the case of Firm X, a high inventory turnover ratio of 10 indicates that the company is efficiently selling its inventory. However, this ratio should be compared to the industry average to ensure it aligns with market standards.

If the inventory turnover ratio is low, this raises the risk of obsolete inventory. This occurs because the longer inventory sits in storage, the higher the likelihood that it will become outdated or less valuable, leading to financial losses.

3) Steps to manage the risk of obsolete inventory:

To manage the risk of obsolete inventory, companies can consider the following steps:

- Implement just-in-time inventory management: This approach involves keeping the minimum level of inventory to fulfill immediate customer demands. By reducing inventory storage, the risk of obsolete inventory can be minimized.
- Monitor inventory regularly and discard obsolete inventory: Companies should frequently evaluate their inventory levels and discard any obsolete inventory. This helps to avoid excess costs associated with storing obsolete inventory, such as storage and disposal costs.
- Optimize demand forecasting: Companies should utilize data and analytics to optimize their demand forecasting. This ensures that they are producing and storing the right kind and amount of inventory, ultimately minimizing the risk of obsolete inventory.

Thus, by monitoring inventory levels, implementing just-in-time inventory management, and optimizing their demand forecasting, firms can effectively manage the risk of obsolete inventory and use the inventory turnover ratio as a tool to avoid such risks.

Cash Conversion Cycle

Problem 13: How does our cash conversion cycle compare to industry standards, and what implications does this have for managing our working capital?

Solution: Firm Y wants to know how their cash conversion cycle (CCC) compares to industry standards and what implications this has for managing their working capital. The financial statements of the company show:

- Days Inventory Outstanding (DIO): 30
- Days Sales Outstanding (DSO): 20
- Days Payables Outstanding (DPO): 15

1) Calculate the cash conversion cycle (CCC) for Firm Y.
2) Compare the CCC to industry standards.
3) What implications does the CCC have for managing Firm Y's working capital?

Solution:

1) Calculation of the cash conversion cycle (CCC) for Firm Y:

$$CCC = DIO + DSO - DPO$$

$$CCC = 30 + 20 - 15 = 35$$

2) Comparing the CCC to industry standards:

A company's CCC measures the time it takes from investing in inventory to receiving cash from sales, and it has to be sufficiently managed to ensure that the company doesn't tie up excess cash into working capital. The ideal CCC varies depending on the industry, business model, and the company's shorter or longer-sighted strategy since a lower CCC relative to industry standards can indicate a more efficient uses of working capital.

Corporate Finance Institute has indicated that CCC standards vary from industry to industry, ranging from negative CCC cycles to over 100 days.

In general, if the CCC is lower than the industry average, it indicates that the company is managing its working capital effectively, while a higher-than-average CCC suggests to job inefficient management of working capital.

3) Implications of the CCC for managing Firm Y's working capital:

For Firm Y, their CCC is 35 days, meaning that it takes an average of 35 days for the company to recover cash from its investments in inventory and payables. The comparison of the CCC of Firm Y with the industry average should be considered along with the nature of the business and the business model that the company conducts.

A lower CCC implies a faster liquidity conversion of inventory to sales and sales to cash, allowing a company to invest the remaining funds into other projects. A higher CCC, on the other hand, affects liquidity and has associated holding costs from inventory, which may lead to cash flow problems.

Therefore, it is essential that Firm Y evaluates its CCC regularly to ensure that the company has an efficient cash conversion cycle to maintain its liquidity and profitability by managing their working capital efficiently, with access to sufficient capital to invest in growth opportunities.

Return on Equity

Problem 14: Is our return on equity within acceptable limits for our industry, and what factors could be driving changes in this ratio?

Solution: Firm Z wants to know if its return on equity (ROE) is within acceptable limits for their industry and what factors could be driving changes in this ratio. The financial statements of the company show:

- Net income: $1,000,000
- Total equity: $10,000,000

1) Calculate the ROE for Firm Z
2) Compare the ROE to industry standards to assess if it's within acceptable limits for the industry.
3) What factors could be driving changes in the ROE for Firm Z?

Solution:

1) Calculation of the ROE for Firm Z:

ROE = (Net income / Total Equity) x 100%

ROE = ($1,000,000 / $10,000,000) x 100% = 10%

2) Comparison of the ROE to industry standards:

The ROE measures the rate of return that shareholders receive on their investment relative to each dollar of equity invested. Industry standards vary by sector and firm size; generally, a higher ROE indicates a company is effectively using its equity to generate profit.

Usually, analyzing ROE over time is a more effective approach to determine what's considered acceptable limit than comparing it to industry's standards. For Firm Z, the historical trend of ROE to is compared to the industry average or benchmark to assess if it's acceptable.

If the ROE is higher than the industry average or benchmark, it may indicate that the company is generating significant profits from its investment relative to its peers. A lower ROE, however, may suggest that the company is not efficiently utilizing its equity to create profits, and if it becomes serious, it may affect the company's long-term growth and profitability.

3) Factors that could be driving changes in the ROE for Firm Z:

Changes in the ROE of a company can be driven by several factors, including:

- Profit margins: Profit margins are the ratio of net income to sales, which indicates a company's profitability. An increase in profit margins can drive an increase in ROE.

- Financial leverage: By taking on more debt or repurchasing shares, a company can increase its financial leverage, which can drive up the ROE.
- Asset turnover: Asset turnover is a measure of how efficiently a company utilizes its assets to generate sales. A company that can generate more sales per dollar of assets will have a higher ROE.
- Changes in the equity capital: Any movement in the equity capital, such as the issuance of new shares, can impact the ROE.

Therefore, to properly evaluate the ROE and identify potential factors driving changes in this ratio, Firm Z should focus on analyzing key performance metrics, financial statements, and external market factors that impact the industry, comparing trends over time with industry benchmarks.

Trend Analysis on Debt-to-Assets Ratio Prediction

Problem 15: How does trend analysis inform our ability to predict changes in our debt-to-assets ratio, and what steps might we take to manage this risk?

Solution:

Problem: Firm ABC has been growing rapidly over the past few years. In 2020, their debt-to-assets ratio was at 30%, but it increased to 40% in 2021, and further to 45% in 2022. How does trend analysis inform our ability to predict changes in our debt-to-assets ratio, and what steps might we take to manage this risk?

Solution: Trend analysis in ratio analysis allows us to identify patterns and understand changes over time. In the case of Firm ABC, the overall trend shows that their debt-to-assets ratio is increasing. This suggests that the company is relying more heavily on debt financing, which poses a potential risk to the company's long-term sustainability.

To manage this risk, Firm ABC should take several steps. Firstly, they should consider reducing their reliance on debt financing and seek alternative funding sources, such as equity financing or using their profits to fund growth. Additionally, they should closely monitor their financial performance and leverage ratios regularly to identify trends and ensure that they are on track to achieve their financial goals.

In conclusion, trend analysis provides us with essential insights into a company's financial performance over time. In the case of Firm ABC, the trend of increasing debt-to-assets ratio requires a course of action to manage the risk of over-reliance on debt financing. By taking proactive steps to reduce their reliance on debt financing, Firm ABC can ensure that they remain sustainable in the long term.

Total Shareholder Return (TSR):

Total Shareholder Return (TSR) refers to the overall gain or loss an investor receives from owning a company's stock, considering both capital gain or loss, dividends, and any other related distributions. There are two common formulas to measure TSR:

1. The first formula considers the starting and ending price of a stock with the addition of any dividends paid during the period being measured. The formula is calculated by subtracting the beginning price from the ending price and adding any dividends paid during that period, then dividing the result by the beginning price.

2. The second formula also considers the stock price and dividends but is calculated as a ratio. The ending price is added to any dividends, and the result is divided by the beginning price to determine the TSR.

It's important to note that TSR can be calculated over any time period, such as a year, quarter, or month, and it's a valuable metric for analyzing a company's overall performance from an investor's viewpoint.

Problem 1: ABC Inc

Let's assume that you have invested in a company called ABC Inc. You have bought 1,000 shares of the company at a stock price of $50 per share, and you plan to hold the stock for a year. The company announces that it will pay a dividend of $2 per share at the end of the year.

Using the first formula to calculate the Total Shareholder Return (TSR) for your investment in ABC Inc., we have:

TSR = (Ending stock price - Beginning stock price + Dividends) / Beginning stock price

The ending stock price, assuming it appreciates by 10%, would be:

Ending stock price = $50 + ($50 x 10%) = $55 per share

So, the total value of your investment at the end of the year would be:

Ending value = 1,000 shares x $55 per share = $55,000

Adding the dividend of $2 per share, the total dividend received would be:

Total Dividend = 1,000 shares x $2 per share = $2,000

Therefore, using the formula, the TSR for the investment in ABC Inc. is:

TSR = ($55 - $50 + $2) / $50 = 14%

Now, let's assume that your financial management problem is to determine whether your investment in ABC Inc. is meeting your desired rate of return. If your desired rate of return is 12%, based on the formula, the solution is to compare your desired rate of return to the calculated TSR. In this case, since the calculated TSR of 14% is higher than the desired rate of return of 12%, the investment in ABC Inc. is meeting your financial expectations.

Thus, the formula for calculating TSR helps investors understand the actual return on their investment by considering stock price appreciation, dividends, and other distributions. It can be used as a financial management tool to compare actual returns to desired rates of return and help investors make informed investment decisions.

Problem 2: XYZ Corporation

Let's consider a real-life business case of an investor who purchased 500 shares of XYZ Corporation for $25 per share on January 1, 2021. The investor received a dividend of $1.50 per share at the end of the year, and the stock price increased to $30 per share by December 31, 2021.

Using the second formula to calculate the Total Shareholder Return (TSR) for the investment in XYZ Corporation, we have:

TSR = (Ending stock price + Dividends) / Beginning stock price

The ending value of the investment in XYZ Corporation is:

Ending value = 500 shares x $30 per share = $15,000

Adding the dividend of $1.50 per share, the total dividend received would be:

Total Dividend = 500 shares x $1.50 per share = $750

Therefore, using the formula, the TSR for the investment in XYZ Corporation is:

$$TSR = (\$15,000 + \$750) / (\$25 \times 500) = 66\%$$

Now, let's assume that the financial management problem is to determine whether this investment meets the investor's desired rate of return of 60%. The solution is to compare the calculated TSR of 66% to the desired rate of return. Since the calculated TSR is higher than the desired rate of return, the investor has earned higher returns than expected on this investment. On the other hand, if the calculated TSR was 55%, which is lower than the desired rate of return, then the financial management problem would be to consider other investment options that could generate higher returns.

To sum up, both formulas for calculating TSR are useful financial management tools for evaluating investments from a shareholder's perspective. They help investors understand the performance of their investments by considering stock price appreciation, dividends, and other distributions. By comparing the calculated TSR with the desired rate of return, investors can make informed investment decisions.

Interest Rate in Macroeconomic Policy Targets: Problems

If the central bank increases the interest rate by 1%, what effect will this have on the affordability of home loans for consumers? Calculate the new monthly payment for a 30-year mortgage of $200,000 at an interest rate of 4% before the rate increase, assuming a fixed rate, and after the rate increase.
Solution: If the central bank increases the interest rate by 1%, it will have a negative impact on the affordability of home loans for consumers, because borrowing money to purchase a home becomes more expensive due to higher interest rates.
To calculate the new monthly payment for a 30-year mortgage of $200,000 at an interest rate of 4% before the rate increase, we can use a mortgage calculator. Using a standard mortgage calculator, the monthly payment to repay the $200,000 at 4% interest over 30 years would be $955. The same calculator can be used to calculate the monthly payment after the rate increase.
After the interest rate is increased by 1%, the new interest rate will be 5%. Using the same mortgage calculator, the new monthly repayment would be $1,073. This represents a $118 increase in monthly payments, or an annual increase of $1,416.
So, the increase in the interest rate by 1% makes a significant difference in the affordability of a home loan for consumers, as it increases the monthly mortgage payment by nearly $118 for our given loan of $200,000 at a fixed rate of 30 years.

Problem 2

A country is experiencing low economic growth and high unemployment. To stimulate the economy, the central bank decides to lower the interest rate by 2%. If businesses take advantage of the reduced borrowing costs and increase their investment spending by $50 million, by how much will the GDP of the country increase in the short run? Assume a marginal propensity to consume of 0.75.

Solution: When the central bank lowers the interest rate by 2%, businesses can take advantage of lower borrowing costs and increase their investment spending.

The increase in investment of $50 million will have a short-term effect on the GDP of the country. To calculate the impact on GDP, we need to use the concept of the multiplier.

The multiplier tells us how much an initial injection of money into the economy increases the overall level of economic activity. In this case, the multiplier can be calculated using the marginal propensity to consume (MPC). MPC is the percentage of each additional dollar of income that households consume.

If the MPC is 0.75, then $0.75 of each additional dollar of income will be consumed and $0.25 will be saved. Therefore, the multiplier can be calculated as:

$$\text{Multiplier} = 1 / (1 - \text{MPC})$$
$$\text{Multiplier} = 1 / (1 - 0.75)$$
$$\text{Multiplier} = 4$$

This means that the initial investment of $50 million will eventually lead to an increase in GDP of $50 million x 4 = $200 million.

So, when the central bank lowers interest rate by 2%, and businesses take advantage of the reduced borrowing costs and increase their investment spending by $50 million, the GDP of the country will increase by $200 million in the short run, assuming a marginal propensity to consume of 0.75.

Problem 3

A central bank aims to maintain an inflation rate of 2% annually. If the inflation rate is currently at 3% and the bank decides to implement a contractionary monetary policy, what change in the interest rate is required to bring inflation down to the target level? Assume a negative relationship between the interest rate and inflation.

Solution: When the inflation rate exceeds the target level, the central bank can use a contractionary monetary policy to reduce inflationary pressures. One way to implement a contractionary policy is to increase the interest rate.

In this case, to bring inflation down to the target level of 2%, the central bank needs to increase the interest rate as there is a negative relationship between the interest rate and inflation.

If the inflation rate is currently at 3%, then the central bank needs to decrease the money supply to reduce spending in the economy, which will decrease inflation. This can be achieved by increasing the interest rate.

To determine how much the central bank should increase the interest rate, it needs to assess the impact that the change in interest rate will have on inflation. If the central bank has empirical evidence on the exact relationship between the interest rate and inflation for their economy, then that can be used to estimate how much to increase the interest rate.

However, in general, we know that when interest rates rise, borrowing costs for businesses and consumers increase, which results in a decrease in spending and economic activity, which in turn helps to decrease inflation. Therefore, the central bank would need to increase the interest rate sufficiently to reduce loans and bring down inflation back to the target level of 2%.

Therefore, the exact amount by which the interest rate needs to be increased to bring inflation down to the target level depends on the specifics of the economy and the relationship between interest rates and inflation in that country.

Problem 4

A country is experiencing high exchange rate volatility due to capital flows. The central bank decides to increase the interest rate by 1% to attract foreign investors and stabilize the exchange rate. If $10 billion in foreign capital flows into the country as a result of the policy, what is the effect of this increase in capital on the money supply of the economy?

Solution: When a country experiences high exchange rate volatility due to capital flows, the central bank can use monetary policy, specifically changes in interest rates, to attract foreign investors and stabilize the exchange rate.

In this case, the central bank decides to increase the interest rate by 1% to attract foreign investors. As a result of the policy, $10 billion in foreign capital flows into the country.

When foreign capital flows in, it adds to the reserves of the country's central bank. The central bank may use these reserves to increase the money supply in the economy by using the reserves to purchase domestic currency in the foreign exchange market.

When the central bank purchases domestic currency, it increases the domestic money supply, which can lead to inflation in the economy if the increase in the money supply is too large.

However, the effect of the $10 billion in foreign capital flows on the money supply depends on what the central bank does with the new reserves. If the central bank does not purchase domestic currency, then there will be no change in the money supply.

On the other hand, if the central bank does use the reserves to purchase domestic currency, then it will increase the money supply in the economy, and the effect on the money supply will depend on the amount of reserves used to purchase currency.

Overall, the effect of the increase in capital flows on the money supply of the economy will depend on the specific actions taken by the central bank with the new reserves.

Problem 5

A developing country has a high debt-to-GDP ratio and is struggling to meet its debt payments. The central bank decides to increase the interest rate by 3% to reduce government borrowing and contain the growth of public debt. If the country's annual debt payment is $5 billion and the increase in interest rate leads to a reduction in debt-to-GDP ratio from 0.8 to 0.75, by how much is the government able to reduce its debt payment in the first year?

Solution: A high debt-to-GDP ratio can negatively impact a country's creditworthiness and economic stability, which can make it difficult to meet debt payments. Monetary policy, specifically changes in interest rates, is one tool that the central bank can use to reduce government borrowing and contain the growth of public debt.

In this case, if the central bank decides to increase the interest rate by 3%, it will make government borrowing more expensive, which can reduce the growth of public debt. If the increase in interest rates leads to a reduction in debt-to-GDP ratio from 0.8 to 0.75, then the government should be able to reduce its debt payment by a certain amount.

To calculate the reduction in the debt payment, we need to first calculate how much the debt payment would be without the interest rate increase. If the debt-to-GDP ratio was originally 0.8, this means that the country's debt was 80% of its annual GDP. Therefore, the country's annual GDP can be calculated as:

$$GDP = Debt / Debt\text{-to-}GDP \text{ ratio}$$
$$GDP = \$5 \text{ billion} / 0.8$$
$$GDP = \$6.25 \text{ billion}$$

With an interest rate of 3%, the new debt payment would be calculated as:

$$\text{New Debt Payment} = Debt \times (1 + \text{Interest Rate})$$
$$\text{New Debt Payment} = \$5 \text{ billion} \times (1 + 0.03)$$
$$\text{New Debt Payment} = \$5.15 \text{ billion}$$

Now that we have the new debt payment, we can calculate how much it reduces by subtracting it from the old payment:

$$\text{Debt Payment Reduction} = \text{Old Debt Payment} - \text{New Debt Payment}$$
$$\text{Debt Payment Reduction} = \$5 \text{ billion} - \$5.15 \text{ billion}$$
$$\text{Debt Payment Reduction} = -\$150 \text{ million}$$

Therefore, the government's debt payment will be reduced by $150 million in the first year due to the 3% increase in interest rate, assuming that the debt-to-GDP ratio is reduced from 0.8 to 0.75.

Exchange Rate in Macroeconomic Policy Targets:

Problem 1: How can the central bank use the exchange rate to manage inflation in the economy? If the economy is experiencing high inflation, how can the central bank use an appreciation of the currency to lower inflation? Provide a step-by-step calculation of how a 10% appreciation of the currency can lower the inflation rate from 5% to 2%.

Solution: The exchange rate is one of the tools that central banks can use to manage inflation in an economy. An appreciation of the currency can lead to lower inflation, while a depreciation can lead to higher inflation, assuming all other factors remain constant.

If an economy is experiencing high inflation, the central bank can use an appreciation of the currency to lower inflation. A stronger currency can make imports cheaper and, therefore, decrease the cost of production for domestic firms, which helps to lower the price level in the economy.

To calculate how a 10% appreciation of the currency can lower the inflation rate from 5% to 2%, one can use the following steps:

1. Assume that the inflation rate is currently at 5%.
2. Assume that the exchange rate is currently at X units of domestic currency per one unit of foreign currency.
3. Increase the exchange rate by 10% to 1.1X, which represents a 10% appreciation of the currency.
4. Calculate the change in the cost of imports due to the change in exchange rates. If the exchange rate increases by 10%, imported goods become 10% cheaper. Therefore, domestic firms can buy inputs more cheaply, which will decrease their costs of production.
5. This decrease in the cost of production will lead to a decrease in the price level of goods and services in the economy.
6. Assuming all other factors remain constant, a 10% appreciation of the currency can lead to a decrease in the inflation rate by 3 percentage points, from 5% to 2%.

Therefore, the central bank can use the exchange rate as a tool to manage inflation in the economy, and a 10% appreciation in the currency can lead to a significant decrease in inflation rates, assuming all other variables remain constant.

Problem 2

A country is experiencing weak economic growth and high unemployment. How can the central bank use the exchange rate to improve economic conditions? If the central bank decides to devalue the currency by 5%, how much must exports increase to offset the devaluation, assuming a price elasticity of demand of -0.5?

Solution: When a country's economy is experiencing slow growth and high unemployment, the central bank can use various macroeconomic policies to improve economic conditions. One such policy is to manage the exchange rate.

If a central bank decides to devalue its currency by 5%, it means that the value of its currency will decrease by 5% compared to other currencies in the forex market. This deliberate decrease in currency value will make the country's exports cheaper to foreign buyers, thus increasing demand for exports.

To determine how much exports must increase to offset the 5% devaluation, we need to consider the price elasticity of demand for exports. If the price elasticity of demand for exports is -0.5, it means that for every 1% drop in price, there will be a 0.5% increase in demand.

Therefore, to offset the 5% devaluation caused by the central bank, exports must increase by (5%/0.5) x 100, which is equal to 10%. This means that if the central bank devalues the currency by 5%, the country's exports must increase by 10% to offset the devaluation.

In conclusion, the central bank can use exchange rate management policies like devaluation to improve economic conditions, increase economic growth, and reduce unemployment. If the central bank decides to devalue the currency by 5%, exports must increase by 10% to offset the devaluation, assuming a price elasticity of demand of -0.5.

Problem 3

A country is experiencing a trade deficit due to high imports and low exports. How can interest rates be adjusted to stabilize the exchange rate and improve the trade balance? Assuming an increase in interest rates by 2% leads to a 10% appreciation of the currency, calculate the reduction in the trade deficit, given that the country's trade balance is currently $10 billion in the red.

Solution: When a country is experiencing a trade deficit, it means that the value of imports is higher than the value of exports. To improve the trade balance and stabilize the exchange rate, the central bank can use macroeconomic policies such as adjusting interest rates.

Increasing interest rates can encourage foreign investors to invest in domestic assets, which will increase the demand for the domestic currency, leading to an appreciation of the exchange rate. This appreciation of the exchange rate will make imports more expensive, thus reducing demand for imports, and increasing demand for exports, thus improving the trade balance.

Assuming an increase in interest rates by 2% leads to a 10% appreciation of the currency, it means that a 1% increase in interest rates results in a 5% appreciation of the currency. Therefore, if the central bank increases the interest rates by 4%, the currency will appreciate by 20%.

To calculate the reduction in the trade deficit, we need to use the income approach to measure the trade balance. If the trade balance is currently $10 billion in the red, it means that the country has a trade deficit of $10 billion.

Assuming that the income elasticity of demand for imports and exports is equal to one, a 20% appreciation of the currency will lead to a 20% reduction in imports and a 20% increase in exports. Therefore, the trade balance will improve by $4 billion, which is equal to 20% of the initial trade deficit of $10 billion.

In conclusion, to stabilize the exchange rate and improve the trade balance, the central bank can adjust interest rates. Assuming an increase in interest rates by 2% leads to a 10% appreciation of the currency, a 4% increase in interest rates will lead to a 20% appreciation of the currency. With the assumption that the income elasticity of demand for imports and exports is equal to one, the trade deficit will reduce by $4 billion, which is equivalent to 20% of the initial trade deficit of $10 billion.

Problem 4

A country is experiencing high exchange rate volatility due to speculative capital flows. How can the central bank use exchange rates to stabilize the economy? If the central bank decides to increase the interest rate by 3%, by how much must the currency appreciate to offset the capital outflows, which are currently at $5 billion?

Solution: High exchange rate volatility due to speculative capital flows can destabilize an economy. To stabilize the economy, a central bank can use exchange rate management policies.

If the central bank decides to increase the interest rate by 3%, it can encourage foreign investors to invest in domestic assets, which will cause an appreciation in the currency value, thus offsetting the capital outflows caused by the speculative capital flows.

To determine by how much the currency must appreciate to offset the capital outflows, we need to consider the capital account balance. If the capital outflows are currently at $5 billion, it means that the country has a net capital outflow of $5 billion.

Assuming that the interest rate elasticity of capital flows is equal to one, a 3% increase in interest rates should lead to an appreciation in the currency value that will offset the capital outflows. This is equivalent to saying that a 1% increase in interest rates should lead to an appreciation in the currency by the same percentage.

Therefore, to offset the $5 billion capital outflows caused by the speculative capital flows, the currency must appreciate by 3.33%, which is equal to ($5 billion/0.03) x 100, based on the assumption that the interest rate elasticity of capital flows is equal to one.

In conclusion, the central bank can use exchange rate management policies like increasing interest rates to stabilize the economy and offset the capital outflows caused by speculative capital flows. Assuming a 3% increase in interest rates, the currency must appreciate by 3.33% to offset the $5 billion capital outflows, assuming the interest rate elasticity of capital flows is equal to one.

Problem 5

A developing country has a high external debt and is struggling to meet its payments. How can the central bank adjust exchange rates to improve the country's creditworthiness? If the central bank decides to devalue the currency by 4%, how much will the country's external debt (in US dollars) decrease if the total external debt is $50 billion and the exchange rate originally was 1 to 2 US dollars?

Solution: A developing country with high external debt struggles to pay off its debts. The central bank can use exchange rate management policies to improve the country's creditworthiness and make the debt more manageable.

If the central bank decides to devalue the currency by 4%, it means that the value of the country's currency will decrease by 4% relative to other currencies. This decrease in the value of the currency will reduce the external debt burden in terms of the domestic currency, making it easier for the central bank to pay off the debt in the long run.

To calculate the decrease in the country's external debt in US dollars, we need to convert the original external debt in terms of the original exchange rate. If the original exchange rate was 1 to 2 US dollars, and the total external debt is $50 billion, then the original external debt in terms of the domestic currency is 100 billion units.

After the 4% devaluation, the new exchange rate is 1 to 1.92 US dollars (since the currency value decreased by 4%). Therefore, the new external debt in US dollars is equal to 1.92 times the domestic currency value of $100 billion, which is equal to $192 billion.

Comparing the new external debt in US dollars to the original debt of $50 billion, we can see that the external debt decreased by 62.4% ($50 billion/$192 billion) due to the 4% devaluation of the currency.

Hence, the central bank can use exchange rate management policies like devaluation to improve the country's creditworthiness and reduce the external debt burden. In this case, a 4% devaluation led to a 62.4% decrease in external debt in US dollars, thereby making the debt more manageable for the central bank of the developing country.

Stock in Financial Markets: Case Studies

A country's economy has been experiencing high inflation for the past few quarters. The central bank plans to adjust the stock market as part of its macroeconomic policy to lower inflation. To do so, the central bank will increase the interest rate by 1%. Assuming stocks are currently valued at $20 per share, and the expected returns on a stock are 8%, calculate the fair value of the stock if the interest rate increases to 3%.

Solution:

The fair value of a stock using the dividend discount model is calculated as follows:

Fair value of stock = Expected return / (Interest rate - Expected growth rate)

Given that the expected return on the stock is 8%, and the central bank increases the interest rate to 3%, we can calculate the fair value of the stock as follows:

Fair value of stock = 8% / (3% - 0%)

Fair value of stock = $266.67 per share

Therefore, assuming the interest rate increases by 1%, the fair value of the stock would decrease to $266.67 per share from $750 per share. This would reduce the demand for stocks and help lower inflation.

Case 2

A country's economy is experiencing high unemployment due to the recent recession. The central bank plans to adjust the stock market as part of its macroeconomic policy to reduce unemployment rates. To do so, the central bank will decrease the interest rate by 1%. Assuming stocks are currently valued at $50 per share, and the expected returns on a stock are 10%, calculate the fair value of the stock if the interest rate decreases to 2%.

Solution:

The fair value of a stock using the dividend discount model is calculated as follows:

Fair value of stock = Expected return / (Interest rate - Expected growth rate)

Given that the expected return on the stock is 10%, and the central bank decreases the interest rate to 2%, we can calculate the fair value of the stock as follows:

Fair value of stock = 10% / (2% - 0%)

Fair value of stock = $500 per share

Therefore, assuming the interest rate decreases by 1%, the fair value of the stock would increase to $500 per share from $50 per share. This would increase the demand for stocks and help reduce unemployment rates.

Corporate Bond in Financial Markets:

A company wants to issue corporate bonds to raise capital to expand its business operations. However, before issuing the bonds, the company's management wants to evaluate the risk-return tradeoff associated with the issuance. Assume that the current yield on a bond with similar characteristics and risk profile is 5%, and the management estimates that the required return on the company's bond is 7%. What must be the coupon rate on the bond to make it attractive to investors?

Solution:

The coupon rate on a bond refers to the annual percentage payment that a bond issuer pays to the bondholder.

To calculate the coupon rate required for the bond, we need to use the formula:

Yield to maturity = (Annual interest payment + (Bond price - Face value) / Time to maturity) / ((Bond price + Face value) / 2)

Given that the current yield on a similar bond is 5%, and the management estimates that the required return on the company's bond is 7%, we can estimate the price of the bond as follows:

Price of bond = Annual interest payment / Required yield

Price of bond = $70 / 0.07

Price of bond = $1,000

Now using the above values in the formula, the coupon rate required for the bond would be:

Coupon rate = (70 + (1000-1000)/10) / ((1000+1000)/2)

Coupon rate = 7.70%

Therefore, the coupon rate required for the bond to be issued by the company is 7.70%.

Case 2

A company issued a bond with a face value of $1,000 and a coupon rate of 6% three years ago, when interest rates were at 8%. Now, due to the recession in the economy, the central bank has lowered interest rates to 3%, and the company is considering issuing new bonds. The company wants to know what the new bond's coupon rate should be to match the current yield on similar bonds. What must be the new bond's coupon rate to make it equivalent to a bond with a similar risk profile?

Solution:

The current yield on a bond with a similar risk profile will depend on current market interest rates.

To calculate the new bond's coupon rate required to match the current yield, we need to use the formula:

Bond price = Annual interest payment / Yield to maturity

Since the current yield on a bond with a similar risk profile is not given, we will assume that it's equivalent to the current market rate of 3%.

Using the above values in the formula, the new bond's coupon rate required would be:

Coupon rate = (Bond price x Yield to maturity) / Face value

Coupon rate = ($1,000 x 0.03) / $1,000

Coupon rate = 3%

Therefore, the new bond's coupon rate required to match the current yield on similar bonds is 3%, which is lower than the original bond's coupon rate of 6%. This shows that as interest rates decline, the value of previously issued bonds increases, making new bond issuances more expensive.

Manage Exposure to Foreign Currency Risk: Case Studies

You are a financial manager of a multinational corporation that imports raw materials from Japan to produce goods to sell in the United States. The company expects to import JPY 125 million worth of raw materials next quarter, and the current spot exchange rate is 1 USD = 110 JPY. If the U.S. Federal Reserve decides to raise interest rates to combat inflation, causing the U.S. dollar to appreciate, and the new exchange rate becomes 1 USD = 114 JPY, what is the impact on your company's cost of importing raw materials, and what hedging strategies could you utilize to manage the exposure to foreign currency risk?

Solution:

Given:
Amount of raw materials imported next quarter = JPY 125 million
Current spot exchange rate = 1 USD = 110 JPY
Expected new exchange rate after the U.S. Federal Reserve raises interest rates = 1 USD = 114 JPY

To find:
Impact on the company's cost of importing raw materials and hedging strategies that can be utilized to manage exposure to foreign currency risk

Step 1: Calculate the company's cost of importing raw materials under the current exchange rate
125 million JPY / 110 = USD 1,136,364.00

The cost of importing raw materials with the current exchange rate is USD 1,136,364.00.

Step 2: Calculate the new cost of raw materials if the exchange rate changes to 1 USD = 114 JPY
125 million JPY / 114 = USD 1,096,491.00

If the exchange rate changes to 1 USD = 114 JPY, the new cost of importing raw materials would be USD 1,096,491.00.

Step 3: Calculate the impact of the exchange rate change on the company's cost of importing raw materials
1,136,364.00 - 1,096,491.00 = USD 39,873.00 (decrease)

The company would save USD 39,873.00 on the cost of importing raw materials if the exchange rate changes to 1 USD = 114 JPY.

Step 4: Hedging strategies to manage exposure to foreign currency risk

There are various hedging strategies that can be used to manage exposure to foreign currency risk. Some of the common strategies are:

- Forward contract: In a forward contract, the company agrees to buy or sell foreign currency at a predetermined exchange rate at a future date. This helps to lock in the exchange rate and reduce the risk of exchange rate fluctuations.
- Option contract: An option contract gives the company the right, but not the obligation, to buy or sell foreign currency at a predetermined exchange rate at a future date. This provides flexibility and helps to reduce the risk of unfavorable exchange rate movements.
- Money market hedge: A money market hedge involves borrowing or investing in a foreign currency to offset the risk of exchange rate movements. This can be a cost-effective way to manage exposure to foreign currency risk.

In conclusion, the company's cost of importing raw materials would decrease if the exchange rate changes to 1 USD = 114 JPY due to the U.S. Federal Reserve's decision to raise interest rates. Hedging strategies such as forward contracts, option contracts, and money market hedges can be utilized to manage exposure to foreign currency risk.

Case Based on Trade Policy Target

Your company is a Swiss exporter selling goods to customers in the United Kingdom. The company has GBP 2 million in receivables due in 6 months, and the current spot exchange rate is 1 CHF = 0.85 GBP. The United Kingdom and the European Union are in the process of negotiating a trade agreement, and a no-deal Brexit scenario is looming. If the trade negotiations fail, and the sterling plummets, becoming 1 CHF = 0.75 GBP, what impact does this have on the Swiss company's profitability, and what strategies can the company use to manage exposure to foreign currency risk?

Solution:

Given:
Amount of receivables due in 6 months = GBP 2 million
Current spot exchange rate = 1 CHF = 0.85 GBP
Expected new exchange rate if the no-deal Brexit happens = 1 CHF = 0.75 GBP

To find:
Impact on Swiss company's profitability and strategies to manage exposure to foreign currency risk

Step 1: Calculate the value of the receivables due in 6 months under the current exchange rate
2 million GBP x 0.85 CHF/GBP = 1.7 million CHF

The value of the receivables due in 6 months under the current exchange rate is 1.7 million CHF.

Step 2: Calculate the new value of the receivables if the exchange rate changes to 1 CHF = 0.75 GBP
2 million GBP x 0.75 CHF/GBP = 1.5 million CHF

If the exchange rate changes to 1 CHF = 0.75 GBP due to the no-deal Brexit scenario, the new value of the receivables due in 6 months would be 1.5 million CHF.

Step 3: Calculate the impact of the exchange rate change on the Swiss company's profitability
1.7 million CHF - 1.5 million CHF = 0.2 million CHF (decrease)

The Swiss company would lose 0.2 million CHF of profitability if the exchange rate changes to 1 CHF = 0.75 GBP due to the no-deal Brexit scenario.

Step 4: Strategies to manage exposure to foreign currency risk
Some of the hedging strategies that the Swiss company can use to manage exposure to foreign currency risk in this situation include:

- Forward contract: Entering into a forward contract with a bank or a counterparty to protect against unfavorable exchange rate movements for the receivables due in 6 months.
- Option contract: Buying a put option on GBP/CHF to hedge against the potential decline in the value of the GBP due to the no-deal Brexit scenario.
- Invoice in CHF: Converting the invoices from GBP to CHF to eliminate foreign currency risk.

In conclusion, the Swiss company's profitability would decrease if the sterling plummets and the exchange rate changes to 1 CHF = 0.75 GBP due to the no-deal Brexit scenario. The hedging strategies that can be used to manage exposure to foreign currency risk include forward contracts, option contracts, and invoicing in CHF.

Case Based on Monetary Policy Target

Your company has acquired a Canadian subsidiary and expects to collect CAD 10 million in dividends next year. The current spot exchange rate is 1 USD = 1.25 CAD. The Bank of Canada has decided to increase the money supply and lower interest rates to stimulate the economy, causing the Canadian dollar to depreciate, and the new exchange rate becomes 1 USD = 1.33 CAD. What is the impact of the Bank of Canada's decision on your company's cash inflow, and what financial instruments could be used to mitigate exposure to foreign currency risk?

Solution:

Given:
Dividends due in CAD next year = CAD 10 million
Current spot exchange rate = 1 USD = 1.25 CAD
Expected new exchange rate after the Bank of Canada's decision = 1 USD = 1.33 CAD

To find:
Impact on the company's cash inflow and financial instruments that can be used to mitigate exposure to foreign currency risk

Step 1: Convert CAD 10 million to USD at the current exchange rate
10 million CAD x 1.25 USD/CAD = USD 8,000,000

The amount of dividends due in CAD next year is USD 8,000,000 at the current exchange rate.

Step 2: Convert CAD 10 million to USD at the expected new exchange rate
10 million CAD x 1.33 USD/CAD = USD 7,518,796.99

If the Bank of Canada's decision causes the Canadian dollar to depreciate and the exchange rate changes to 1 USD = 1.33 CAD, the amount of dividends due would decrease to USD 7,518,796.99.

Step 3: Calculate the impact of the exchange rate change on the company's cash inflow
8,000,000 - 7,518,796.99 = USD 481,203.01 (loss)

The company would lose USD 481,203.01 in cash inflow due to the depreciation of the Canadian dollar caused by the Bank of Canada's decision.

Step 4: Financial instruments to manage exposure to foreign currency risk
To manage exposure to foreign currency risk, the company can use the following strategies:

- Forward contract: Entering into a forward contract with a bank or a counterparty to lock in the exchange rate for the dividends due, thereby eliminating foreign currency risk.
- Swap contract: Entering into a currency swap, where the company exchanges CAD for USD at the current exchange rate, and then exchanges USD for CAD at a fixed rate in the future to eliminate foreign currency risk.
- Option contract: Buying a call option on CAD/USD to hedge against the potential appreciation of the Canadian dollar, or buying a put option on USD/CAD to hedge against the potential depreciation of the Canadian dollar.

In conclusion, the Bank of Canada's decision to increase the money supply and lower interest rates would cause the Canadian dollar to depreciate and affect the company's cash inflow from its Canadian subsidiary. Hedging strategies such as forward contracts, swap contracts, and option contracts can be used to mitigate exposure to foreign currency risk.

Interest-Bearing Instruments of the Money Market

Treasury Bills: Suppose the inflation rate is expected to rise from 2% to 4%, and an investor wants to purchase a T-bill with a face value of $100,000 and a maturity of 91 days. If the current risk-free rate of return is 1%, what is the price of the T-bill?

Solution:
The current risk-free rate of return = 1%
Annual inflation rate = 4%
Number of days until maturity = 91/365 = 0.2493

The nominal rate of return required to purchase the T-bill can be calculated using the Fisher equation:
Nominal interest rate = (1 + real interest rate) x (1 + inflation rate) - 1
Nominal interest rate = (1 + 0.01) x (1 + 0.04) - 1 = 5.15%

The price of the T-bill can be calculated using the following formula:
Price = Face Value / (1 + (Nominal Interest Rate x Time until Maturity))
Price = 100,000 / (1 + (0.0515 x 0.2493)) = $99,240.80

Therefore, the price of the T-bill is $99,240.80.

Case 2: Monetary Policy Target
Suppose the Federal Reserve decides to increase interest rates to combat inflation, causing the T-bill yield to increase from 2% to 3%. If an investor purchases a T-bill with a face value of $1,000,000 and a maturity of 182 days, what is the investor's yield to maturity?

Solution:
Face value of the T-bill = $1,000,000
T-bill yield = 3%
Number of days until maturity = 182/365 = 0.4986

The yield to maturity on the T-bill can be calculated using the following formula:
Yield to Maturity = Face Value - Purchase Price / Purchase Price x 365 / Days until Maturity

Purchase Price = Face Value / (1 + (T-bill yield x Time until Maturity))
Purchase Price = 1000000 / (1 + (0.03 x 0.4986)) = $985,746.09
Yield to Maturity = 1000000 - 985746.09 / 985746.09 x 365 / 182 = 6.18%

Therefore, the investor's yield to maturity on the T-bill is 6.18%.

Certificates of Deposit (CDs):

Inflation Targeting: Suppose John invests $10,000 in a CD with a maturity of 2 years and an interest rate of 2.5% per annum. The government's central bank is targeting a 2% annual inflation rate. Calculate John's real interest rate after taking inflation into account.

Solution: The inflation rate is 2% per annum, so after two years, the cumulative inflation rate is 4%. The real interest rate formula is: (1 + nominal interest rate) / (1 + inflation rate) - 1. Plugging in the numbers:

(1 + 2.5%) / (1 + 4%) - 1 = -1.44%

Therefore, John's real interest rate after taking inflation into account is -1.44%.

Case 2: Expansionary Monetary Policy

Suppose Sarah invests $5,000 in a CD with a maturity of 1 year and an interest rate of 1.8% per annum. The government's central bank is pursuing an expansionary monetary policy by lowering interest rates. Calculate the new interest rate on Sarah's CD if the central bank cuts interest rates by 0.25%.

Solution: A 0.25% cut in interest rates means Sarah's CD interest rate will decrease by 0.25%. The new interest rate on Sarah's CD after the interest rate cut is:

1.8% - 0.25% = 1.55%

Therefore, the new interest rate on Sarah's CD is 1.55%.

Commercial paper:

Problem 1: The government is implementing contractionary monetary policy, which aims to decrease the money supply and reduce inflation. As a result, interest rates are expected to rise.

ABC Corporation needs to borrow $500,000 to cover its immediate need for working capital. Instead of going to a bank for a loan, ABC decides to issue commercial paper with a 90-day maturity period. The current interest rate on commercial paper is 2.5%. What will be the total interest cost for ABC Corporation when the commercial paper is due?

Calculation:
Interest = Principal x Rate x Time
= $500,000 x 2.5% x (90/360)
= $3,125

Answer: The total interest cost for ABC Corporation will be $3,125 when the commercial paper is due.

Scenario 2:

The government is implementing expansionary fiscal policy, which aims to increase spending and stimulate economic growth. As a result, interest rates are expected to decrease. XYZ Corporation has the option to issue commercial paper with a 180-day maturity period to finance its expanding business. The current interest rate on commercial paper is 1.5%. If XYZ Corporation decides to issue the commercial paper, how much interest revenue will the investors earn on a $100,000 investment?

Calculation:
Interest = Principal x Rate x Time
= $100,000 x 1.5% x (180/360)
= $750

Answer: The investors will earn $750 in interest revenue on a $100,000 investment in the commercial paper issued by XYZ Corporation.

Banker's acceptances:

Case 1: The government is implementing expansionary fiscal policy, which aims to increase spending and stimulate economic growth. As a result, interest rates are expected to decrease. ABC Corporation needs to purchase $250,000 worth of raw materials from its supplier. Instead of paying cash, ABC decides to use a banker's acceptance with a discount rate of 3.5%. If the maturity of the banker's acceptance is 60 days, what is the effective interest rate paid by ABC Corporation?

Calculation:
Effective interest rate = (Discount amount / Face value) x (365 / Days to maturity)
Discount amount = Face value x Discount rate x (Days to maturity / 360)
Discount amount = $250,000 x 3.5% x (60/360) = $1,458.33
Face value = $250,000
Days to maturity = 60
Effective interest rate = ($1,458.33 / $250,000) x (365 / 60)
Effective interest rate = 8.91%

Answer: The effective interest rate paid by ABC Corporation is 8.91% when using a banker's acceptance to purchase the raw materials.

Scenario 2

The government is implementing contractionary monetary policy, which aims to decrease the money supply and reduce inflation. As a result, interest rates are expected to rise. XYZ Corporation needs to purchase $150,000 worth of inventory from its supplier. Instead of paying cash, XYZ decides to use a banker's acceptance with a discount rate of 4%. If the maturity of the banker's acceptance is 90 days, what is the amount of funds that XYZ Corporation effectively borrows?

Calculation:
Face value = $150,000

Discount rate = 4%
Days to maturity = 90
Discount amount = Face value x Discount rate x (Days to maturity / 360)
Discount amount = $150,000 x 4% x (90/360) = $1,200
Effective loan amount = Face value - Discount amount
Effective loan amount = $150,000 - $1,200

Answer: The amount of funds that XYZ Corporation effectively borrows is $148,800 when using a banker's acceptance to purchase the inventory.

Repurchase agreements (repos):

Question 1: Assume that the Federal Reserve Bank conducts a repo agreement with a commercial bank. The repo is for a term of 10 days, and the commercial bank purchases Treasury bills from the Fed worth $1,000,000. The agreed repo rate is 2%. What will be the total amount that the commercial bank is required to pay the Fed at the end of the term?

Solution:
Repo interest = Principal x Repo rate x Time
= $1,000,000 x 2% x 10/360 = $5,556

Total amount paid by the commercial bank = Principal + Repo interest
= $1,000,000 + $5,556 = $1,005,556

Question 2

Suppose the government wants to increase the money supply in the economy. To do so, the Fed starts conducting repos with commercial banks. The repo term is 14 days, and the banks purchase Treasury bonds worth $2,500,000 at a repo rate of 1.5%. Calculate how much excess reserves will be created in the banking system due to this repo.

Solution:
Repo interest = Principal x Repo rate x Time
= $2,500,000 x 1.5% x 14/360 = $24,305.56

Excess reserves created = Principal - Repo interest
= $2,500,000 - $24,305.56 = $2,475,694.44

Thus, the excess reserves created in the banking system due to this repo are $2,475,694.44.

Federal funds:

Question 1: Assume that there is excess money supply in the economy due to a slack in demand. For this reason, the Fed wants to reduce the money supply. To do so, it increases the Federal Funds target rate from 1.5% to 2%. If a bank has borrowed $10 million in Federal Funds and the interest rate on the loan is 1.75%, how much interest will the bank need to pay if it rolls over the loan for a period of six months?

Solution:
Interest paid on Federal funds loan = Principal x Federal funds rate x Time
= $10,000,000 x 1.75% x 6/12 = $87,500

Thus, the bank needs to pay an interest of $87,500 on the loan.

Question 2

Suppose there is a slowdown in the economy, unemployment is high, and the government wants to increase the money supply to stimulate economic growth. To achieve this, the Fed lowers the Federal Funds target rate from 2% to 1.5%. If a bank has borrowed $5 million in Federal Funds and the interest rate on the loan is 1.25%, how much will the interest cost be for the bank if it rolls over the loan for 30 days?

Solution:
Interest paid on Federal funds loan = Principal x Federal funds rate x Time
= $5,000,000 x 1.25% x 30/360 = $10,417

Thus, the bank will need to pay an interest of $10,417 on the loan.

Municipal notes:

Question 1: Suppose the government of a particular state wants to finance infrastructure projects such as bridge construction and repair using Municipal Notes. The government issues 1-year Municipal Notes worth $500,000 at an interest rate of 2.5%. After one year, what will be the total payable amount to the investors?

Solution:
Interest on Municipal Notes = Principal x Rate x Time
= $500,000 x 2.5% x 1 = $12,500

Total payable amount at maturity = Principal + Interest
= $500,000 + $12,500 = $512,500

Therefore, the total payable amount to the investors at maturity will be $512,500.

Question 2

Assume that the economy is in a slowdown, and there is a liquidity shortage in the market. To overcome this, the Central Bank decides to lower interest rates. As a result, the interest rates of Municipal Notes issued by state and municipal governments also fall. Suppose the government of a state wants to issue 6-month Municipal Notes worth $1,000,000 at an interest rate of 1.5%. What will be the total interest payments on the Municipal Notes over a 6-month period?

Solution:
Interest on Municipal Notes = Principal x Rate x Time
= $1,000,000 x 1.5% x 6/12 = $7,500

Thus, the total interest payments on the Municipal Notes over a 6-month period will be $7,500.

Negotiable certificates of deposit (NCDs):

Question 1: Assume that an investor purchases an NCD with a face value of $50,000 and a maturity period of six months. The NCD has an interest rate of 1.5%. If the investor decides to sell the NCD after three months on the secondary market to another investor with a buyer's fee of 0.5%, how much will the investor receive from the sale?

Solution:
Interest earned on NCD: Principal x Rate x Time
= $50,000 x 1.5% x 3/12 = $625

Total value of the NCD at the time of sale: Principal + Interest earned
= $50,000 + $625 = $50,625

Buyer's fee: 0.5% of $50,625 = $253.12

Amount received by the investor: $50,625 - $253.12 = $50,371.88

Therefore, the investor will receive $50,371.88 from the sale of the NCD.

Question 2

Suppose the central bank wants to increase the supply of money in the market to stimulate economic growth. It does so by lowering interest rates, which leads to a fall in returns on CDs. Assume that an investor purchases a 1-year NCD with a face value of $100,000 and an interest rate of 2.5%. If the investor sells the NCD after six months to another investor with a seller's fee of 0.75%, how much money will the investor receive from the sale?

Solution:
Interest earned on NCD: Principal x Rate x Time
= $100,000 x 2.5% x 6/12 = $2,500

Total value of the NCD at the time of sale: Principal + Interest earned

$$= \$100{,}000 + \$2{,}500 = \$102{,}500$$

Seller's fee: 0.75% of $102,500 = $768.75

Amount received by the investor: $102,500 - $768.75 = $101,731.25

Thus, the investor will receive $101,731.25 from the sale of the NCD.

Eurodollar deposits:

Question 1: Assume that a U.S. company has a Eurodollar deposit of $500,000 with a foreign bank at an annual interest rate of 1.8%. The company requires the funds in six months to make a payment. How much money will the company receive after interest at the time of maturity if the company has to pay a withholding tax of 20% on the interest earned on the deposit?

Solution:
Interest earned on the deposit: Principal x Rate x Time
= $500,000 x 1.8% x 6/12 = $4,500

Amount of interest after the tax deduction: $4,500 - ($4,500 x 20%) = $3,600

Amount to be received by the company at maturity: Principal + Interest earned after tax deduction
= $500,000 + $3,600 = $503,600

Therefore, the company will receive $503,600 at the end of the deposit term after deducting the withholding tax.

Question 2

Assume that there is a shortage of dollar supply in the market. To address this situation, the Fed reduces the Federal Funds rate, which leads to a decrease in the interest rates on Eurodollar deposits. Suppose a foreign bank offers a 3-year Eurodollar deposit with an interest rate of 2.5% p.a. to U.S bank. If the U.S. bank invests $2 million in the Eurodollar deposit, how much interest will it earn at maturity?

Solution:
Interest earned on the deposit: Principal x Rate x Time
= $2,000,000 x 2.5% x 3 = $150,000

Thus, the U.S. bank will earn an interest of $150,000 at maturity.

Therefore, the U.S. bank's Eurodollar deposit with the foreign bank will yield $150,000 after 3 years based on the interest rate offered during the deposit term.

Money market funds:

Question 1: Suppose a mutual fund company offers a Money Market Fund with an objective to provide higher returns than a savings account while maintaining low risk. The fund invests in short-term, low-risk securities such as Treasury bills and commercial paper. Assume that the Money Market Fund has $2 million in assets and an expense ratio of 0.5%. If the fund earns 2.0% in annual returns after deducting expenses, how much will be the investor's return on investment (ROI)?

Solution:
Amount of deductions due to expenses: $2,000,000 x 0.5% = $10,000

Total earnings: $2,000,000 x 2.0% = $40,000

Net earnings after expenses: $40,000 - $10,000 = $30,000

ROI = Net earnings / Initial investment x 100%

$$= \$30{,}000 / \$2{,}000{,}000 \times 100\% = 1.5\%$$

Therefore, the investor's ROI in the Money Market Fund will be 1.5%.

Question 2

Assume that the economy is booming, and the central bank wants to reduce liquidity in the market to avoid inflation. To achieve this, it increases the interest rates of Treasury bills and commercial paper held by Money Market Funds. An investor has invested $50,000 in a Money Market Fund with a current yield of 2.5%. If the fund adjusts its portfolio and invests in higher-yielding securities with a yield of 3.0%, what will be the increase in earnings of the investor after a year?

Solution:

Current annual earnings with 2.5% yield: $50,000 x 2.5% = $1,250

Future annual earnings with 3.0% yield: $50,000 x 3.0% = $1,500

Increase in earnings after a year: $1,500 - $1,250 = $250

Thus, there will be an increase of $250 in earnings for the investor after a year due to the increase in the yield of the Money Market Fund.

Derivative Products: Scenarios

Suppose you are a trader who is considering a futures contract on crude oil. The current market price for crude oil futures is $90 per barrel, and the contract expires in six months. However, the Federal Reserve has just announced that it intends to decrease interest rates in the coming months in order to boost the economy. Assuming that this policy change will increase demand for oil, you estimate that the market price for crude oil futures will rise by 10% over the next six months. What price should you expect to pay for the futures contract? Show your calculation.

Solution: A step-by-step solution to the given problem

Step 1: Determine the current market price for crude oil futures - It's given in the problem as $90 per barrel.

Step 2: Determine the expected increase in price - It's given in the problem as 10% over the next six months.

Step 3: Calculate the expected future market price - Future market price equals the current market price plus the expected increase in price.

Expected future market price = $90 + (10% of $90) = $99 per barrel

Step 4: Determine the value of the futures contract - The value of the futures contract equals the expected future market price multiplied by the number of barrels covered in the contract.

Assuming that the futures contract covers 100 barrels, its value would be:

Value of the futures contract = $99 per barrel x 100 barrels = $9,900

Therefore, the trader should expect to pay $9,900 for the futures contract.

Scenario 2

Suppose you are a soybean farmer who is considering a futures contract on soybeans. The current market price for soybean futures is $10 per bushel, and the contract expires in three months. However, the government has just announced that it will be implementing tariffs on soybean imports in order to protect domestic farmers. You estimate that this policy will decrease the demand for soybeans by 20% over the next three months. What price should you expect to receive for your soybeans if you sell them in the spot market in three months? Show your calculation.

Solution: A step-by-step solution to the given problem -

Step 1: Determine the current market price for soybean futures - It's given in the problem as $10 per bushel.

Step 2: Determine the expected decrease in demand - It's given in the problem as 20% over the next three months.

Step 3: Calculate the expected future market price - Future market price equals the current market price minus the percentage decrease in demand.

Expected future market price = $10 - (20% of $10) = $8 per bushel

Step 4: Determine the spot market price - The spot market price is the price that the farmer will receive for selling the soybeans in the open market.

Assuming that the spot market price is equal to the expected future market price, the farmer can expect to receive $8 per bushel for the soybeans.

Please note that this is a simplified calculation and does not consider factors such as transaction costs, margin requirements, and other risks associated with futures trading. It is important to thoroughly understand the concepts and calculations involved in futures contracts before engaging in trading activities.

Options Contracts:

Question 1: Suppose you are an investor who is considering an options contract on a tech company's stock. The current market price for the stock is $100 per share, and the options contract expires in three months. However, the Federal Reserve has just announced that it will be raising interest rates in order to combat inflation. Assuming that this policy change will decrease demand for stocks, you estimate that the market price for the company's stock will decline by 5% over the next three months. What would be your profit or loss if you purchase a put option with a strike price of $95 per share for a premium of $2 per share? Show your calculation.

Solution: A step-by-step solution to the given problem

Step 1: Determine the current market price for the tech company's stock - It's given in the problem as $100 per share.

Step 2: Estimate the expected decline in the market price - It's given in the problem as 5% over the next three months.

Step 3: Calculate the expected future price for the stock - Future price equals the current market price minus the expected decline.

Expected future price = $100 - (5% of $100) = $95 per share

Step 4: Determine the value of the put option - The value of the put option equals the strike price minus the expected future price.

Value of the put option = $95 - $95 = $0 per share

Step 5: Calculate the total cost of the put option - The total cost of the put option is the premium paid multiplied by the number of shares covered in the option contract.

Assuming that the put option covers 100 shares, its total cost would be:

Total cost of the put option = $2 per share x 100 shares = $200

Step 6: Determine the profit or loss - The profit or loss equals the value of the option minus the total cost of the option.

Profit or loss = $0 - $200 = -$200 (Loss)

Therefore, in this scenario, the investor would incur a loss of $200 if they purchase a put option with a strike price of $95 per share for a premium of $2 per share.

Scenario 2

Suppose you are a business owner who is considering an options contract on gold. The current market price for gold futures is $1,500 per ounce, and the options contract expires in six months. The government has just announced that it intends to implement monetary stimulus in order to boost economic growth. Assuming that this policy change will increase demand for gold, you estimate that the market price for gold futures will rise by 10% over the next six months. What would be your profit or loss if you purchase a call option with a strike price of $1,700 per ounce for a premium of $50 per ounce? Show your calculation.

Solution: A step-by-step solution to the given problem:

Step 1: Determine the current market price for gold futures - It's given in the problem as $1,500 per ounce.

Step 2: Estimate the expected increase in the market price - It's given in the problem as 10% over the next six months.

Step 3: Calculate the expected future market price for gold - Future market price equals the current market price plus the expected increase.

Expected future market price = $1,500 + (10% of $1,500) = $1,650 per ounce

Step 4: Determine the value of the call option - The value of the call option equals the expected future market price minus the strike price.

Value of the call option = $1,650 - $1,700 = $0 per ounce (since the strike price is higher than the expected future market price)

Step 5: Calculate the total cost of the call option - The total cost of the call option is the premium paid multiplied by the number of ounces covered in the option contract.

Assuming that the call option covers 100 ounces, its total cost would be:

Total cost of the call option = $50 per ounce x 100 ounces = $5,000

Step 6: Determine the profit or loss - The profit or loss equals the value of the option minus the total cost of the option.

Profit or loss = $0 - $5,000 = -$5,000 (Loss)

Therefore, in this scenario, the business owner would incur a loss of $5,000 if they purchase a call option with a strike price of $1,700 per ounce for a premium of $50 per ounce.

Forward Contracts:

Scenario 1: Suppose you are an importer who needs to purchase a raw material for your business six months from now. The current market price for the raw material is $100 per unit, and you estimate that the market price will increase by 12% over the next six months due to a tightening supply chain caused by government regulations. What should be the forward price for the raw material to ensure that you would break even on this transaction? Show your calculation.

Solution: As an importer, you need to purchase a raw material six months from now, and you are concerned that the market price will rise by 12%. To protect yourself from the increase, you can enter into a forward contract with a supplier to purchase the raw material at a fixed price.

To determine the forward price that would cause you to break even on this transaction, you must first calculate the future market price of the raw material. If the current price is $100, and it will increase by 12%, the future price will be:

Future Price = Current Price x (1 + Rate of Increase)
Future Price = $100 x (1 + 0.12)
Future Price = $112

Now that you have determined the future market price of the raw material, you can calculate the forward price that would allow you to break even.

Break Even Forward Price = Future Price / (1 + Risk-free Rate)^(Time to Delivery)

Assuming a risk-free rate of 2% and a delivery time of 6 months, the break-even forward price would be:

Break Even Forward Price = $112 / (1 + 0.02)^(6/12)
Break Even Forward Price = $106.81

Therefore, if you enter into a forward contract to purchase the raw material at $106.81 per unit, you will break even on this transaction, since the future market price is expected to be $112. If the market price ends up being higher than $112, you will have saved money by locking in a lower price through the forward contract. However, if the market price ends up being lower than $112, you will have lost the opportunity to purchase the raw material at a lower price.

Scenario 2

Suppose you are an exporter who needs to sell a product abroad in one year. The current market price for the product is $500 per unit, but you estimate that the market price will decrease by 8% over the next year due to a decrease in global demand as a result of high tariffs imposed by the government. You enter into a forward contract with a buyer at a price of $510 per unit. What will be your profit or loss on this transaction when you sell the product in a year? Show your calculation.

Solution: As an exporter, you are concerned about a potential decrease in the market price of your product due to global demand decreasing as a result of high tariffs imposed by the government. You have entered into a forward contract with a buyer to sell the product at a fixed price of $510 per unit, which is higher than the current price of $500 per unit.

To determine your profit or loss on this transaction, you need to compare the forward price of $510 with the future market price of the product. If the market price decreases as you estimate, you would make a profit on this transaction.

Future Price = Current Price x (1 - Rate of Decrease)
Future Price = $500 x (1 - 0.08)
Future Price = $460

The future market price of the product is expected to be $460.

To calculate your profit or loss on this transaction, you can subtract the forward price from the future market price:

$$\text{Profit/Loss} = \text{Future Price} - \text{Forward Price}$$
$$\text{Profit/Loss} = \$460 - \$510$$
$$\text{Profit/Loss} = -\$50$$

Your profit or loss on this transaction is -$50 per unit, which means that you will incur a loss of $50 per unit when you sell the product in a year. This is because the future market price is lower than the price you agreed to in the forward contract.

Swaps Contracts

Suppose you are a multinational corporation based in the United States and you have a subsidiary in the Eurozone. Your subsidiary is concerned about the currency risk associated with receiving payments in Euros and wants to hedge against currency fluctuations. You decide to enter into a currency swap agreement with a counterparty who agrees to exchange payments denominated in Euros for payments denominated in US dollars over the next three years. Assume that the current spot exchange rate is $1.20 per Euro, and the agreed-upon exchange rate for the currency swap is $1.15 per Euro. After one year, the spot exchange rate becomes $1.25 per Euro. What is the net cash flow that you will pay or receive at the end of the year?

Solution:

The multinational corporation has a subsidiary in the Eurozone that is concerned about the currency risk associated with receiving payments in Euros. To protect themselves, they enter into a currency swap contract with a counterparty, agreeing to exchange payments in Euros for payments in US dollars over a period of three years.

Assuming the current spot exchange rate between Euros and US dollars is $1.20 per Euro, the agreed-upon exchange rate for the currency swap contract must be lower than $1.20 per Euro for it to be profitable for the corporation.

After one year, the spot exchange rate increases from $1.20 to $1.25 per Euro. This means that the value of the Euro has increased relative to the US dollar.

To calculate the net cash flow at the end of the year, we need to compare the spot exchange rate with the agreed-upon exchange rate in the currency swap.

In the currency swap, the multinational corporation agreed to exchange Euros for US dollars at an exchange rate of $1.15 per Euro. However, due to the change in the spot exchange rate, they can now exchange Euros for US dollars at a spot exchange rate of $1.25 per Euro.

To calculate their net cash flow, we need to subtract the value of the payments that they will receive in US dollars from the value of the payments that they must make in Euros.

Net Cash Flow = Payments Received − Payments Made
Net Cash Flow = (Amount of Euros x Spot Exchange Rate) − (Amount of Euros x Agreed-upon Exchange Rate)
Net Cash Flow = (Amount of Euros x $1.25 per Euro) − (Amount of Euros x $1.15 per Euro)

Assuming that the amount of Euros in the currency swap is 100,000 Euros, the calculation would be:

Net Cash Flow = (100,000 Euros x $1.25 per Euro) − (100,000 Euros x $1.15 per Euro)
Net Cash Flow = $125,000 − $115,000
Net Cash Flow = $10,000

Therefore, the net cash flow that the multinational corporation will receive from the currency swap at the end of the year is $10,000. They benefit from the currency swap agreement because they exchanged Euros for US dollars at a more favorable exchange rate of $1.25 per Euro instead of the agreed-upon exchange rate of $1.15 per Euro, and the counterparty takes on the currency risk.

Interest Rate Derivatives

Suppose the central bank of a country decides to reduce interest rates in order to stimulate economic growth. As a financial manager, you know that this policy may impact your company's cash flows, particularly if you have fixed-rate debt. To mitigate this risk, you decide to enter into an interest rate swap with a counterparty. Your company agrees to pay a fixed interest rate of 4% per year on a notional amount of $10 million, in exchange for receiving a floating interest rate based on the 3-month LIBOR rate. The current 3-month LIBOR rate is 2.5%. If the central bank reduces interest rates by 50 basis points, what would be the net cash flow impact on your company in the next quarter and how much would you save through the interest rate swap?

Solution:

To solve this problem, we need to first calculate the floating interest rate that the company will receive under the swap agreement. Since the 3-month LIBOR rate is used as the benchmark, the floating rate for the next quarter would be 2.5% - 0.5% = 2.0%.

Next, we need to calculate the net cash flow impact on the company. If the company had not entered into the swap agreement, it would have to pay fixed interest at a rate of 4%. However, since the floating interest rate has decreased to 2.0%, the company would now save 4.0% - 2.0% = 2.0% on the notional amount of $10 million. The company, therefore, would save a total of $10 million x 2.0% = $200,000 in the next quarter through the interest rate swap.

Credit Derivatives

Your company has invested in corporate bonds issued by a telecommunication company that has a credit rating of BB. You are worried about the potential default risk of the company, particularly after the central bank of the country has announced an increase in interest rates. To protect your investment, you decide to buy credit default swaps (CDS) on the telecommunication company's bonds. Assuming the fair value of the 5-year CDS is 250 basis points per year, and the notional value of the bonds is $5 million, what would be the net cash flow impact on your company if the telecommunication company defaults within the next 3 years?

Solution:

To solve this problem, we first need to calculate the premium payment on the CDS. The fair value of the CDS is given as 250 basis points per year, which translates to a premium payment of 2.5% x $5 million = $125,000 per year.

Assuming the telecommunication company defaults in year 2, the net cash flow impact on your company would be as follows:

- The telecommunication company would default on the bond, which has a market value of $5 million.
- As the bondholder, your company would receive a payout of $5 million from the CDS seller.
- However, you would have paid $125,000 x 2 = $250,000 in premium payments for the CDS.
- Therefore, your net cash flow impact would be $5 million - $250,000 = $4.75 million.

If the telecommunication company defaults after 3 years, then the CDS would have expired and your company would have lost the premium payments paid for the CDS. In such a case, the net cash flow impact would be zero as your company would not receive any payout from the CDS seller.

Currency Derivatives

Your company is a US-based exporter that sells goods to customers in Europe. You are worried about currency exchange rate fluctuations, particularly after the central bank of Europe has announced a quantitative easing (QE) program which may lead to a depreciation of the euro. To hedge your currency risk, you decide to enter into a forward contract to sell euros at a fixed exchange rate of $1.20 per euro in 3 months' time. The spot exchange rate is currently $1.15 per euro, and the 3-month interest rate in the US and Europe are 2% and 1.5% per annum, respectively. Assuming there is no counterparty default risk, what would be the total hedging cost for your company?

Solution:

To solve this problem, we first need to calculate the forward exchange rate using the interest rate parity formula:

Forward exchange rate = Spot exchange rate x (1 + foreign interest rate) / (1 + domestic interest rate)

Plugging in the numbers, we get:

Forward exchange rate = $1.15 x (1 + 0.015) / (1 + 0.02) = $1.1475 per euro

Since your company has entered into a forward contract to sell euros at $1.20 per euro, the hedging gain would be $1.20 - $1.1475 = $0.0525 per euro.

Assuming your company has exported 100,000 euros, then the total hedging gain would be $0.0525 x 100,000 = $5,250.

However, we also need to take into account the hedging cost, which is the interest rate differential between the US and Europe. Assuming the notional amount of the forward contract is 100,000 euros, then the interest rate cost for 3 months would be:

Interest rate cost = Notional amount x interest rate differential x (time period in days / 360)

Plugging in the numbers, we get:

Interest rate cost = 100,000 x (0.02 - 0.015) x (90 / 360) = $125

Therefore, the total hedging cost for your company would be $5,375 ($5,250 hedging gain - $125 interest rate cost).

Commodity Derivatives

Your company is a manufacturer that uses crude oil as a raw material in its production process. You are worried about the potential increase in oil prices, particularly after the central bank of the country has announced a policy to tighten liquidity in order to combat inflation. To hedge your commodity risk, you decide to enter into a futures contract to purchase crude oil at a fixed price. The current spot price of oil is $60 per barrel, and the futures contract has a delivery date of 3 months from now. The contract size is for 1,000 barrels of oil, and the futures price for 3-month delivery is $62 per barrel. If your company needs to purchase 20,000 barrels of oil in 3 months' time, what would be the total hedging cost for your company?

Solution:

To solve this problem, we first need to determine the total cost of purchasing 20,000 barrels of oil at the current spot price of $60 per barrel.

Total cost = Number of barrels x Spot price per barrel

Total cost = 20,000 x $60 = $1,200,000

Next, we need to determine the total cost of purchasing the same amount of oil through the futures contract. Assuming the futures price remains constant at $62 per barrel, the total cost would be:

Total cost = Number of barrels x Futures price per barrel

Total cost = 20,000 x $62 = $1,240,000

However, we also need to factor in the cost of carrying the futures contract until delivery. Assuming the annualized cost of carry for crude oil is 5% and the time to delivery is 3 months, the cost of carrying the futures contract would be:

Cost of carry = Futures price x Annualized cost of carry x (time period in days / 365)

Cost of carry = $62 x 0.05 x (90 / 365) = $3.03 per barrel

Total carrying cost = Number of barrels x Cost of carry per barrel

Total carrying cost = 20,000 x $3.03 = $60,600

Therefore, the total hedging cost for your company would be the sum of the futures price and the carrying cost:

Total hedging cost = Total cost + Total carrying cost

Total hedging cost = $1,240,000 + $60,600 = $1,300,600

By entering into the futures contract, your company would be able to hedge its price risk at a cost of $1,300,600, which is higher than the current spot price but provides certainty against any price increase that may occur due to tightening liquidity policies.

Investment Appraisal Techniques

Payback Period: ABC Corporation is considering a new project that requires an initial investment of $100,000. The project is expected to generate cash inflows of $20,000 annually for 7 years. The company has a target payback period of 5 years. Will ABC Corporation be able to recover their initial investment within the target payback period?

Solution:

1. Calculate the net cash inflow for each year by subtracting the initial investment from the annual cash inflow.

Year 1: $20,000 - $100,000 = -$80,000
Year 2: $20,000 - $100,000 = -$80,000
Year 3: $20,000 - $100,000 = -$80,000
Year 4: $20,000 - $100,000 = -$80,000
Year 5: $20,000 - $100,000 = -$80,000
Year 6: $20,000
Year 7: $20,000

2. Determine the cumulative cash inflow for each year by adding up the net cash inflows until the total is equal to or greater than the initial investment.

Year 1: -$80,000
Year 2: -$160,000
Year 3: -$240,000
Year 4: -$320,000
Year 5: -$400,000

Year 6: -$360,000
Year 7: -$320,000

3. Since the cumulative cash inflow is equal to or greater than the initial investment ($100,000) in Year 7, the payback period is 6 years (the end of Year 6). The project does not meet the company's target payback period of 5 years, so the project may not be considered feasible.

Net Present Value (NPV)

XYZ Corporation is considering a new investment in a project that requires an initial cost of $500,000. The project is expected to generate cash inflows of $150,000 annually for 5 years. The cost of capital is 10%. Will the project be accepted if it meets the policy target of the government's positive impact on the inflation rate?

Solution:

1. Find the present value of the expected cash inflows using the formula:

$$PV = CF / (1 + r)^t$$

where CF is the expected future cash flow, r is the discount rate, and t is the time period.

Year 1: $150,000 / (1 + 0.1)^1 = $136,364
Year 2: $150,000 / (1 + 0.1)^2 = $123,967
Year 3: $150,000 / (1 + 0.1)^3 = $112,697
Year 4: $150,000 / (1 + 0.1)^4 = $102,448
Year 5: $150,000 / (1 + 0.1)^5 = $93,141

2. Compute the sum of the present values of all anticipated cash inflows

Total present value of cash inflows = $568,617

3. Calculate the Net Present Value by subtracting the initial investment from the total present value of cash inflows.

NPV = Total present value of cash inflows - Initial investment
NPV = $68,617 - $500,000 = -$431,383

4. Since the NPV is negative, the project is not feasible as it does not meet the government's inflation policy target for capital investments.

Internal Rate of Return (IRR)

Sample Question: DEF Corporation is considering a new investment in a project that requires an initial cost of $750,000. The project is expected to generate cash inflows of $175,000 annually for 5 years. The company wants to assess whether the project will generate a minimum IRR of 20%. Will the project be accepted according to that criteria?

Solution:

1. Calculate the net present value (NPV) of the project at different discount rates, starting at 0% and increasing until the NPV changes sign from positive to negative.

Discount rate of 0%:
NPV = -$750,000 + $175,000 / (1 + 0%)^1 + $175,000 / (1 + 0%)^2 + $175,000 / (1 + 0%)^3 + $175,000 / (1 + 0%)^4 + $175,000 / (1 + 0%)^5
NPV = $425,000

Discount rate of 20%:
NPV = -$750,000 + $175,000 / (1 + 20%)^1 + $175,000 / (1 + 20%)^2 + $175,000 / (1 + 20%)^3 + $175,000 / (1 + 20%)^4 + $175,000 / (1 + 20%)^5
NPV = $72,897

Discount rate of 30%:

$$NPV = -\$750{,}000 + \$175{,}000 / (1 + 30\%)^1 + \$175{,}000 / (1 + 30\%)^2 + \$175{,}000 / (1 + 30\%)^3 + \$175{,}000 / (1 + 30\%)^4 + \$175{,}000 / (1 + 30\%)^5$$
$$NPV = -\$166{,}561$$

2. Since the NPV changes sign between 20% and 30%, this indicates that the Internal Rate of Return (IRR) is between these two discount rates. To find the IRR, interpolate between these two rates by using the following formula:

IRR = Lower Discount Rate + [(Lower NPV / (Lower NPV - Higher NPV)) x (Higher Discount Rate - Lower Discount Rate)]

$$IRR = 20\% + [(\$72{,}897 / (\$72{,}897 - (-\$166{,}561))) \times (30\% - 20\%)]$$
$$IRR = 20\% + [(\$72{,}897 / \$239{,}458) \times 10\%]$$
$$IRR = 22.3\%$$

3. Considering the minimum IRR requirement of 20%, this project can be accepted as its IRR is 22.3%, indicating a good rate of return on the investment.

Profitability Index

Sample Question: MNO Corporation is considering two projects. Project A requires an initial investment of $300,000 and is expected to generate cash inflows of $75,000 per year for 5 years. Project B requires an initial investment of $400,000 and is expected to generate cash inflows of $100,000 per year for 6 years. The company wants to compare the two projects using the profitability index and determine which one is more efficient. Assume a cost of capital of 12%.

Solution:

1. Calculate the present value of future cash inflows for each project using the formula:

$$PV = CF / (1 + r)^t$$

where CF is the expected cash flows, r is the discount rate, and t is the time period.

Project A:
PV = $75,000 / (1 + 0.12)^1 + $75,000 / (1 + 0.12)^2 + $75,000 / (1 + 0.12)^3 + $75,000 / (1 + 0.12)^4 + $75,000 / (1 + 0.12)^5
PV = $225,147

Project B:
PV = $100,000 / (1 + 0.12)^1 + $100,000 / (1 + 0.12)^2 + $100,000 / (1 + 0.12)^3 + $100,000 / (1 + 0.12)^4 + $100,000 / (1 + 0.12)^5 + $100,000 / (1 + 0.12)^6
PV = $425,308

2. Determine the Profitability Index by dividing the present value of future cash inflows by the initial investment for each project.

Project A: Profitability Index = $225,147 / $300,000 = 0.75
Project B: Profitability Index = $425,308 / $400,000 = 1.06

3. Since the Profitability Index for Project A is 0.75 and for Project B is 1.06, Project B is more efficient and will generate more for the company's investment.

Modified Internal Rate of Return (MIRR)

Sample Question: PQR Corporation is considering a new project that requires an initial investment of $200,000. The project is expected to generate cash inflows of $60,000 annually for 6 years. The company has a reinvestment rate of 8% and seeks to determine the Modified Internal Rate of Return (MIRR) for the investment.

Solution:

1. Calculate the future value of all cash inflows using a future value formula and the expected interest rate (reinvestment rate).

Year 1: $60,000 \times (1 + 8\%)^5 = \$90,874$
Year 2: $60,000 \times (1 + 8\%)^4 = \$84,209$
Year 3: $60,000 \times (1 + 8\%)^3 = \$78,093$
Year 4: $60,000 \times (1 + 8\%)^2 = \$72,492$
Year 5: $60,000 \times (1 + 8\%)^1 = \$67,368$
Year 6: $60,000

2. Calculate the total future value of the cash inflows by adding up the future values.

Total future value of cash inflows = $453,046

3. Calculate the Present Value of the Terminal Value (PVTV) by discounting the future value of the last cash inflow to the present time.

$PVTV = \$60,000 / (1 + 8\%)^6$
PVTV = $35,225

4. Calculate the Modified Internal Rate of Return (MIRR) using the formula:

MIRR = [(PVTV + Total present value of cash inflows)^(1/n)] / (Initial investment)^(1/n) - 1
where n is the number of cash flow periods.

MIRR = [($453,046 + $35,225)^(1/6) / ($200,000)]^(1/6) - 1
MIRR = 14.38%

5. Since the MIRR is 14.38%, it is higher than the cost of capital or required rate of return. Therefore, the investment can be considered feasible.

Discounted Payback Period

Suppose Company A is considering investing in a new project that will generate a consistent cash flow stream of $50,000 per year for the next 5 years. The initial investment required for the project is $200,000, and the discount rate is 10%. Compute the Discounted Payback Period of the investment, and determine whether it meets the macroeconomic policy target of keeping inflation low and stable.

Solution:

Using the discounted payback formula:
Discounted Payback Period (Years) = Number of Years before the Investment Recovers its Initial Cost

Annual Cash Flow / (1 + Discount Rate) ^ Year

Year 0: - $200,000
Year 1: $50,000 / (1 + 10%) ^ 1 = $45,454.55
Year 2: $50,000 / (1 + 10%) ^ 2 = $41,322.31
Year 3: $50,000 / (1 + 10%) ^ 3 = $37,563.01
Year 4: $50,000 / (1 + 10%) ^ 4 = $34,134.55
Year 5: $50,000 / (1 + 10%) ^ 5 = $31,004.13

The cumulative cash flow at the end of Year 3 is $159,339.87, which is greater than the initial investment. Therefore, the discounted payback period is between 3 and 4 years. Since Company A can recover its initial investment in less than 4 years, it satisfies the macroeconomic policy target of promoting sustainable economic growth.

2. Company B is evaluating a project that generates cash flows of $40,000, $60,000, and $80,000 at the end of Years 1, 2 and 3 respectively. The initial investment required is $150,000 and the discount rate is 8%. Compute the Discounted Payback Period of the investment, and determine whether it meets the macroeconomic policy target of minimizing unemployment rate.

Solution:

Using the discounted payback formula:
Discounted Payback Period (Years) = Number of Years before the Investment Recovers its Initial Cost

Cumulative Discounted Cash Flow / Initial Investment

Year 0: - $150,000
Year 1: $40,000 / (1 + 8%) ^ 1 = $37,037.04
Year 2: $60,000 / (1 + 8%) ^ 2 = $52,018.26
Year 3: $80,000 / (1 + 8%) ^ 3 = $63,111.54

The cumulative discounted cash flow at the end of Year 3 is $152,166.84, which is less than the initial investment. Therefore, the discounted payback period is more than 3 years. Since Company B cannot recover its initial investment in less than 3 years, it may not be able to hire additional workers, which may lead to higher unemployment rate. Hence, the project does not meet the macroeconomic policy target of minimizing the unemployment rate.

Discounted Cash Flow Analysis

Assuming the government implements a tight monetary policy by increasing the interest rate to curb inflation, how will this affect the valuation of an investment in a firm's cash flows using Discounted Cash Flow (DCF) analysis?

Solution:

An increase in interest rates reduces the present value of future cash flows. For instance, a company forecasts cash flows of $100,000 per year for 5 years. Under the given scenario, with an interest rate of 10%, the calculation would be:

DCF = (100,000/(1+10%)^1) + (100,000/(1+10%)^2) + (100,000/(1+10%)^3) + (100,000/(1+10%)^4) + (100,000/(1+10%)^5)

DCF= $100,000/1.10 + $100,000/1.21 + $100,000/1.33 + $100,000/1.46 + $100,000/1.61
DCF = $85,714 + $ 82,645 + $75,188 + $68,493 + $62,827
DCF = $374,698

In this scenario, the investment's present value is $374,698, indicating a drop in the valuation of the investment due to the higher discount rate resulting from the tight monetary policy.

Question 2

Suppose there is an expansionary fiscal policy, which results in a decline in tax rates. Assume that the company's cash flows are anticipated to grow due to the resulting increase in consumers' disposable income. How would this affect the investment's valuation using Discounted Cash Flow analysis?

Solution:

Lower tax rates increase disposable income, resulting in increased purchasing power for customers, and, as a result, higher earnings for the company. If it is anticipated that the company's cash flows will grow at a stable rate as a result of the expansionary fiscal policy, the present value of the investment will increase. For instance, consider an investment with expected cash flows of $150,000 per year for 5 years with a discount rate of 8%. By utilizing the DCF formula, the calculation would be:

$$DCF = (150,000/(1+8\%)^1) + (150,000/(1+8\%)^2) + (150,000/(1+8\%)^3) + (150,000/(1+8\%)^4) + (150,000/(1+8\%)^5)$$

DCF= $150,000/1.08 + $150,000/1.17 + $150,000/1.26 + $150,000/1.36 + $150,000/1.47
DCF = $138,889 + $128,205 + $118,343 + $109,247 + $100,877
DCF = $596,561

Here, the investment's present value is $596,561, indicating an increase in value due to the expansionary fiscal policy as it has resulted in a consistent increase in cash flows.

Allowing for inflation in Discounted Cash flow

Suppose a company is considering an investment in a new plant, and the inflation rate is expected to be 3% per year for the next five years. If the company forecasts that the cash flows from the plant will be $50,000 in the first year, growing by 5% each year for the next five years, with a discount rate of 8%, what will be the present value of the investment's future cash flows after adjusting for inflation?

Solution:

To incorporate inflation into the Discounted Cash Flow (DCF) analysis, we need to use a real discount rate that takes into account both the nominal discount rate and the inflation rate. Assuming an expected inflation rate of 3%, and a nominal discount rate of 8%, the real discount rate would be 8% - 3% = 5%.

Now, let's calculate the present value of the plant's cash flows using the adjusted real discount rate. The calculation would be:

$$DCF = (\$50,000 * (1+0.05)^1) / (1+0.05)^1 + (\$50,000 * (1+0.05)^2) / (1+0.05)^2 + (\$50,000 * (1+0.05)^3) / (1+0.05)^3 + (\$50,000 * (1+0.05)^4) / (1+0.05)^4 + (\$50,000 * (1+0.05)^5) / (1+0.05)^5$$

DCF = $52,500 / 1.05 + $55,125 / 1.1025 + $57,881.25 / 1.1576 + $ 60,775.31 / 1.2155 + $63,813.07 / 1.2763
DCF = $50,000 + $50,025 + $48,432 + $46,970 + $45,626
DCF = $240,053

Therefore, the present value of the investment's future cash flows, after adjusting for inflation with the real discount rate, is $240,053. This indicates the real worth of the investment after accounting for inflation.

Allowing for taxation in DCF

Suppose a company is considering investing in a new project that will generate cash flows of $100,000 per year for 5 years. The project requires an initial investment of $300,000 and will be taxed at a flat rate of 35%. If the discount rate is 10%, what is the net present value (NPV) of the project after accounting for taxation?

Solution:

To determine the net present value of the project, we first need to calculate the after-tax cash flows for a single year by subtracting the tax liability (based on the cash flows and tax rate) from the gross cash flows. So, in this case, the after-tax cash flows for the first year would be:

After-tax cash flow = ($100,000 - ($100,000 * 35%)) = $65,000

Similarly, we can find the after-tax cash flows for each year of the project's life. The calculation of the after-tax cash flows for year two would be:

After-tax cash flow = ($100,000 * (1+0.05) - ($100,000 * (1+0.05) * 35%)) = $69,750

To calculate the net present value (NPV), we need to compute the present value of all future after-tax cash flows, and the initial investment. We can then subtract the initial investment to determine the project's net present value. Let's use the DCF formula to determine the NPV:

NPV = [(65,000/(1+0.1)^1) + (69,750/(1+0.1)^2) + (73,238/(1+0.1)^3) + (77,312/(1+0.1)^4) + (81,977/(1+0.1)^5)] - 300,000

NPV = $59,090 - $300,000

$$NPV = -\$240{,}910$$

The negative net present value shows that the project would not be profitable after accounting for taxation, investment cost, and the required level of return required by the investors. Thus, the company should reconsider its investment decision considering all these factors.

Analysis

Leasing and Borrowing to Buy – Before – and After Tax Costs of Debt: A firm is deciding between leasing and borrowing to buy a new machine, with costs and tax implications to consider. The machine has a cost of $100,000, and the firm can either lease it for five years at an annual cost of $25,000, or purchase it using a loan at a 7% floating interest rate. The firm's marginal tax rate is 35%. What is the comparative before- and after-tax cost of debt for the lease and the loan options?

Solution:
Leasing Option:
The total cost of leasing the machine for five years would be $25,000 * 5 = $125,000. Since the lease payments are fully deductible as a business expense, we can determine the after-tax cost of leasing by multiplying the lease payment by (1 - tax rate). This is because the lease payment is a pre-tax expense that would decrease the firm's taxable income. So, the after-tax cost of the lease would be:

After-Tax Lease Cost = $25,000 * (1 - 35%) = $16,250

Borrowing Option:
If the firm decides to borrow to buy the machine, they would need to take out a loan of $100,000 with a 7% floating interest rate. The interest payments on the loan would be tax-deductible as a business expense, which would reduce the before-tax cost of the loan. So, we can determine the before-tax cost of the loan as:

Before-Tax Loan Cost = $100,000 * 7% = $7,000

To find the after-tax cost of the loan, we need to consider the tax benefit of the deduction for interest expense. The tax benefit reduces the after-tax cost of the loan. The calculation of the after-tax cost of borrowing would be:

After-Tax Loan Cost = $7,000 * (1 - 35%) = $4,550

Comparing Before- and After-Tax Costs of Debt:
The before-tax cost of the loan is $7,000, while the after-tax cost of the lease is $16,250. Therefore, the borrowing option appears more favorable from a before-tax cost standpoint. However, when we consider the tax benefit of the interest deduction, the after-tax cost of borrowing reduces to $4,550. This result shows that borrowing is less costly than leasing the machine, even after accounting for the tax-deductible expenses in each option.

Thus, borrowing is the more sensible option for the firm to finance the purchase of the machine.

Analyzing Asset Replacement Decisions Using Equivalent Annual Cost and Equivalent Annual Benefit Methods

A company is considering whether to replace an aging machine used in its manufacturing process with a new one. The existing machine costs $10,000 per year to maintain and repair, and it is estimated to have a salvage value of $5,000 at the end of its useful life (10 years). The new machine is expected to cost $50,000 and will have a useful life of 10 years, after which it is expected to have a salvage value of $10,000. The new machine will also require $2,000 in maintenance and repair costs per year. Assuming the company's cost of capital is 8%, what is the equivalent annual cost of the new machine? Should the company replace the existing machine?

Solution:
We can determine the equivalent annual cost of the new machine using the formula:

Equivalent Annual Cost = (Initial cost - Salvage value) * (Present value of annuity factor) + Annual maintenance cost

To find the present value of annuity factor, we use the formula:

$$PVAF = (1 - (1 / (1 + r)^n)) / r$$

where r is the discount rate (8%), and n is the useful life of the machine.

The equivalent annual cost of the new machine would be:

Equivalent Annual Cost = ($50,000 - $10,000 - $10,000) * (6.7100) + $2,000
Equivalent Annual Cost = $19,086

To determine if the replacement is financially viable, we compare the equivalent annual cost of the new machine with that of maintaining the existing machine.

Equivalent Annual Cost of existing machine = Maintenance + Repair cost - Salvage Value) * PVAF
Equivalent Annual Cost of existing machine = ($10,000 - $5,000) * (6.7100)
Equivalent Annual Cost of existing machine = $33,550

Comparing the equivalent annual costs, it is less expensive to maintain the existing machine with an equivalent annual cost of $33,550 than to replace it with a new machine with an equivalent annual cost of $19,086. Therefore, the company should keep the old machine as replacing it with a new one does not make financial sense.

Alternatively, we can use the equivalent annual benefit method to solve this problem. In this method, we subtract the equivalent annual maintenance costs of the new machine from its expected annual savings or benefits.

Annual savings = Old machine annual cost - New machine annual cost
Annual savings = $10,000 - ($50,000 - $10,000)/10 - $2,000
Annual savings = $4,000

Equivalent Annual Benefit = Annual savings / Present Value of Annuity Factor
Equivalent Annual Benefit = $4,000 / 6.7100
Equivalent Annual Benefit = $595.25

Comparing the equivalent annual benefit of $595.25 to the equivalent annual cost of maintaining the old machine of $33,550 shows that it is still financially prudent to maintain the old machine. Therefore, the company should continue to maintain its old machine instead of replacing it with a new one.

Profitability Indexes for Divisible Investment Projects under Single-Period Capital Rationing

Assume that a company has a budget of $1,000,000 to invest in several projects. The company is operating under a single-period capital rationing policy, which means that it can only invest in projects that have a positive NPV and a PI of 1.2 or higher. The company is considering two investment projects: Project A and Project B. The expected cash flows for each project are as follows:

Project A
Initial investment: $500,000
Expected cash flows:
Year 1: $200,000
Year 2: $300,000
Year 3: $400,000

Project B
Initial investment: $600,000
Expected cash flows:
Year 1: $250,000
Year 2: $350,000
Year 3: $450,000

Assuming a discount rate of 10%, which project(s) should the company invest in and calculate the Profitability Index (PI) for each project?

Solution:

To calculate the PI, we'll divide the present value of the expected cash flows by the initial investment. Let's calculate the present value of each project's cash flows first:

Project A
Year 1: $200,000 / (1 + 0.10) ^ 1 = $181,818.18
Year 2: $300,000 / (1 + 0.10) ^ 2 = $247,933.88
Year 3: $400,000 / (1 + 0.10) ^ 3 = $318,781.70
Present value of expected cash flows: $181,818.18 + $247,933.88 + $318,781.70 = $748,533.76

Project B
Year 1: $250,000 / (1 + 0.10) ^ 1 = $227,272.73
Year 2: $350,000 / (1 + 0.10) ^ 2 = $247,933.88
Year 3: $450,000 / (1 + 0.10) ^ 3 = $286,778.37
Present value of expected cash flows: $227,272.73 + $247,933.88 + $286,778.37 = $761,984.99

Now we can calculate the PI for each project:

Project A: PI = $748,533.76 / $500,000 = 1.50
Project B: PI = $761,984.99 / $600,000 = 1.27

Since both projects have a PI of 1.2 or higher, we can invest in both of them. Project A has a higher PI, so it is the better investment.

NPV of Combinations of Non-Divisible Investment Projects under Single-Period Capital Rationing

Assume that a company has a budget of $500,000 to invest in several projects. The company is operating under a single-period capital rationing policy, which means that it can only invest in projects that have a positive NPV and a combined NPV that is less than or equal to the company's budget. The company is considering three investment projects: Project X, Project Y, and Project Z. The expected cash flows for each project and their initial investments are as follows:

Project X
Initial investment: $200,000
Expected cash flows:
Year 1: $80,000
Year 2: $100,000
Year 3: $110,000
Discount rate: 8%

Project Y
Initial investment: $150,000
Expected cash flows:
Year 1: $60,000
Year 2: $70,000
Year 3: $90,000
Discount rate: 8%

Project Z
Initial investment: $250,000
Expected cash flows:
Year 1: $90,000
Year 2: $110,000
Year 3: $130,000
Discount rate: 8%

Which projects should the company invest in to maximize the total NPV and what is the maximum total NPV?

Solution:

We need to calculate the NPV for each project and then choose the combination of projects that has the highest combined NPV that is within the company's budget of $500,000.

Let's start by calculating the NPV of each project using the given discount rate:

NPV of Project X = -$200,000 + $80,000/(1+0.08) + $100,000/(1+0.08)^2 + $110,000/(1+0.08)^3 = $27,844.92

NPV of Project Y = -$150,000 + $60,000/(1+0.08) + $70,000/(1+0.08)^2 + $90,000/(1+0.08)^3 = $16,050.59

NPV of Project Z = -$250,000 + $90,000/(1+0.08) + $110,000/(1+0.08)^2 + $130,000/(1+0.08)^3 = $47,925.91

Now we can test which combinations of projects are within the budget constraint and have the highest combined NPV. One way to do this is to test all the possible combinations.

Possible combinations of projects and their NPVs:

- X: $27,844.92
- Y: $16,050.59
- Z: $47,925.91
- X+Y: $43,895.51
- X+Z: $75,770.83
- Y+Z: $64,976.50
- X+Y+Z: $91,820.42 (not feasible due to budget constraint)

The best combination of projects that we can afford are X and Z, which have a combined NPV of $75,770.83, well within the budget of $500,000. Therefore, the company should invest in Projects X and Z to maximize the NPV of their investment portfolio.

Cost of Capital

Assume that a company is considering a new investment project that costs $2,000,000. The company estimates that the project will generate annual cash flows of $400,000 for the next 10 years. The company needs to determine its cost of capital in order to evaluate the profitability of this project. Given the following information, what is the company's cost of capital?

- Risk-free rate: 2%
- Market risk premium: 8%
- Beta: 1.5
- Tax rate: 30%

Solution:

The cost of capital is the minimum rate of return that the company requires in order to undertake an investment project. It is the weighted average of the cost of debt and the cost of equity, where the weights are the proportion of debt and equity in the company's capital structure.

Let's start by calculating the cost of equity using the CAPM (Capital Asset Pricing Model) formula:

Cost of equity = Risk-free rate + Beta * Market risk premium
Cost of equity = 2% + 1.5 * 8% = 14%

Next, we need to calculate the cost of debt. We can assume that the company's debt has an interest rate of 5%. To calculate the after-tax cost of debt, we need to adjust for the tax shield:

After-tax cost of debt = Pre-tax cost of debt * (1 - Tax rate)
After-tax cost of debt = 5% * (1 - 30%) = 3.5%

Computing Weighted average cost of capital (WACC):

WACC = (Weight of equity * Cost of equity) + (Weight of debt * After-tax cost of debt)
Weight of equity = Market value of equity / Total market value
Weight of debt = Market value of debt / Total market value
Total market value = Market value of equity + Market value of debt

Assuming that the market value of equity is $4,000,000 and the market value of debt is $2,000,000, we can calculate the total market value:

Total market value = $4,000,000 + $2,000,000 = $6,000,000

Using these values, we can calculate the weights:

Weight of equity = $4,000,000 / $6,000,000 = 0.67
Weight of debt = $2,000,000 / $6,000,000 = 0.33

Now we can calculate the WACC:

WACC = (0.67 * 14%) + (0.33 * 3.5%) = 10.505%

Therefore, the company's cost of capital is 10.505%, which is the minimum rate of return that this investment project should generate in order to be profitable.

Cost of equity

Assume that a company is considering issuing new common stock to finance a new project. The company wants to estimate the cost of equity to determine the appropriate discount rate for this project. Given the following information, what is the company's cost of equity?

- The company's stock price is $50 per share.
- The company pays an annual dividend of $2 per share, which is expected to grow at a constant rate of 5% per year.
- The risk-free rate is 3%.
- The market risk premium is 8%.

Solution:

The cost of equity is the minimum rate of return that the company's shareholders require in order to invest in the company's stock. We can estimate the cost of equity using the dividend discount model (DDM) formula:

Cost of equity = (Dividend / Stock price) + Dividend growth rate

Let's first calculate the dividend growth rate using the information given:

Dividend growth rate = 5%

Now we can calculate the cost of equity:

Dividend = Dividend in the current year = $2.00
Stock price = $50.00

Cost of equity = ($2.00 / $50.00) + 5% = 9%

Therefore, the company's cost of equity is 9%, which means that the company needs to achieve a return of at least 9% in order to satisfy its shareholders and attract new investors. The cost of equity is a critical input in the calculation of the company's weighted average cost of capital (WACC), which is used to evaluate the attractiveness of different projects and investment opportunities.

Dividend growth model

Assume that a company is planning to invest in a new project that requires a total funding of $2,000,000. The company is considering to finance the project by issuing new common stock. The company's stock is currently trading at $40 per share, and they paid a dividend of $1.5 per share last year. The company is expecting to pay an annual dividend of $1.75 next year. If the company is expecting a constant growth rate of 6% in its dividends, what is the common equity cost of financing the new project?

Solution:

The common equity cost of financing is represented by the cost of equity, which can be calculated using the dividend growth model (DGM) formula. The formula is:

Cost of equity = [dividend next year/ current stock price] + expected dividend growth rate

We can use the following equation to find out the expected dividend for any year:

Dividend for a year = Dividend for the previous year x (1 + dividend growth rate)

Using this equation, we can calculate the expected dividends for the next three years:

Year 1: $1.75
Year 2: $1.75 x (1 + 6%) = $1.855
Year 3: $1.855 x (1 + 6%) = $1.9683

Now we can use the DGM formula to calculate the cost of equity:

Cost of equity = [$1.855 / $40] + 6% = 10.64%

Therefore, the cost of equity is 10.64%, which indicates that the company needs to earn at least that return in order to satisfy its shareholders and attract new investors. The cost of equity is a critical metric in evaluating the attractiveness of various funding sources and investment opportunities.

Systematic risk

Assume that a company is planning to issue new bonds to raise funds for a new project. The company's current beta is 1.8, and the current yield-to-maturity (YTM) of the 10-year Treasury bond is 2.5%. If the market risk premium is 7%, what is the systematic risk associated with the new bonds?

Solution:

The systematic risk associated with a security is its sensitivity to changes in the overall market. The beta coefficient is a measure of systematic risk that is used to compare the volatility of an individual security or portfolio to the volatility of the market as a whole. The market risk premium is the additional return that investors require to invest in a risky asset over and above the risk-free rate.

We can use the following formula to calculate the expected return on an asset:

Expected return on an asset = Risk-free rate + [Beta x Market risk premium]

Let's first calculate the expected return on the market:

Expected return on the market = Risk-free rate + Market risk premium
Expected return on the market = 2.5% + 7% = 9.5%

Now we can use the beta coefficient and the expected return on the market to calculate the expected return on the new bonds:

Expected return on the new bonds = 2.5% + (1.8 x 7%) = 14.1%

Therefore, the systematic risk associated with the new bonds is 14.1%. This is the minimum return that the company must provide to its bondholders in order to compensate them for the systematic risk associated with the bonds. If the expected return on the new bonds is lower than 14.1%, then the bonds will be considered unattractive to investors.

Unsystematic risk

Company XYZ, a manufacturing business, is considering investing in a new production line for its latest product. The business needs to decide on the amount of investment and what percentage of the project they are willing to finance through equity issuance. The company estimates that the project will generate an annual cash flow of $500,000, with a standard deviation (σ) of cash flows of $50,000. The equity market risk premium is 6%, while the risk-free rate of return is 3%. The beta of Company XYZ is 1.2.

Assume the unsystematic risk of the project is 10%. Calculate the following:

a) The required rate of return (RRR) for the project
b) The cost of equity using CAPM method
c) The expected return on investment for the company
d) The maximum amount of money that the company should invest in the project to be financially feasible
e) The percentage of the project that the company should finance through equity issuance.

Solution:

a) The RRR for the project can be calculated using the formula:
RRR = Risk-free rate + (Beta of the company * Market risk premium)
RRR = 3% + (1.2 * 6%) = 10.2%

b) The cost of equity can be calculated using the CAPM method as follows:

Cost of equity = Risk-free rate + (Beta of the company * Market risk premium)

Cost of equity = 3% + (1.2 * 6%) = 10.2%

c) The expected return on investment for the company can be calculated as follows:

Expected return on investment = (Cash flow * (1 - Unsystematic risk)) / Investment amount

Expected return on investment = ($500,000 * (1 - 0.1)) / Investment amount

d) The maximum amount of money that the company should invest in the project to be financially feasible can be calculated using the following formula:

Max investment = (Expected cash flows - Required Return) / Risk Factor

Risk factor = 1 / (1 + (β * (1 - Unsystematic risk)))

Max investment = ($500,000 - 10.2%) / (1 + (1.2 * (1-0.1))) = $3,766,314.70 (rounded to the nearest dollar)

e) The percentage of the project that the company should finance through equity issuance can be calculated using the following formula:

Percentage of financing by Equity = 1 - (Investment amount / Total project cost)

Percentage of financing by Equity = 1 - (Amount invested / (Amount invested + Equity))

where, Total project cost = Amount invested + Equity

By setting the above equation equal to 0.5 (50%), it can be determined that the company should finance 50% of the project through equity issuance for it to be financially feasible.

Capital Asset Pricing Model (CAPM)

Company ABC is planning to invest in a new project which is expected to generate an expected return of 12% per annum. The project's beta is 1.5 and the risk-free rate is 4%. The equity market risk premium is 8%.

Assume that the current market return is 11.5%, use the CAPM formula to calculate the required return on this project.

Solution:

The Capital Asset Pricing Model (CAPM) is used to estimate the required return on an investment. The formula is:

Required return = Risk-free rate + (Beta x Equity market risk premium)

To answer the above question, we substitute the values given in the formula:

Required return = 0.04 + (1.5 x 0.08)

Required return = 0.04 + 0.12

Required return = 0.16 (or 16%)

The required return is 16%, which means that Company ABC must achieve a return of 16% on the project in order to compensate for the risk they are taking by investing in the project. Since the expected return of the project is 12%, the project is not financially feasible at this point. The company should consider adjusting the investment amount or adjusting the project's risk to make it financially more feasible.

Cost of Debt

Company MNO is planning to issue a bond with a face value of $1,000 and a coupon rate of 8%. The bond will mature in 10 years and will pay interest every year. The company's income tax rate is 30%. The bond has a market value of $950.

Use the cost of debt formula to calculate the cost of debt for this bond.

Solution:

The cost of debt is the rate of return required to borrow funds. It is calculated as follows:

Cost of debt = (Interest expense x (1 - Tax rate)) / Amount of debt after tax

To answer the above question, we substitute the values given in the formula:

Interest expense = Annual coupon payment = Face value of bond x Coupon rate
Interest expense = $1,000 x 0.08 = $80

Amount of debt after tax = Market value of bond = $950

Cost of debt = ($80 x (1 - 0.30)) / $950
Cost of debt = $56 / $950
Cost of debt = 5.89%

The cost of debt for Company MNO is 5.89%. This means that the company must earn a return of at least 5.89% on its investment projects, as this is the interest rate that the company is paying for its debt financing. If the company's expected return on its investment projects is less than the cost of debt, it may indicate that the company should consider other financing options or choose different investment projects.

Irredeemable debt

Company PQR has issued an irredeemable debenture with a face value of $1,000, a coupon rate of 9%, and a yield to maturity of 10%. The company has an income tax rate of 35%.

a) What is the market price of the debenture?
b) What is the pre-tax cost of this irredeemable debt to the company?
c) What is the after-tax cost of this irredeemable debt to the company?

Solution:

a) The market price of the debenture can be calculated using the present value formula as follows:

Market price = Coupon payment / Yield to maturity
Market price = 0.09 x $1,000 / 0.1
Market price = $900

b) The pre-tax cost of debt is the yield to maturity. Therefore, the pre-tax cost of this irredeemable debt to the company is 10%.

c) The after-tax cost of debt can be calculated using the formula:

After-tax cost of debt = Pre-tax cost of debt x (1 - Tax rate)

After-tax cost of debt = 10% x (1 - 0.35)
After-tax cost of debt = 6.5%

The after-tax cost of this irredeemable debt to the company is 6.5%. This means that Company PQR must earn a return of at least 6.5% on its investment projects, as this is the interest rate that the company is paying for its debt financing. If the company's expected return on its investment projects is less than the after-tax cost of debt, it may indicate that the company should consider other financing options or choose different investment projects.

Redeemable debt

Company XYZ issued a redeemable bond with a face value of $1,000, a coupon rate of 7% and a maturity period of 5 years. The bond will be redeemed at a premium of 10% above its face value. The current market price of the bond is $1,100. The company's income tax rate is 30%.

a) What is the yield to maturity of the bond?
b) What is the pre-tax cost of this redeemable debt to the company?
c) What is the after-tax cost of this redeemable debt to the company?

Solution:

a) The yield to maturity of the bond is the rate of return that the investor would earn if he/she held the bond until maturity. The formula to calculate the yield to maturity is:

Yield to maturity = Annual interest payment + (Bond redemption price - Bond purchase price) ÷ Number of years until redemption + Bond purchase price ÷ 2.

Annual interest payment = Face value x Coupon rate = $1,000 x 0.07 = $70
Bond redemption price = Face value x (1 + Premium rate) = $1,000 x (1 + 0.10) = $1,100
Number of years until redemption = 5
Bond purchase price = $1,100

$$\text{Yield to maturity} = \$70 + (\$1{,}100 - \$1{,}100) / 5 + \$1{,}100 / 2$$
$$\text{Yield to maturity} = \$70 + \$110 / 5 + \$550$$
$$\text{Yield to maturity} = \$820 / 5 = 164\%$$

The yield to maturity of the bond is 16.4%

b) The pre-tax cost of debt is the yield to maturity. Therefore, the pre-tax cost of this redeemable debt to the company is 16.4%.

c) The after-tax cost of debt can be calculated using the formula:
After-tax cost of debt = Pre-tax cost of debt x (1 - Tax rate)

$$\text{After-tax cost of debt} = 16.4\% \times (1 - 0.30)$$
$$\text{After-tax cost of debt} = 11.48\%$$

The after-tax cost of this redeemable debt to the company is 11.48%. This means that Company XYZ must earn a return of at least 11.48% on its investment projects, as this is the interest rate that the company is paying for its debt financing. If the company's expected return on its investment projects is less than the after-tax cost of debt, it may indicate that the company should consider other financing options or choose different investment projects.

Convertible debt

Company ABC Corporation issued a convertible bond with a face value of $1,000, a coupon rate of 6%, and a maturity date of 5 years. The conversion price is $50 per share for 50 shares of common stock. The stock is currently selling for $48. The company's income tax rate is 30%.

a) What is the conversion ratio and the conversion premium?
b) What is the yield-to-maturity of the bond?
c) What is the current yield-to-maturity (CYTM) of the bond?
d) What is the cost of debt before the conversion option is considered?
e) What is the cost of debt after the conversion option is considered?

Solution:

a) The conversion ratio is calculated as the par value of the bond divided by the conversion price of the common stock:

Conversion ratio = Par value ÷ Conversion price = $1,000 ÷ $50 = 20

The conversion premium is calculated as the difference between the market price of the convertible bond and the market value of the bond's conversion feature:

Conversion premium = Conversion ratio x Market price of the convertible bond - Market value of one share x Conversion ratio
Conversion premium = (20 x $1,000) - (20 x $48)
Conversion premium = $20,000 - $960
Conversion premium = $19,040

b) Yield-to-maturity measures the total return that an investor will receive from the bond over its life. We can calculate the yield-to-maturity of the bond using the present value formula. We need to find the rate of discount that makes the present value of the bond's cash flows equal to the current market price of the bond ($1,000 + (0.06 x $1,000) / (1 + Yield-to-maturity) ^ 1 + ... + ($1,000 + (0.06 x $1,000) / (1 + Yield-to-maturity) ^ 5 = $1,065.51).

We can calculate the yield-to-maturity using numerical methods or a financial calculator, which gives us 6.7%.

c) The current yield-to-maturity (CYTM) measures the return that an investor would receive if they purchased the bond at the current market price. The CYTM is calculated by dividing the annual coupon payment by the current market price of the bond and multiplying by 100:

CYTM = Annual coupon payment ÷ Current market price x 100%
CYTM = $60 ÷ $1,000 x 100%
CYTM = 6%

d) The cost of the debt before the conversion option is considered is the yield-to-maturity of the convertible bond, which is 6.7%.

e) The cost of the debt after the conversion option is considered is the lower of the yield-to-maturity of the convertible bond or the yield on the common shares. Assuming the company issues new common shares to the bondholders on conversion:

Yield on common shares = Annual dividend ÷ Market price of common shares
Yield on common shares = 0 ÷ $48 x 100% = 0%

The cost of debt after the conversion option is considered is still 6.7%, as it is lower than the yield on the common shares. The conversion option adds value to the bond, making it more attractive to investors. Companies can use the conversion option to reduce the cost of debt financing, as investors are willing to accept a lower return in exchange for the potential upside that comes with the common shares.

Preference shares

Company PQR is considering issuing preference shares to raise capital. The company offers 8% preference shares with a face value of $100. The dividend is paid semi-annually, and current market value is $110. The company's income tax rate is 30%.

a) What is the current dividend yield of the preference shares?
b) What is the cost of preference shares to the company before considering tax savings?
c) What is the cost of preference shares to the company after considering tax savings?
d) If the company's ordinary shares have a cost of equity of 12%, what is the after-tax cost of preference shares?

Solution:

a) The current dividend yield measures the return that an investor would earn if they purchased the preference shares at the current market price. The dividend yield can be calculated as follows:

Dividend yield = Annual dividend / Current market price x 100%

Annual dividend = Face value x Dividend rate = $100 × 8% = $8
Current market price = $110

Dividend yield = $8 / $110 x 100%
Dividend yield = 7.27%

b) The cost of preference shares to the company before considering tax savings is equal to the preference dividend rate, which is 8%.

c) The cost of preference shares to the company after considering tax savings is equal to the preference dividend rate multiplied by (1 - tax rate), which is 5.6%.

Cost of preference shares after tax = 8% × (1 - 30%) = 5.6%

d) The after-tax cost of preference shares can be compared to the company's cost of equity to determine the most appropriate source of financing. The cost of equity is typically higher than the cost of preference shares because equity investors demand a higher return to compensate for the greater risk of holding equity.

After-tax cost of preference shares = Dividend rate / Market price × (1 - Tax rate)
After-tax cost of preference shares = 8% / $110 × (1 - 30%)
After-tax cost of preference shares = 5.6%

Since the cost of equity is 12%, the company should prefer to finance its operations using the preference shares, as this will help in reducing its weighted average cost of capital (WACC).

Bank debt

A company is planning to apply for a bank debt of $500,000 to finance its expansion project. The loan has an annual interest rate of 7% and a term of 5 years. The company intends to repay the loan at the end of the term with a lump sum payment. The expansion project is expected to increase the company's annual net income by $120,000.

What is the minimum yearly cash flow that the company needs to generate to cover the annual interest expense and pay off the loan at the end of the term?

Solution:

Step 1: Calculate the annual interest expense
Annual interest expense = Loan amount x Annual interest rate
Annual interest expense = $500,000 x 7% = $35,000

Step 2: Calculate the lump sum payment at the end of the term
Lump sum payment = Loan amount + (Loan amount x Annual interest rate x Loan term)
Lump sum payment = $500,000 + ($500,000 x 7% x 5) = $675,000

Step 3: Calculate the total cash flow needed to cover the interest expense and the lump sum payment at the end of the term
Total cash flow = Annual interest expense + Lump sum payment - Net income from the expansion project
Total cash flow = $35,000 + $675,000 - $120,000 = $590,000

Therefore, the minimum yearly cash flow that the company needs to generate to cover the annual interest expense and pay off the loan at the end of the term is $590,000.

Average and Marginal Cost of Capital

ABC Ltd. is considering raising funds through debt and equity for a new project. The company's current capital structure consists of 60% equity and 40% debt. The cost of equity is 14% and the cost of debt is 8%. The marginal tax rate is 30%. The company plans to raise $500,000 by issuing new equity shares and $300,000 by issuing new debt.

What is the average cost of capital and marginal cost of capital for the company, assuming that the company's beta is 1.5 and the risk-free rate is 5%?

Solution:

Step 1: Calculate the cost of equity
Cost of equity = Risk-free rate + Beta x Equity risk premium
Equity risk premium = Cost of equity - Risk-free rate
Equity risk premium = 14% - 5% = 9%
Cost of equity = 5% + 1.5 x 9% = 18.5%

Step 2: Calculate the after-tax cost of debt
After-tax cost of debt = Cost of debt x (1 - Marginal tax rate)
After-tax cost of debt = 8% x (1 - 30%) = 5.6%

Step 3: Calculate the weighted average cost of capital (WACC)
WACC = (Weight of equity x Cost of equity) + (Weight of debt x After-tax cost of debt)
Weight of equity = 60% and Weight of debt = 40%
WACC = (60% x 18.5%) + (40% x 5.6%) = 13.24%

Step 4: Calculate the new weighted average cost of capital after raising funds
The new capital structure will be 65% equity and 35% debt.
Weight of equity = 65% and Weight of debt = 35%
New WACC = (65% x 18.5%) + (35% x 5.6%) = 14.45%

Step 5: Calculate the marginal cost of capital (MCC)
MCC = (New WACC - WACC) / (Total new capital - Total old capital)
Total new capital = $500,000 + $300,000 = $800,000
Total old capital = $800,000
MCC = (14.45% - 13.24%) / ($800,000 - $800,000) = N/A

In this case, the marginal cost of capital is not applicable because the total new capital raised is equal to the total old capital.

Weighted Average Cost of Capital (WACC) Using Book Value and Market Value Weightings

XYZ Inc. is evaluating a new project that requires a total investment of $1,000,000. The company's current capital structure consists of 40% debt and 60% equity. The before-tax cost of debt is 6% and the cost of equity is 12%. The marginal tax rate is 25%. The company's book value of equity is $2,000,000 and the market value of equity is $4,000,000. The book value of debt is $600,000 and the market value of debt is $550,000.

What is the weighted average cost of capital (WACC) of XYZ Inc. using both book value and market value weightings?

Solution:

Step 1: Calculate the after-tax cost of debt
After-tax cost of debt = Cost of debt x (1 - Marginal tax rate)
After-tax cost of debt = 6% x (1 - 25%) = 4.5%

Step 2: Calculate the market value weight of equity and debt
Market value weight of equity = Market value of equity / Total market value
Market value weight of equity = $4,000,000 / ($4,000,000 + $550,000) = 0.879
Market value weight of debt = Market value of debt / Total market value

Market value weight of debt = $550,000 / ($4,000,000 + $550,000) = 0.121

Step 3: Calculate the book value weight of equity and debt
Book value weight of equity = Book value of equity / Total book value
Book value weight of equity = $2,000,000 / ($2,000,000 + $600,000) = 0.769
Book value weight of debt = Book value of debt / Total book value
Book value weight of debt = $600,000 / ($2,000,000 + $600,000) = 0.231

Step 4: Calculate the weighted average cost of capital (WACC) using market value weightings
WACC using market value weightings = (Market value weight of equity x Cost of equity) + (Market value weight of debt x After-tax cost of debt)
WACC using market value weightings = (0.879 x 12%) + (0.121 x 4.5%) = 10.88%

Step 5: Calculate the weighted average cost of capital (WACC) using book value weightings
WACC using book value weightings = (Book value weight of equity x Cost of equity) + (Book value weight of debt x After-tax cost of debt)
WACC using book value weightings = (0.769 x 12%) + (0.231 x 4.5%) = 10.15%

Therefore, the weighted average cost of capital (WACC) using both book value and market value weightings is 10.88% and 10.15%, respectively.

Traditional View of Capital Structure

ABC Ltd. is a company in the manufacturing industry that is considering raising funds to finance a new project. The company has a traditional view of capital structure and follows the use of debt financing. The company is currently financed with 70% debt and 30% equity. The before-tax cost of debt is 9% and the cost of equity is 16%. The company is planning to raise $500,000 by issuing new debt.

What is the new debt-to-equity ratio after the new debt is issued and what will be the weighted average cost of capital (WACC) of the company after the new debt is issued?

Solution:

Step 1: Calculate the total amount of debt and equity before issuing new debt
Total amount of debt = 70% of Total capital
Total amount of equity = 30% of Total capital
Let's assume that the total capital of the company is $1,000,000
Total amount of debt = 70% x $1,000,000 = $700,000
Total amount of equity = 30% x $1,000,000 = $300,000

Step 2: Calculate the new debt-to-equity ratio after issuing new debt
The company is planning to raise $500,000 by issuing new debt. Therefore, the total amount of debt after issuing new debt will be $700,000 + $500,000 = $1,200,000
The total amount of equity will remain the same at $300,000. Therefore, the new debt-to-equity ratio will be $1,200,000 / $300,000 = 4:1

Step 3: Calculate the weighted average cost of capital (WACC) after issuing new debt
WACC = (Weight of debt x Cost of debt) + (Weight of equity x Cost of equity)
Weight of debt = Total amount of debt / Total capital

Weight of equity = Total amount of equity / Total capital
Total capital = Total amount of debt + Total amount of equity
Total capital = $1,200,000 + $300,000 = $1,500,000
Weight of debt = $1,200,000 / $1,500,000 = 0.8
Weight of equity = $300,000 / $1,500,000 = 0.2
WACC = (0.8 x 9%) + (0.2 x 16%) = 10.6%

Therefore, the new debt-to-equity ratio after issuing new debt will be 4:1 and the weighted average cost of capital (WACC) of the company after issuing new debt will be 10.6%.

Miller-Modigliani Theory of Capital Structure Under Different Tax Regimes

ABC Inc. is a company with an unlevered cost of capital of 12%. The company is operating in a country that has a corporate tax rate of 30%. The company is evaluating two financing options for a new project. Option A is to issue only equity securities, while Option B is to issue 50% debt and 50% equity securities. The before-tax cost of debt will be 8%, and the after-tax cost of debt will be 5.6%.

What is the value of ABC Inc. and which financing option should the company choose according to the Miller-Modigliani theory of capital structure?

Solution:

Step 1: Calculate the value of ABC Inc. without the use of debt
Value of the company (VU) = EBIT / Unlevered cost of capital
EBIT = $1,000,000
Unlevered cost of capital (Ku) = 12%
VU = $1,000,000 / 12% = $8,333,333

Step 2: Calculate the value of ABC Inc. under Option B with debt

Value of the company (VL) = (EBIT - Interest expense) / (Unlevered cost of capital x (1 - Tax rate)) + (Debt / (Unlevered cost of capital x (1 - Tax rate)))

EBIT = $1,000,000
Interest expense = $500,000 x 8% = $40,000
Debt = $500,000
Tax rate = 30%
Unlevered cost of capital (Ku) = 12%
After-tax cost of debt (Kd) = 5.6%
VL = (($1,000,000 - $40,000) / (12% x (1 - 30%))) + ($500,000 / (5.6% x (1 - 30%)))
VL = $8,994,152.54

Step 3: Calculate the value of ABC Inc. under Option A with only equity

Since there is no debt, the after-tax cost of debt is not applicable.
Value of the company (VE) = EBIT / (Unlevered cost of capital x (1 - Tax rate))
EBIT = $1,000,000
Tax rate = 30%
Unlevered cost of capital (Ku) = 12%
VE = $1,000,000 / (12% x (1 - 30%)) = $10,714,285.71

According to the Miller-Modigliani theory of capital structure, the value of the company is independent of its capital structure. However, the choice between Option A and Option B depends on the tax shield benefits of debt financing. In this case, the value of the company under Option B ($8,994,152.54) is less than the value of the company under Option A ($10,714,285.71). Therefore, ABC Inc. should choose Option A, which is to issue only equity securities, as per the Miller-Modigliani theory of capital structure.

Miscellaneous

Working Capital Management: A company is considering taking out a $100,000 loan with a 10% annual interest rate to finance their working capital needs. If the company has an operating profit margin of 20%, what is the minimum sales level required to cover the interest expense?

Solution: The interest expense can be calculated as follows:
Interest expense = Loan amount x Annual interest rate = $100,000 x 0.10 = $10,000

The minimum sales level can be calculated using the following formula:
Minimum sales level = Interest expense / Operating profit margin

Minimum sales level = $10,000 / 0.20 = $50,000

Therefore, the company needs to generate a minimum of $50,000 in sales to cover the interest expense.

Problem 2

A company has a working capital requirement of $60,000 for their operations. They are considering two financing options: (1) to take out a $60,000 loan with a 9% annual interest rate and (2) to sell $70,000 of accounts receivables with a 2% factoring fee. Assuming the company has a 25% tax rate, which financing option should they choose based on lower financing costs?

Solution: The total financing cost for each option can be calculated as follows:

Option 1: Interest expense = Loan amount x Annual interest rate
= $60,000 x 0.09 = $5,400
After-tax interest expense = $5,400 x (1 - 0.25) = $4,050

Option 2: Factoring fee = Accounts Receivables x Factoring rate = $70,000 x 0.02 = $1,400
After-tax factoring fee = $1,400 x (1 - 0.25) = $1,050

Therefore, the company should choose Option 2 to sell $70,000 of accounts receivables with a 2% factoring fee based on lower financing costs.

Problem 3

A company has a cash conversion cycle of 60 days and an average daily operating expense of $10,000. If the company is considering to implement a new inventory management policy that will reduce the inventory holding period from 40 days to 30 days, how much savings can the company achieve?

Solution: The cash conversion cycle can be calculated as follows:
CCC = Inventory holding period + Accounts receivable collection period - Accounts payable payment period

Given that the CCC is 60 days, the accounts receivable collection period must be 50 days (60 - 40 + 50 - AP payment period = 60 days)
The inventory holding period can be reduced from 40 days to 30 days, hence the CCC would be 50 days (30 + 50 - AP payment period = 50 days)

Therefore, the accounts payable payment period must be 20 days (30 + 50 - 20 = 60 days)
The company can achieve savings of $200,000 (20 days x $10,000 per day) by implementing the new inventory management policy.

Problem 4

A company is considering to implement a dynamic discount policy to encourage customers to pay their invoices earlier. The company offers credit terms of 30 days with a 2% discount if paid within 10 days. If a customer purchases $10,000 worth of goods and pays within 10 days, how much will the company receive after taking into account the discount and the factoring fee of 1%?

Solution: The discount rate can be calculated as follows:
Discount rate = Discount amount / Invoice amount

Discount rate = $10,000 x 0.02 / $10,000 = 0.02

The factoring fee can be calculated as follows:
Factoring fee = Invoice amount x Factoring rate
Factoring fee = $10,000 x 0.01 = $100

The amount received by the company after taking into account the discount and the factoring fee can be calculated as follows:
Amount received = Invoice amount x (1 - Discount rate) x (1 - Factoring rate)
Amount received = $10,000 x (1 - 0.02) x (1 - 0.01) = $9,800

Therefore, the company will receive $9,800 after taking into account the discount and the factoring fee.

Problem 5

A company is considering a trade credit offer from a supplier for a purchase of $30,000. The supplier offers credit terms of 2/10, net 30. If the company pays within the discount period, what is the cost of trade credit in terms of effective annual interest rate?

Solution: The discount rate can be calculated as follows:
Discount rate = Discount amount / Purchase amount
Discount rate = $30,000 x 0.02 / $30,000 = 0.02

The effective annual interest rate can be calculated using the following formula:
Effective annual interest rate = (Discount percentage / Discount period) x (365 / (Total credit period - Discount period))
Effective annual interest rate = (2% / 10) x (365 / (30 - 10))
Effective annual interest rate = 0.40 x 18.25 = 7.3%

Therefore, the cost of trade credit is 7.3% in terms of effective annual interest rate if the company pays within the discount period.

Free cash flow to firm:

Problem 1: A company generated a net income of $500,000 for the year ended 2022, with depreciation and amortization expenses of $100,000. If the company's tax rate is 30%, and they have capital expenditures of $100,000 and interest expense of $50,000, what is the FCFF for the year ended 2022?

Solution: FCFF can be calculated using the following formula:
FCFF = Net Income + Depreciation and Amortization - Capital Expenditures - Change in Working Capital - (Interest Expense x (1 - Tax Rate))

FCFF = $500,000 + $100,000 - $100,000 - Change in Working Capital - ($50,000 x (1 - 0.30))
Assuming Change in Working Capital is zero for simplicity purposes:
FCFF = $450,000

Therefore, the FCFF for the year ended 2022 is $450,000.

Problem 2

A company generated a net income of $1,000,000 for the year ended 2021, with depreciation and amortization expenses of $200,000. If the company's tax rate is 35%, and they have capital expenditures of $250,000 and interest expense of $100,000, what is the maximum amount of dividends that the company can distribute for the year ended 2021 if they want to maintain a constant level of debt?

Solution: The maximum amount of dividends that the company can distribute and maintain a constant level of debt can be calculated using the following formula:
Maximum dividends = FCFF - (Net Borrowing - Repayment of Debt)

FCFF can be calculated as follows:

FCFF = Net Income + Depreciation and Amortization - Capital Expenditures - Change in Working Capital - (Interest Expense x (1 - Tax Rate))
FCFF = $1,000,000 + $200,000 - $250,000 - Change in Working Capital - ($100,000 x (1 - 0.35))
Assuming Change in Working Capital is zero for simplicity purposes:
FCFF = $715,000

Net borrowing can be calculated as follows:
Net borrowing = Change in Debt - Repayment of Debt

Since the company wants to maintain a constant level of debt, the net borrowing is zero.

Therefore, the maximum amount of dividends that the company can distribute for the year ended 2021 is $715,000.

Problem 3

A company's financial statements show the following information:
- Net Income: $600,000
- Depreciation and Amortization: $150,000
- Capital Expenditures: $100,000
- Change in Working Capital: $50,000
- Interest Expense: $75,000
- Tax Rate: 30%

What is the FCFF for the year ended 2020?

Solution: FCFF can be calculated using the following formula:
FCFF = Net Income + Depreciation and Amortization - Capital Expenditures - Change in Working Capital - (Interest Expense x (1 - Tax Rate))
FCFF = $600,000 + $150,000 - $100,000 - $50,000 - ($75,000 x (1 - 0.30))
FCFF = $522,500

Therefore, the FCFF for the year ended 2020 is $522,500.

Problem 4

A company's financial statements show the following information:
- Net Income: $450,000
- Depreciation and Amortization: $100,000
- Capital Expenditures: $75,000
- Change in Working Capital: $25,000
- Interest Expense: $50,000
- Tax Rate: 25%

What is the ratio of FCFF to total debt for the year ended 2021?

Solution: FCFF can be calculated using the following formula:
FCFF = Net Income + Depreciation and Amortization - Capital Expenditures - Change in Working Capital - (Interest Expense x (1 - Tax Rate))
FCFF = $450,000 + $100,000 - $75,000 - $25,000 - ($50,000 x (1 - 0.25))
FCFF = $372,500

Total debt can be obtained from the company's financial statements. Assuming total debt is $1,500,000:
FCFF to Total debt ratio = FCFF / Total debt
FCFF to Total debt ratio = $372,500 / $1,500,000
FCFF to Total debt ratio = 0.25 or 25%

Therefore, the ratio of FCFF to total debt for the year ended 2021 is 25%.

Problem 5

A company's financial statements show the following information:
- Net Income: $800,000
- Depreciation and Amortization: $200,000
- Capital Expenditures: $150,000
- Change in Working Capital: $50,000
- Interest Expense: $100,000
- Tax Rate: 30%

Assuming a weighted average cost of capital (WACC) of 10%, what is the company's enterprise value (EV) for the year ended 2022?

Solution: FCFF can be calculated using the following formula:
FCFF = Net Income + Depreciation and Amortization - Capital Expenditures - Change in Working Capital - (Interest Expense x (1 - Tax Rate))
FCFF = $800,000 + $200,000 - $150,000 - $50,000 - ($100,000 x (1 - 0.30))
FCFF = $610,000

EV can be calculated using the following formula:
EV = FCFF / WACC
EV = $610,000 / 0.10
EV = $6,100,000

Therefore, the company's EV for the year ended 2022 is $6,100,000.

Firm Cash Flow to Equity:

Problem 1: A company generated $1,000,000 net income for the year ended 2022, with depreciation and amortization expenses of $250,000. If the company's tax rate is 35%, they have capital expenditures of $150,000 and pay $50,000 in dividends, what is the FCFE for the year ended 2022?

Solution: FCFE can be calculated using the following formula:
FCFE = Net Income - (Capital Expenditures - Depreciation) - Change in Working Capital - (Net Borrowing)

FCFE = $1,000,000 - ($150,000 - $250,000) - Change in Working Capital - (Net Borrowing)
Assuming Change in Working Capital is zero for simplicity purposes:
FCFE = $1,100,000 - (Net Borrowing)

Net borrowing can be calculated as follows:
Net borrowing = (Dividends - Net Income x (1 - Tax Rate)) + (Capital Expenditures - Depreciation)

Net borrowing = ($50,000 - $1,000,000 x (1 - 0.35)) + ($150,000 - $250,000)
Net borrowing = -$90,500

FCFE = $1,100,000 - (-$90,500)
FCFE = $1,190,500

Therefore, the FCFE for the year ended 2022 is $1,190,500.

Problem 2

A company has a net income of $800,000, capital expenditures of $200,000, and depreciation and amortization expenses of $100,000 for the year ended 2021. The company paid $50,000 in dividends for the same year. If the company's tax rate is 30%, what is the FCFE for the year ended 2021?

Solution: FCFE can be calculated using the following formula:
FCFE = Net Income - (Capital Expenditures - Depreciation) - Change in Working Capital - (Net Borrowing)

FCFE = $800,000 - ($200,000 - $100,000) - Change in Working Capital - (Net Borrowing)
Assuming Change in Working Capital is zero for simplicity purposes:
FCFE = $700,000 - (Net Borrowing)

Net borrowing can be calculated as follows:
Net borrowing = (Dividends - Net Income x (1 - Tax Rate)) + (Capital Expenditures - Depreciation)

Net borrowing = ($50,000 - $800,000 x (1 - 0.30)) + ($200,000 - $100,000)
Net borrowing = -$216,000

$$FCFE = \$700{,}000 - (-\$216{,}000)$$
$$FCFE = \$916{,}000$$

Therefore, the FCFE for the year ended 2021 is $916,000.

Problem 3

A company has a net income of $500,000, capital expenditures of $150,000, and depreciation and amortization expenses of $100,000 for the year ended 2020. The company paid $50,000 in dividends for the same year. If the company's tax rate is 25%, what is the maximum amount of new debt that the company can issue for the year ended 2020 and still maintain their desired level of dividends?

Solution: The maximum amount of new debt that the company can issue and still maintain their desired level of dividends can be calculated using the following formula:

Maximum net borrowing = Dividends - (Net Income x (1 - Tax Rate)) - (Capital Expenditures - Depreciation)

Maximum net borrowing = $50,000 - ($500,000 x (1 - 0.25)) - ($150,000 - $100,000)
Maximum net borrowing = $50,000 - $300,000
Maximum net borrowing = -$250,000

Therefore, the company cannot issue any new debt for the year ended 2020 if they want to maintain their desired level of dividends.

About Author

I am bestselling author. Data scientist. Cambridge Alumnus. I have proven technical skills (MBA, ACCA (Knowledge Level- FTMS college Malaysia), BBA, several Google certifications such as Google Data Analytics Specialization, Google Digital Marketing & E-commerce Specialization, and Google Project Management Specialization) to deliver insightful books with ten years of business experience. I have written and published 650+ titles.

ORCID: https://orcid.org/0009-0004-8629-830X
Azhar.sari@hotmail.co.uk